ALSO BY RIAD SATTOUF

The Arab of the Future:
A Childhood in the Middle East, 1978–1984

THE ARAB
OF THE FUTURE 2

A GRAPHIC MEMOIR

A Childhood in the Middle East (1984–1985)

RIAD SATTOUF

TRANSLATED BY SAM TAYLOR

METROPOLITAN BOOKS   HENRY HOLT AND COMPANY   NEW YORK

Metropolitan Books
Henry Holt and Company, LLC
Publishers since 1866
175 Fifth Avenue
New York, New York 10010
www.henryholt.com

Metropolitan Books® and m® are registered trademarks of
Henry Holt and Company, LLC.

Distributed in Canada by Raincoast Book Distribution Limited

Originally published in France in 2015 by Allary Éditions

Library of Congress Cataloging-in-Publication data for the first volume is as follows:

Sattouf, Riad, author.
[Arabe du futur. English]
The Arab of the future : growing up in the Middle East (1978–1984) : a graphic memoir / Riad Sattouf ; translated from the French by Sam Taylor.
pages cm
ISBN 978-1-62779-344-5 (hardback)—ISBN (invalid) 978-1-62779-345-2 (electronic book)
1. Sattouf, Riad—Childhood and youth—Comic books, strips, etc. 2. Cartoonists—France—Biography—Comic books, strips, etc. 3. Middle East—Biography—Comic books, strips, etc. 4. Graphic novels.
I. Taylor, Sam, 1970– translator. II. Title.
NC1499.S337A2 2015
741.5'69092–dc23
[B] 2014041152

ISBN: 978-1-62779-351-3

Our books may be purchased in bulk for promotional, educational, or business use. Please contact your local bookseller or the Macmillan Corporate and Premium Sales Department at (800) 221-7945, extension 5442, or by e-mail at MacmillanSpecialMarkets@macmillan.com.

First U.S. Edition 2016

Designed by Kelly S. Too

Printed in China
10 9 8 7 6 5 4 3 2 1

CHAPTER 1

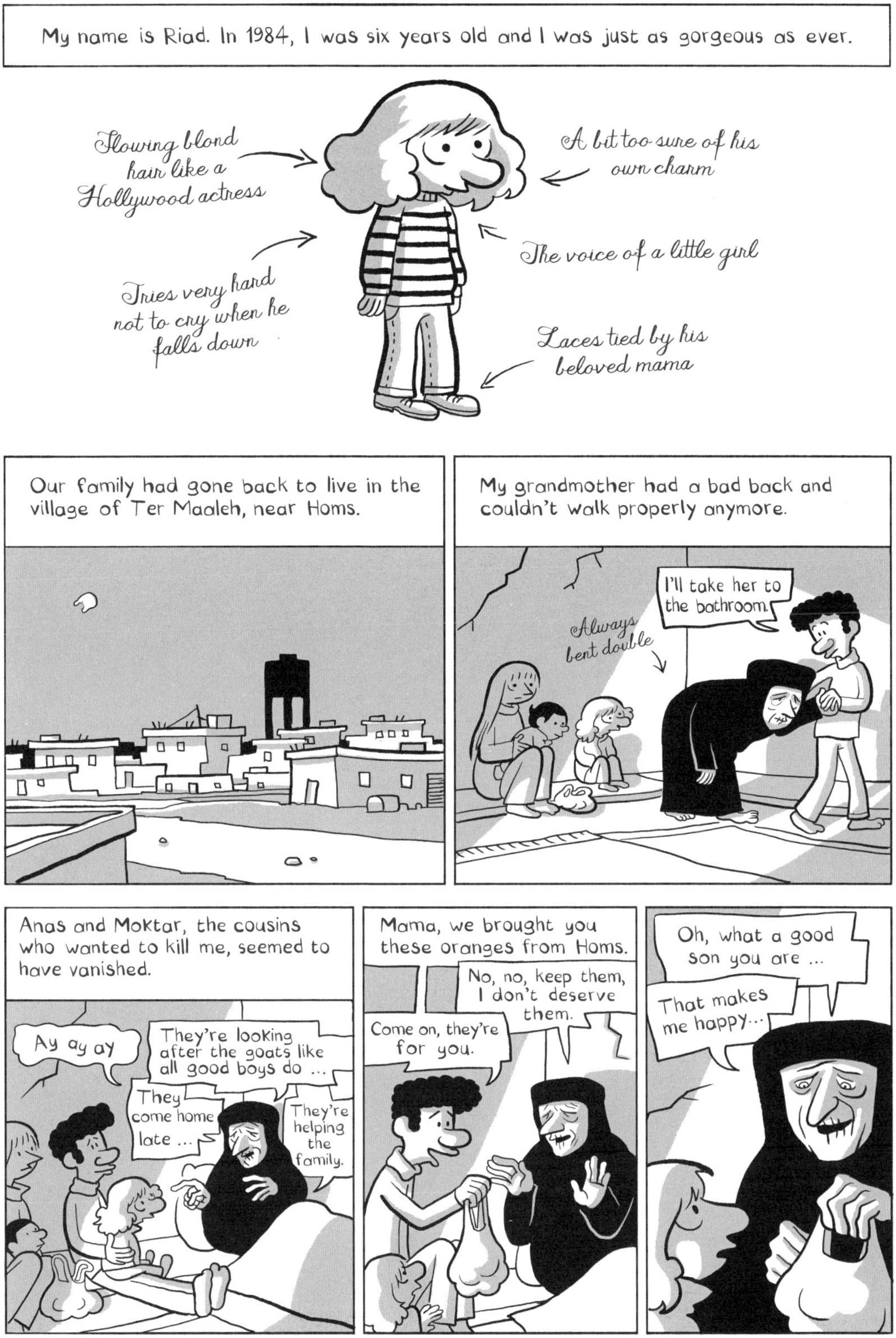

My name is Riad. In 1984, I was six years old and I was just as gorgeous as ever.
Flowing blond hair like a Hollywood actress
A bit too sure of his own charm
The voice of a little girl
Tries very hard not to cry when he falls down
Laces tied by his beloved mama
Our family had gone back to live in the village of Ter Maaleh, near Homs.
My grandmother had a bad back and couldn't walk properly anymore.
Always bent double
I'll take her to the bathroom.
Anas and Moktar, the cousins who wanted to kill me, seemed to have vanished.
Ay ay ay
They're looking after the goats like all good boys do ...
They come home late ...
They're helping the family.
Mama, we brought you these oranges from Homs.
No, no, keep them, I don't deserve them.
Come on, they're for you.
Oh, what a good son you are ...
That makes me happy...

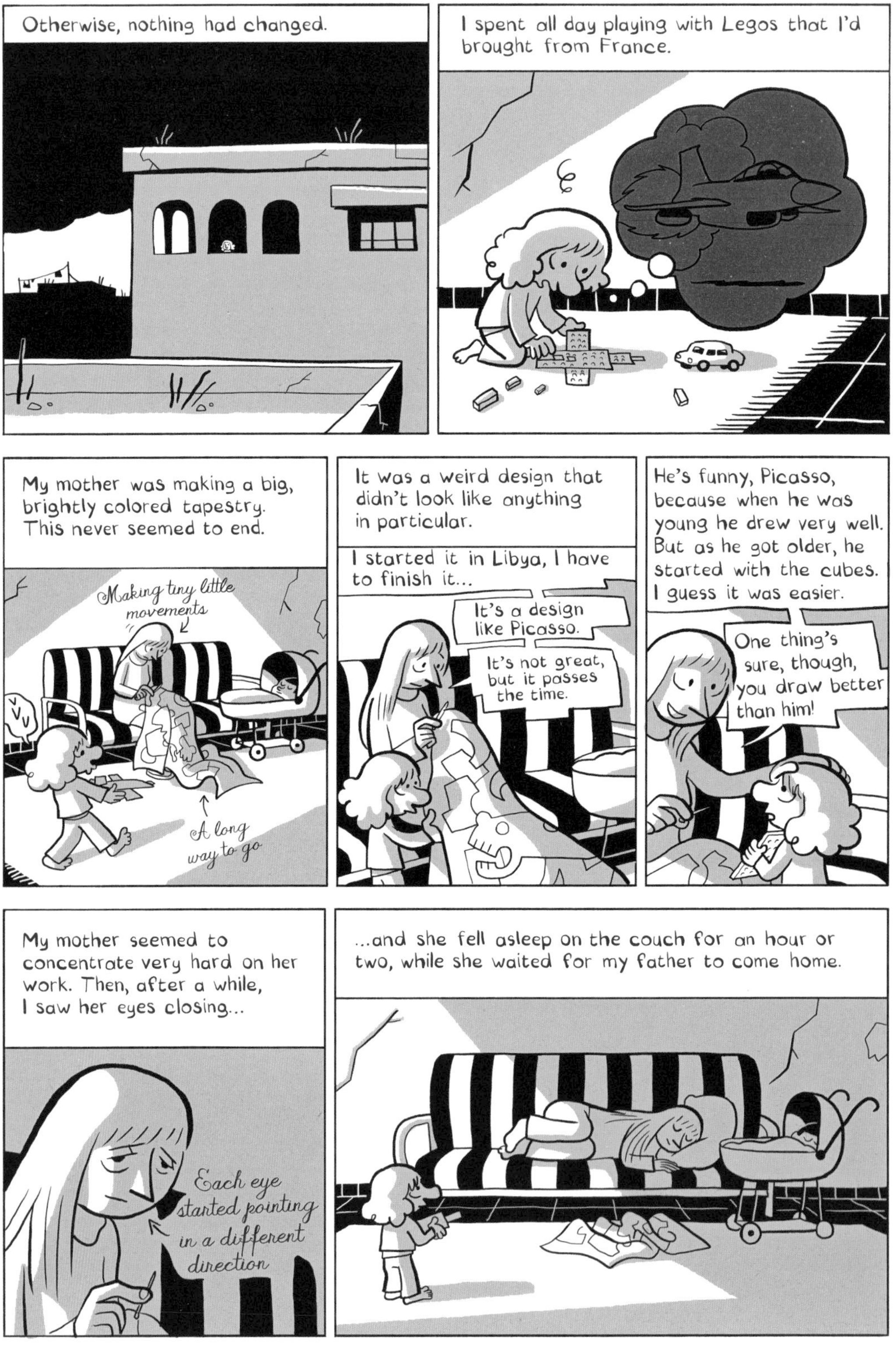
Otherwise, nothing had changed.
I spent all day playing with Legos that I'd brought from France.
My mother was making a big, brightly colored tapestry. This never seemed to end.
Making tiny little movements
A long way to go
It was a weird design that didn't look like anything in particular.
I started it in Libya, I have to finish it...
It's a design like Picasso.
It's not great, but it passes the time.
He's funny, Picasso, because when he was young he drew very well. But as he got older, he started with the cubes. I guess it was easier.
One thing's sure, though, you draw better than him!
My mother seemed to concentrate very hard on her work. Then, after a while, I saw her eyes closing...
Each eye started pointing in a different direction
...and she fell asleep on the couch for an hour or two, while she waited for my father to come home.

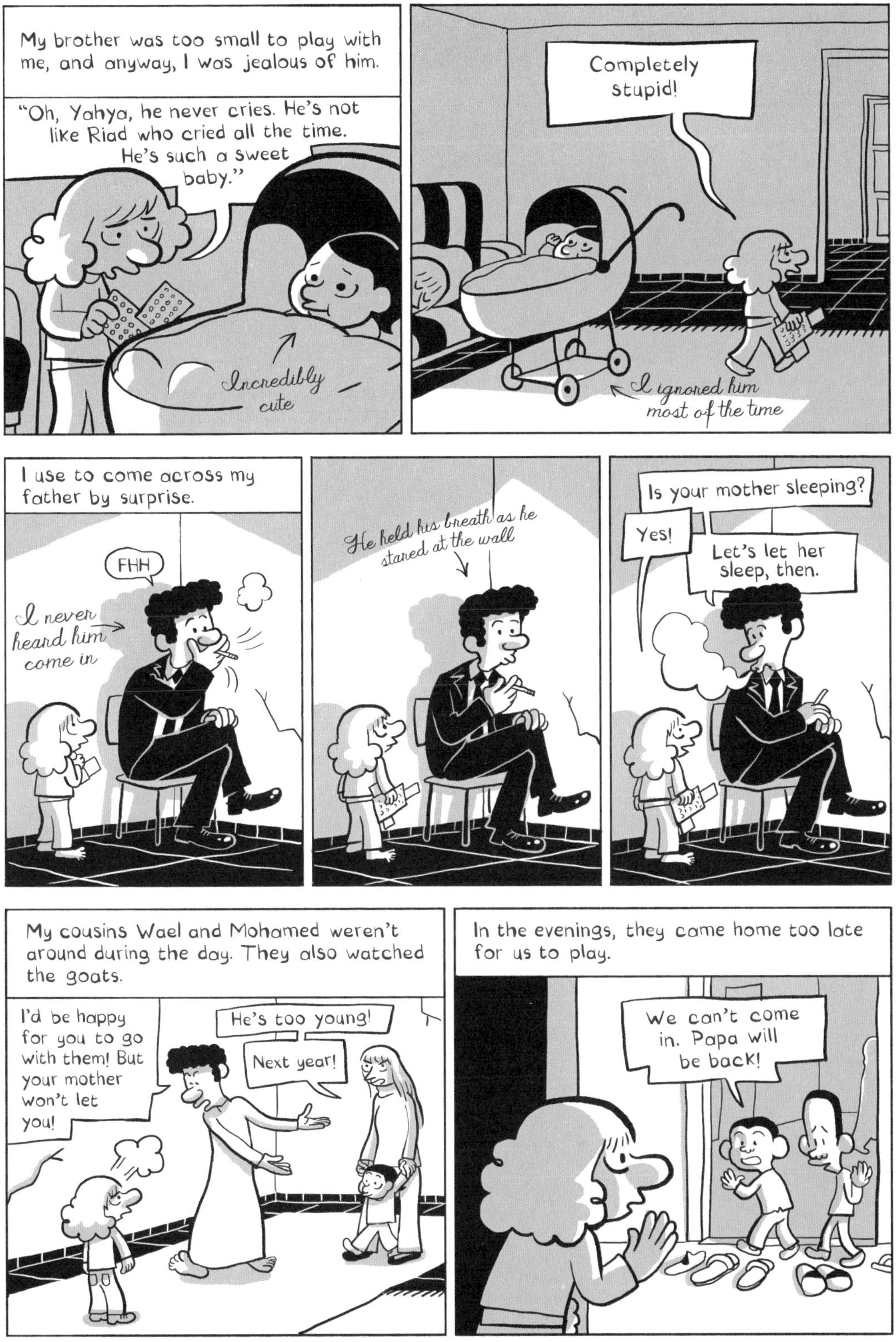
My brother was too small to play with me, and anyway, I was jealous of him.
"Oh, Yahya, he never cries. He's not like Riad who cried all the time. He's such a sweet baby."
Incredibly cute
Completely stupid!
I ignored him most of the time
I use to come across my father by surprise.
FHH
I never heard him come in
He held his breath as he stared at the wall
Is your mother sleeping?
Yes!
Let's let her sleep, then.
My cousins Wael and Mohamed weren't around during the day. They also watched the goats.
I'd be happy for you to go with them! But your mother won't let you!
He's too young!
Next year!
In the evenings, they came home too late for us to play.
We can't come in. Papa will be back!

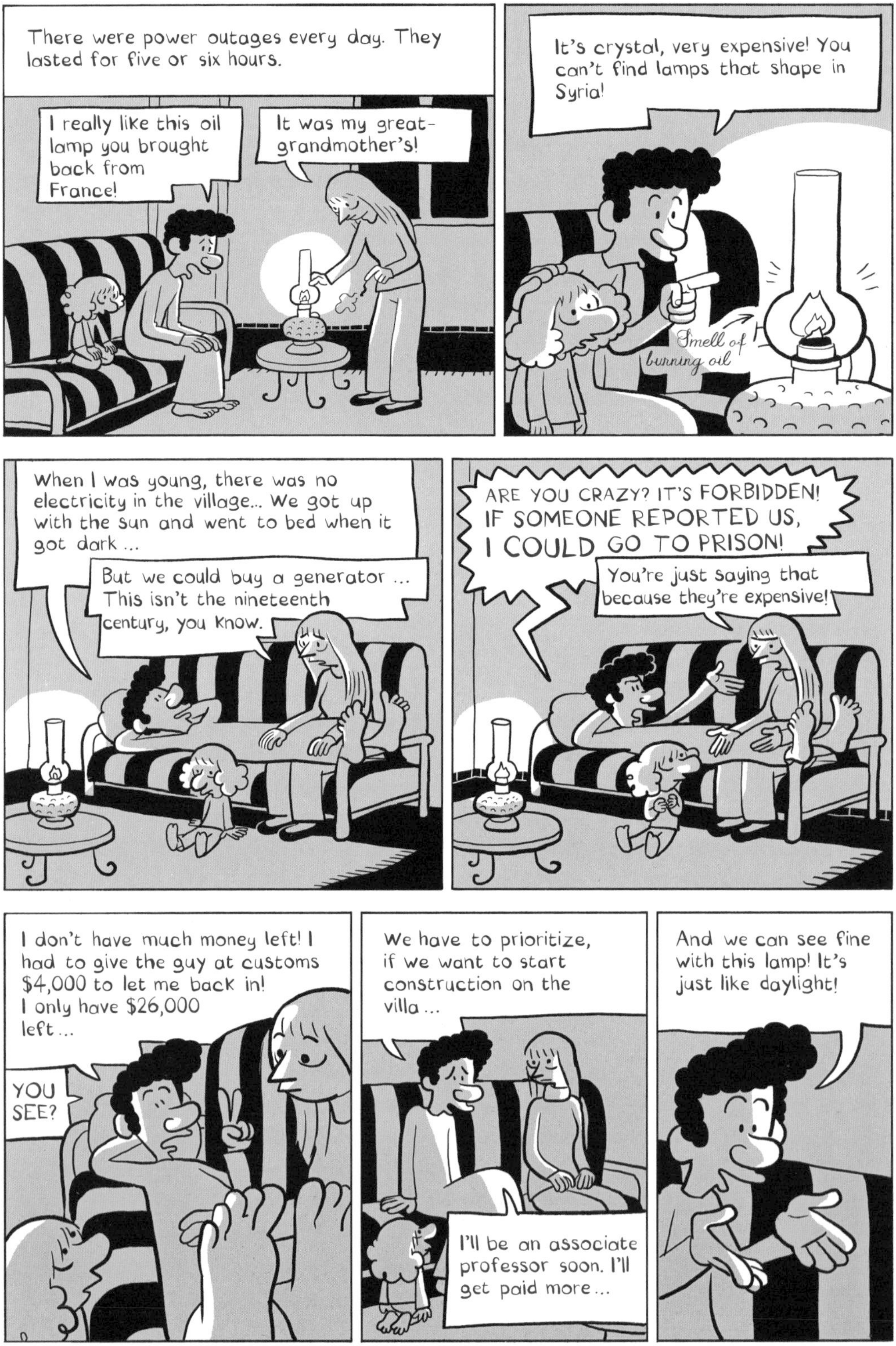

There were power outages every day. They lasted for five or six hours.
I really like this oil lamp you brought back from France!
It was my great-grandmother's!
It's crystal, very expensive! You can't find lamps that shape in Syria!
Smell of burning oil
When I was young, there was no electricity in the village... We got up with the sun and went to bed when it got dark ...
But we could buy a generator ... This isn't the nineteenth century, you know.
ARE YOU CRAZY? IT'S FORBIDDEN! IF SOMEONE REPORTED US, I COULD GO TO PRISON!
You're just saying that because they're expensive!
I don't have much money left! I had to give the guy at customs $4,000 to let me back in! I only have $26,000 left ...
YOU SEE?
We have to prioritize, if we want to start construction on the villa ...
I'll be an associate professor soon. I'll get paid more ...
And we can see fine with this lamp! It's just like daylight!

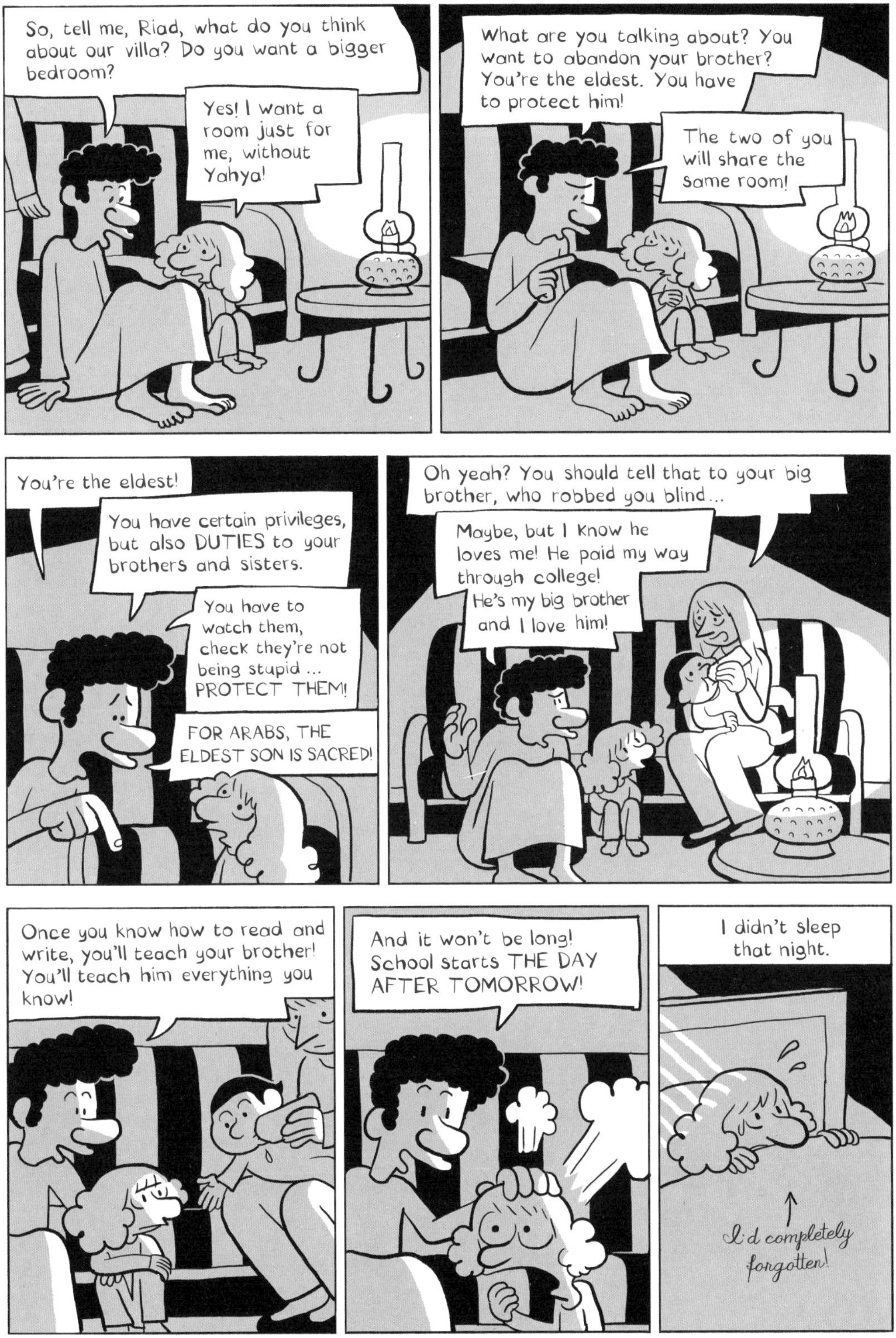
So, tell me, Riad, what do you think about our villa? Do you want a bigger bedroom?
Yes! I want a room just for me, without Yahya!
What are you talking about? You want to abandon your brother? You're the eldest. You have to protect him!
The two of you will share the same room!
You're the eldest!
You have certain privileges, but also DUTIES to your brothers and sisters.
You have to watch them, check they're not being stupid ... PROTECT THEM!
FOR ARABS, THE ELDEST SON IS SACRED!
Oh yeah? You should tell that to your big brother, who robbed you blind...
Maybe, but I know he loves me! He paid my way through college!
He's my big brother and I love him!
Once you know how to read and write, you'll teach your brother! You'll teach him everything you know!
And it won't be long! School starts THE DAY AFTER TOMORROW!
I didn't sleep that night.
I'd completely forgotten!

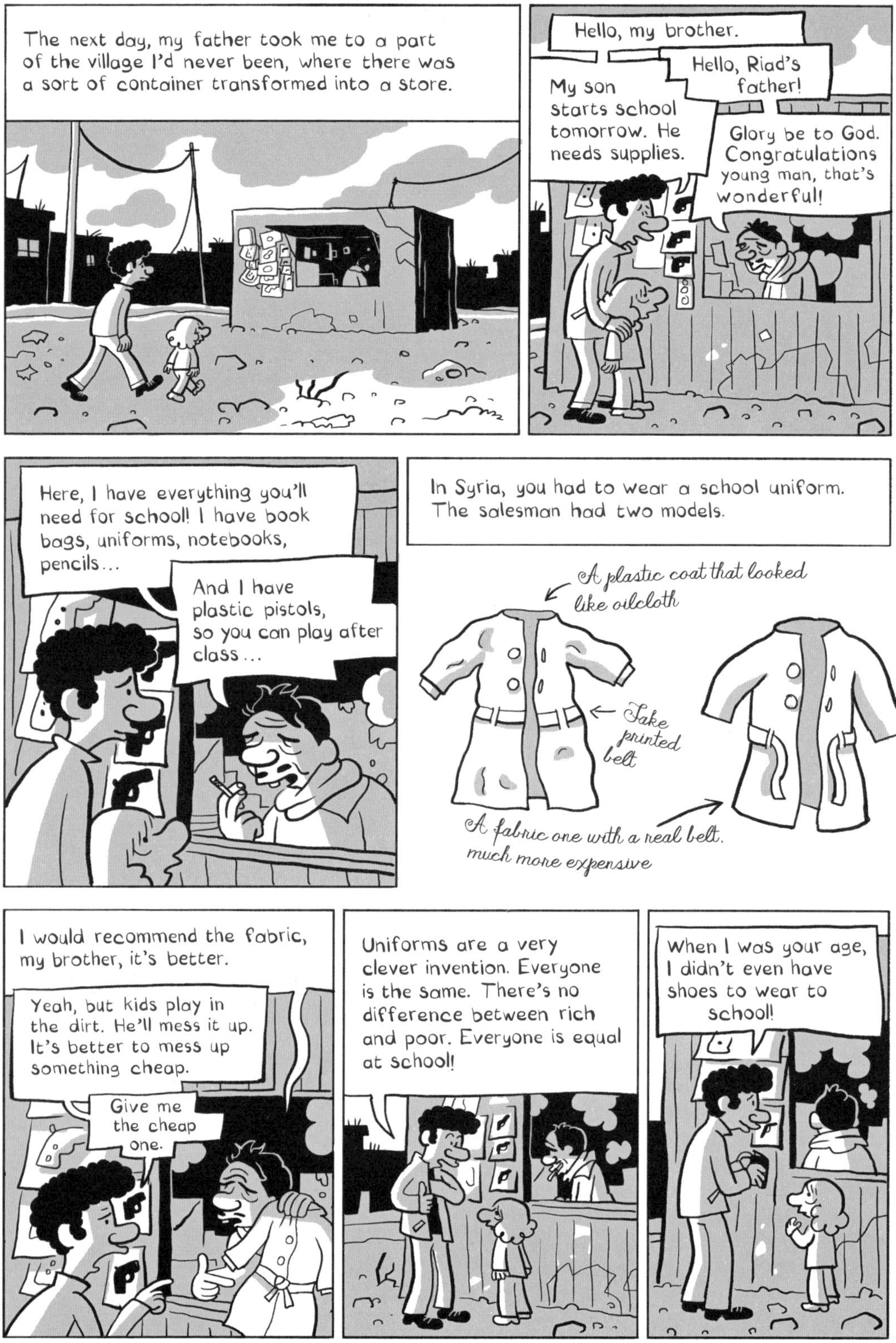
The next day, my father took me to a part of the village I'd never been, where there was a sort of container transformed into a store.
Hello, my brother.
Hello, Riad's father!
My son starts school tomorrow. He needs supplies.
Glory be to God. Congratulations young man, that's wonderful!
Here, I have everything you'll need for school! I have book bags, uniforms, notebooks, pencils...
And I have plastic pistols, so you can play after class...
In Syria, you had to wear a school uniform. The salesman had two models.
A plastic coat that looked like oilcloth
Fake printed belt
A fabric one with a real belt, much more expensive
I would recommend the fabric, my brother, it's better.
Yeah, but kids play in the dirt. He'll mess it up. It's better to mess up something cheap.
Give me the cheap one.
Uniforms are a very clever invention. Everyone is the same. There's no difference between rich and poor. Everyone is equal at school!
When I was your age, I didn't even have shoes to wear to school!

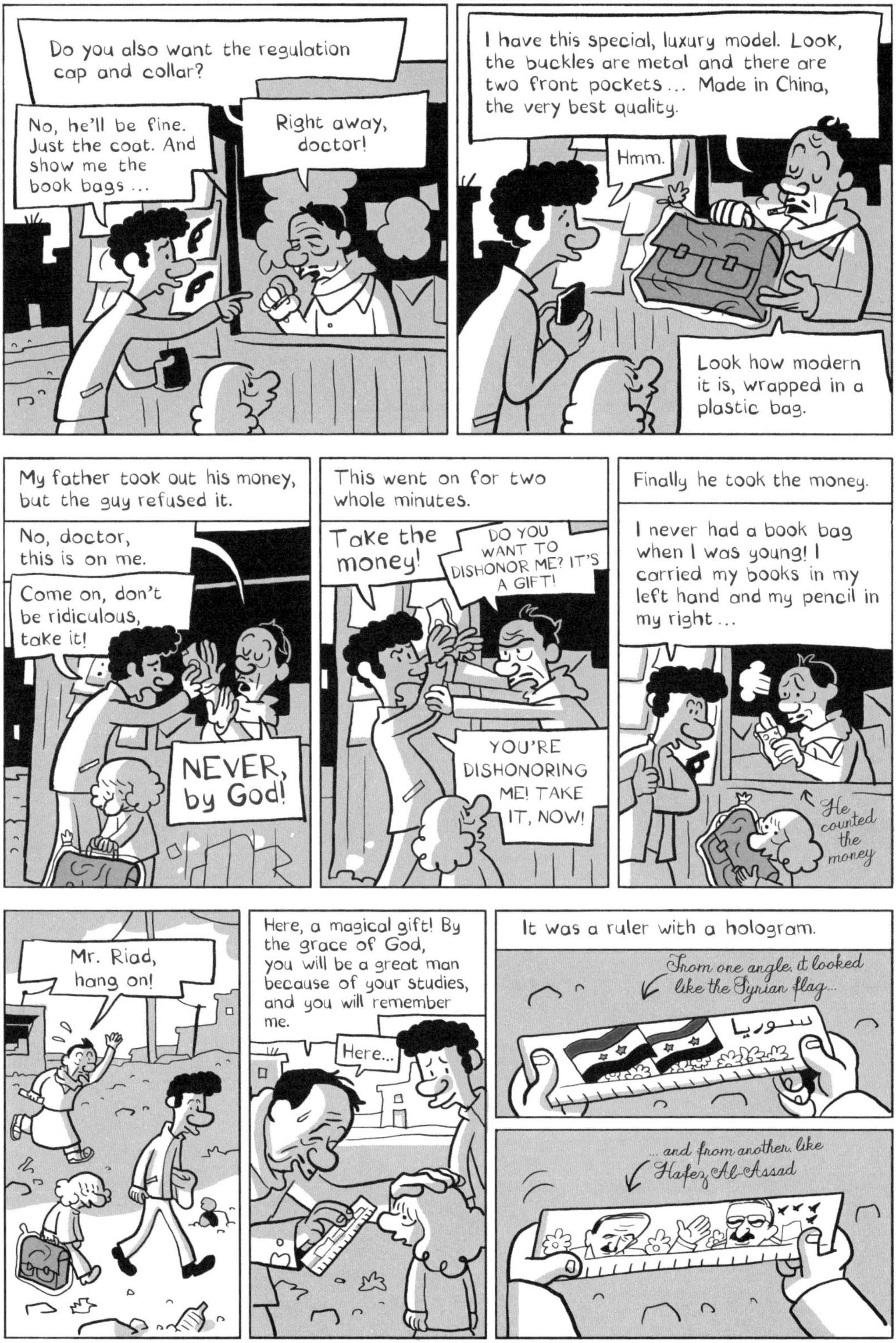
Do you also want the regulation cap and collar?
No, he'll be fine. Just the coat. And show me the book bags ...
Right away, doctor!
I have this special, luxury model. Look, the buckles are metal and there are two front pockets ... Made in China, the very best quality.
Hmm.
Look how modern it is, wrapped in a plastic bag.
My father took out his money, but the guy refused it.
No, doctor, this is on me.
Come on, don't be ridiculous, take it!
NEVER, by God!
This went on for two whole minutes.
Take the money!
DO YOU WANT TO DISHONOR ME? IT'S A GIFT!
YOU'RE DISHONORING ME! TAKE IT, NOW!
Finally he took the money.
I never had a book bag when I was young! I carried my books in my left hand and my pencil in my right ...
He counted the money
Mr. Riad, hang on!
Here, a magical gift! By the grace of God, you will be a great man because of your studies, and you will remember me.
Here...
It was a ruler with a hologram.
From one angle, it looked like the Syrian flag...
سوريا
... and from another, like Hafez Al-Assad

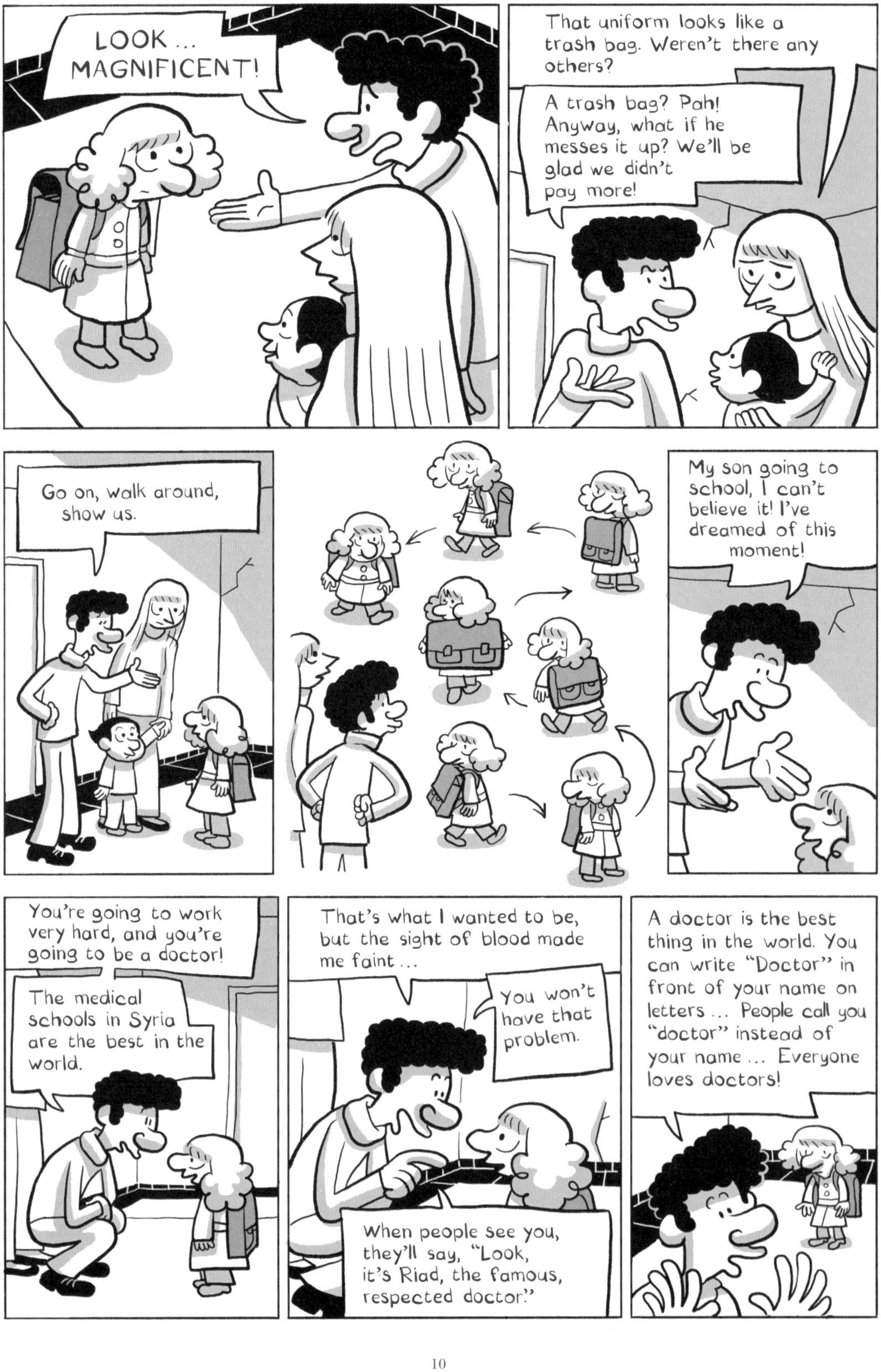
LOOK ... MAGNIFICENT!
That uniform looks like a trash bag. Weren't there any others?
A trash bag? Pah! Anyway, what if he messes it up? We'll be glad we didn't pay more!
Go on, walk around, show us.
My son going to school, I can't believe it! I've dreamed of this moment!
You're going to work very hard, and you're going to be a doctor!
The medical schools in Syria are the best in the world.
That's what I wanted to be, but the sight of blood made me faint ...
You won't have that problem.
When people see you, they'll say, "Look, it's Riad, the famous, respected doctor."
A doctor is the best thing in the world. You can write "Doctor" in front of your name on letters ... People call you "doctor" instead of your name ... Everyone loves doctors!

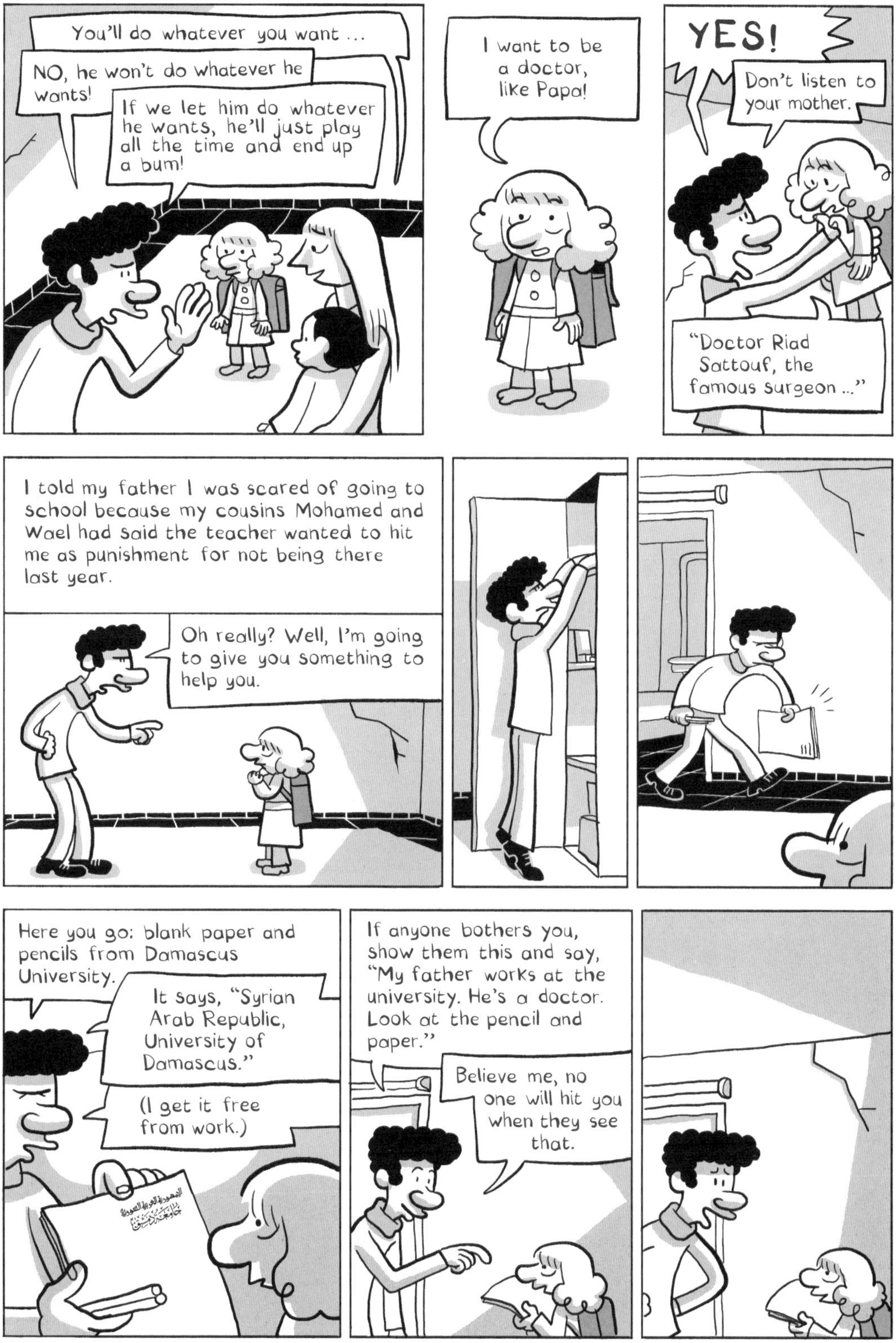

You'll do whatever you want ...
NO, he won't do whatever he wants!
If we let him do whatever he wants, he'll just play all the time and end up a bum!
I want to be a doctor, like Papa!
YES!
Don't listen to your mother.
"Doctor Riad Sattouf, the famous surgeon ..."
I told my father I was scared of going to school because my cousins Mohamed and Wael had said the teacher wanted to hit me as punishment for not being there last year.
Oh really? Well, I'm going to give you something to help you.
Here you go: blank paper and pencils from Damascus University.
It says, "Syrian Arab Republic, University of Damascus."
(I get it free from work.)
If anyone bothers you, show them this and say, "My father works at the university. He's a doctor. Look at the pencil and paper."
Believe me, no one will hit you when they see that.

The next morning, my mother woke me early.

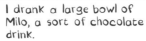
I drank a large bowl of Milo, a sort of chocolate drink.

Will you come with me to school?

I can't take you, I have to look after your brother...

Your father's still asleep... I don't think he was planning to go with you...

...get dressed and ask him...

Sudden terror

Papa!

You sleeping?

Pssst!

Noise of the plastic coat

↓

CRINKLE

Mnng

ZZZ

Papa! Can you take me to school? I don't know how to get there!

Of course you do! You go down the street, and you're there.

Go on your own. You're a man now.

I'm sleeping.

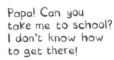
I started crying, and he finally got up. My mother talked to him and made him take me.

Children don't go to school with their parents here!

You have to grow up!

...But it was my first day.

Sniff.

12

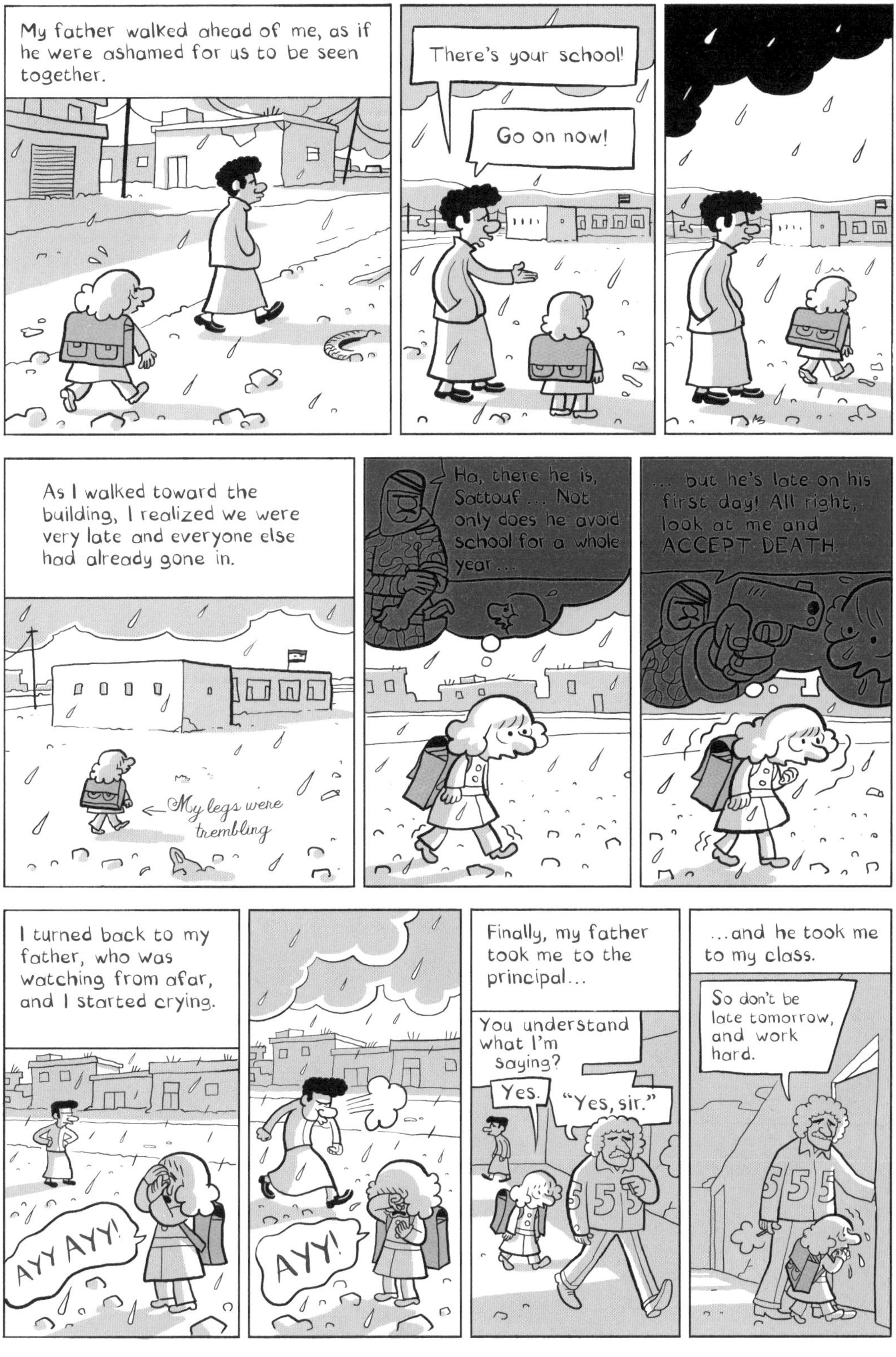
My father walked ahead of me, as if he were ashamed for us to be seen together.
There's your school!
Go on now!
As I walked toward the building, I realized we were very late and everyone else had already gone in.
My legs were trembling
Ha, there he is, Sattouf... Not only does he avoid school for a whole year...
... but he's late on his first day! All right, look at me and ACCEPT DEATH.
I turned back to my father, who was watching from afar, and I started crying.
AYY AYY!
AYY!
Finally, my father took me to the principal...
You understand what I'm saying?
Yes.
"Yes, sir."
...and he took me to my class.
So don't be late tomorrow, and work hard.

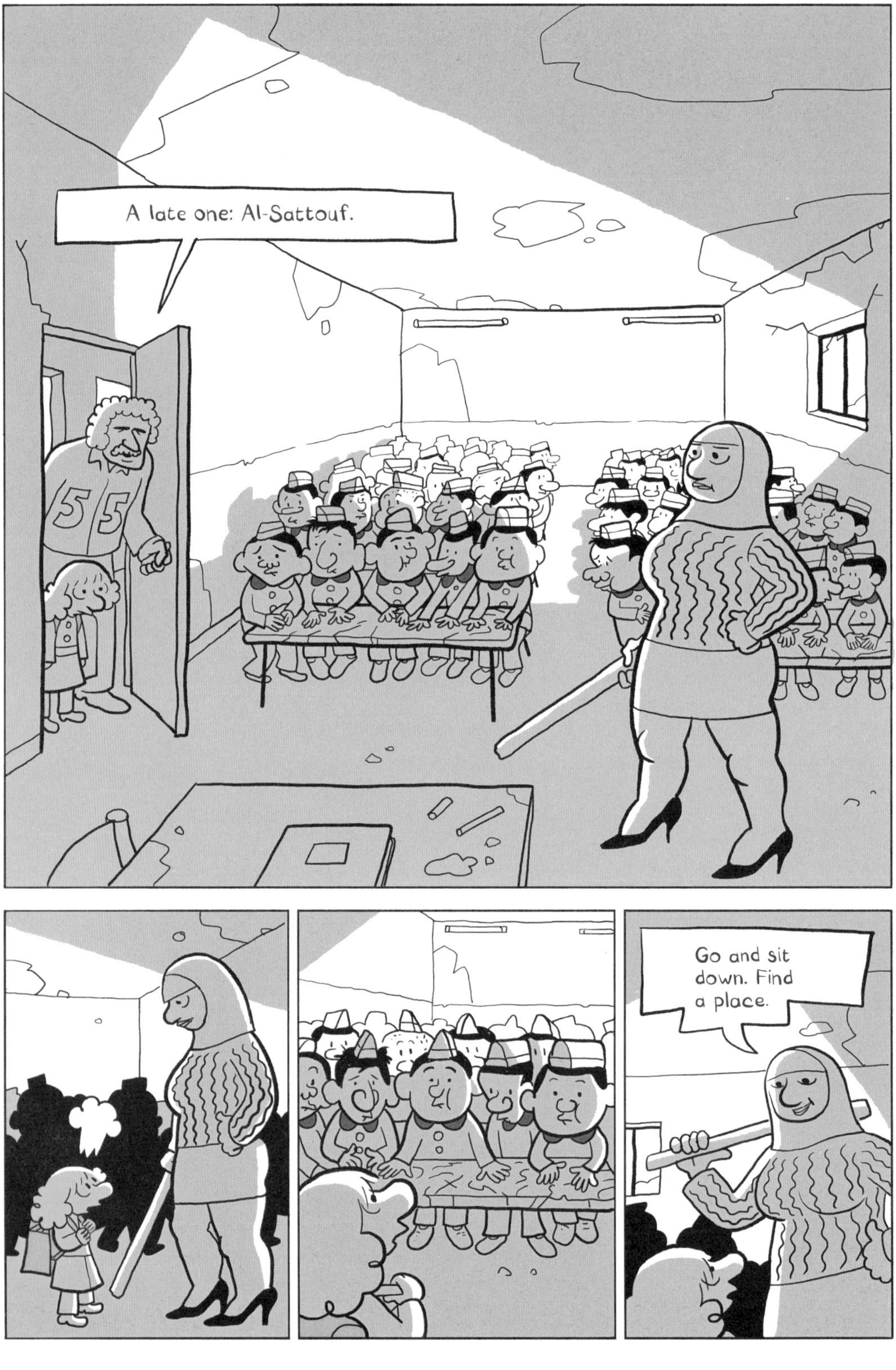
A late one: Al-Sattouf.
Go and sit down. Find a place.

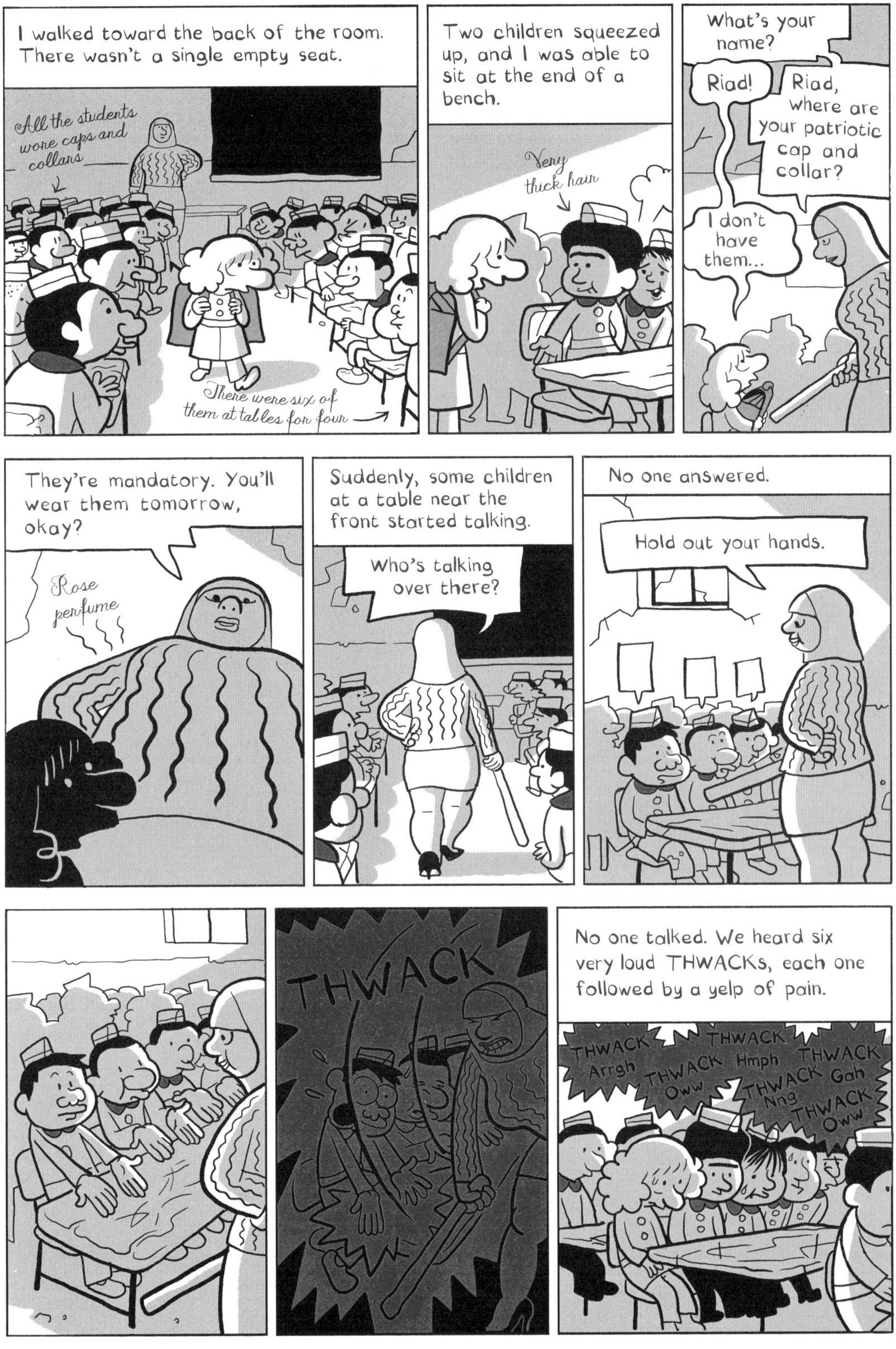
I walked toward the back of the room. There wasn't a single empty seat.
All the students wore caps and collars
There were six of them at tables for four
Two children squeezed up, and I was able to sit at the end of a bench.
Very thick hair
What's your name?
Riad!
Riad, where are your patriotic cap and collar?
I don't have them...
They're mandatory. You'll wear them tomorrow, okay?
Rose perfume
Suddenly, some children at a table near the front started talking.
Who's talking over there?
No one answered.
Hold out your hands.
THWACK
No one talked. We heard six very loud THWACKs, each one followed by a yelp of pain.
THWACK Arrgh
THWACK
THWACK Oww
Hmph
THWACK
THWACK Nng
Gah
THWACK Oww

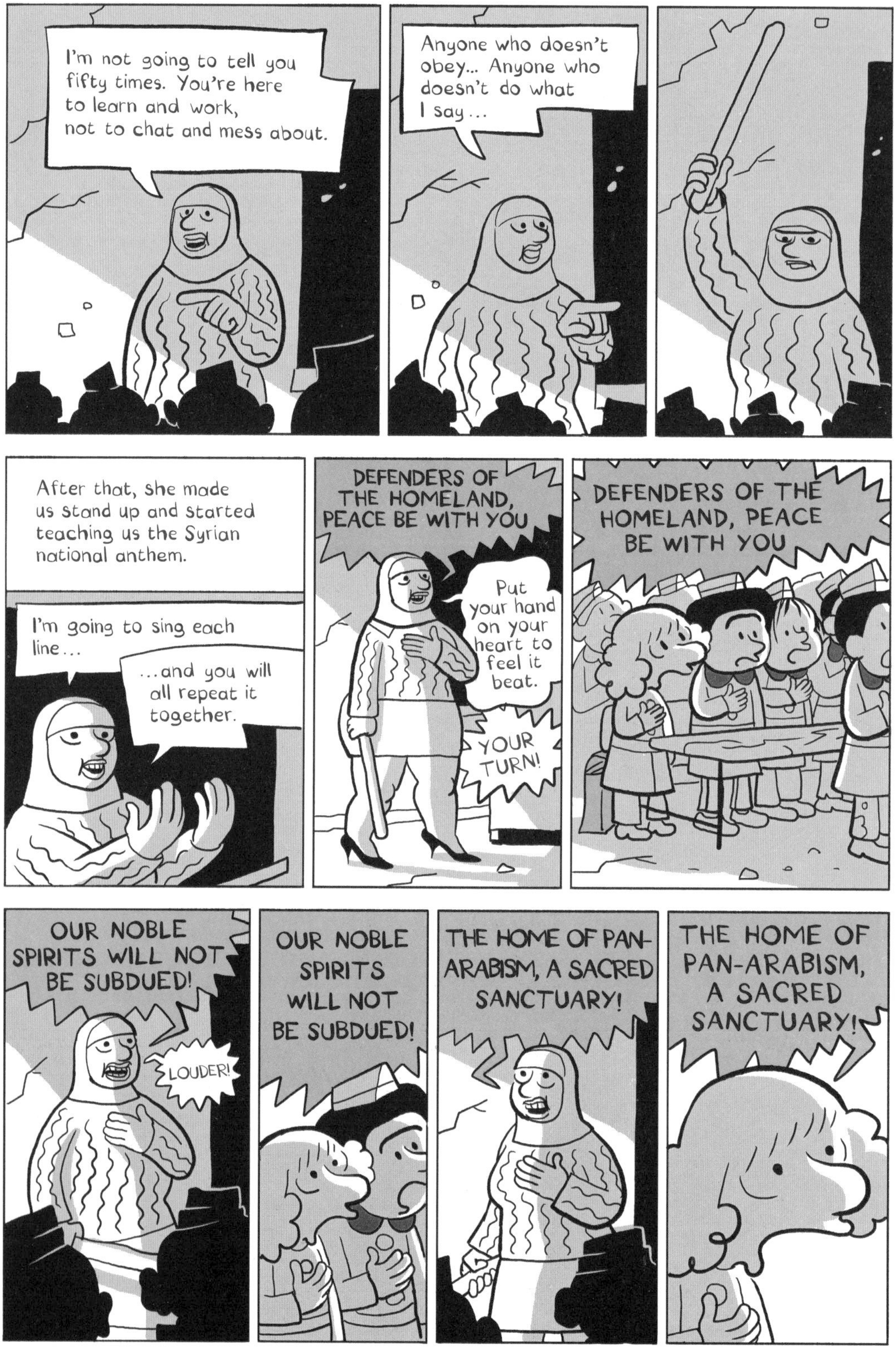
I'm not going to tell you fifty times. You're here to learn and work, not to chat and mess about.
Anyone who doesn't obey... Anyone who doesn't do what I say...
After that, she made us stand up and started teaching us the Syrian national anthem.
I'm going to sing each line...
...and you will all repeat it together.
DEFENDERS OF THE HOMELAND, PEACE BE WITH YOU
Put your hand on your heart to feel it beat.
YOUR TURN!
DEFENDERS OF THE HOMELAND, PEACE BE WITH YOU
OUR NOBLE SPIRITS WILL NOT BE SUBDUED!
LOUDER!
OUR NOBLE SPIRITS WILL NOT BE SUBDUED!
THE HOME OF PAN-ARABISM, A SACRED SANCTUARY!
THE HOME OF PAN-ARABISM, A SACRED SANCTUARY!

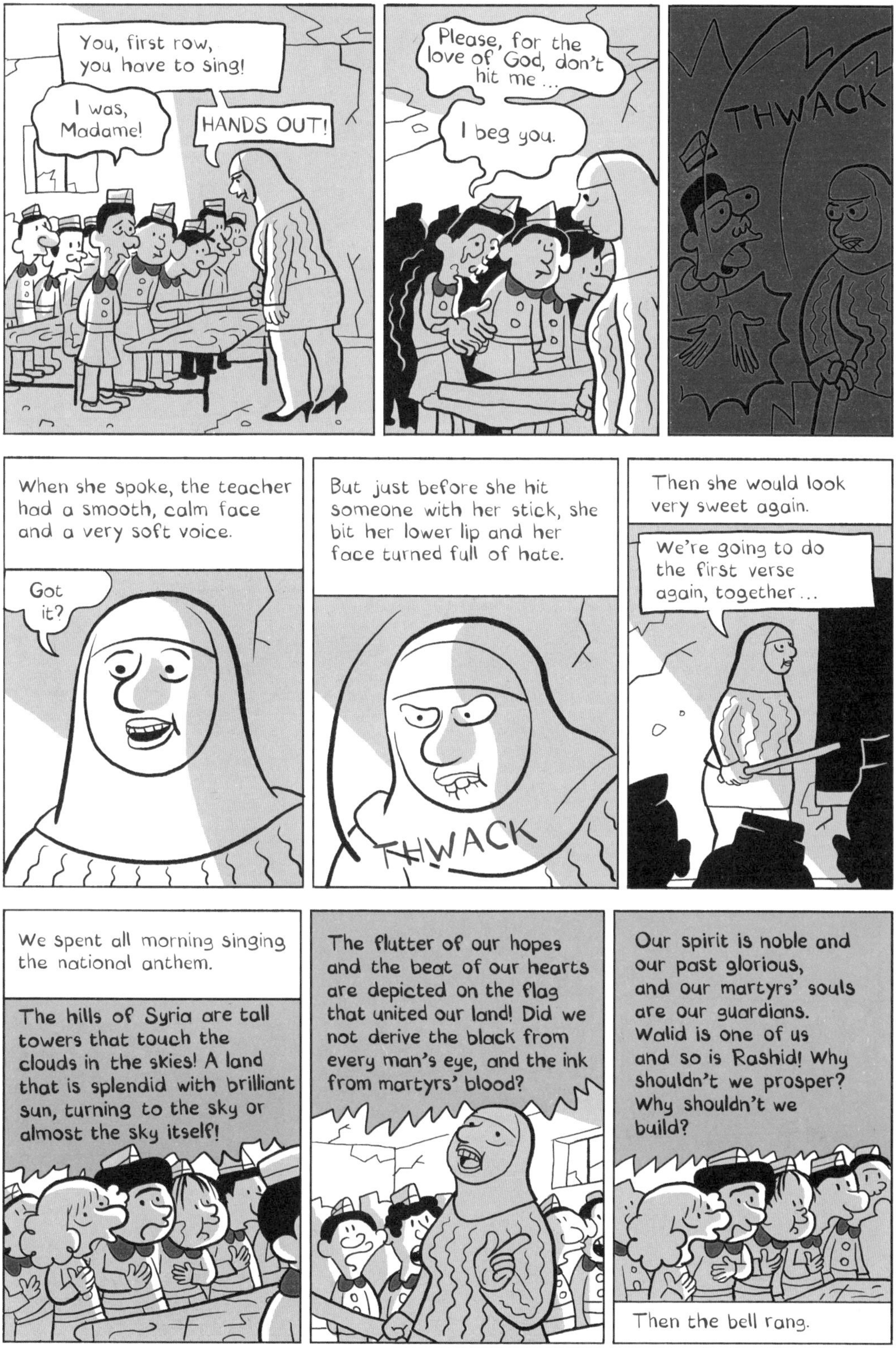
You, first row, you have to sing!
I was, Madame!
HANDS OUT!
Please, for the love of God, don't hit me...
I beg you.
THWACK
When she spoke, the teacher had a smooth, calm face and a very soft voice.
Got it?
But just before she hit someone with her stick, she bit her lower lip and her face turned full of hate.
THWACK
Then she would look very sweet again.
We're going to do the first verse again, together...
We spent all morning singing the national anthem.
The hills of Syria are tall towers that touch the clouds in the skies! A land that is splendid with brilliant sun, turning to the sky or almost the sky itself!
The flutter of our hopes and the beat of our hearts are depicted on the flag that united our land! Did we not derive the black from every man's eye, and the ink from martyrs' blood?
Our spirit is noble and our past glorious, and our martyrs' souls are our guardians. Walid is one of us and so is Rashid! Why shouldn't we prosper? Why shouldn't we build?
Then the bell rang.

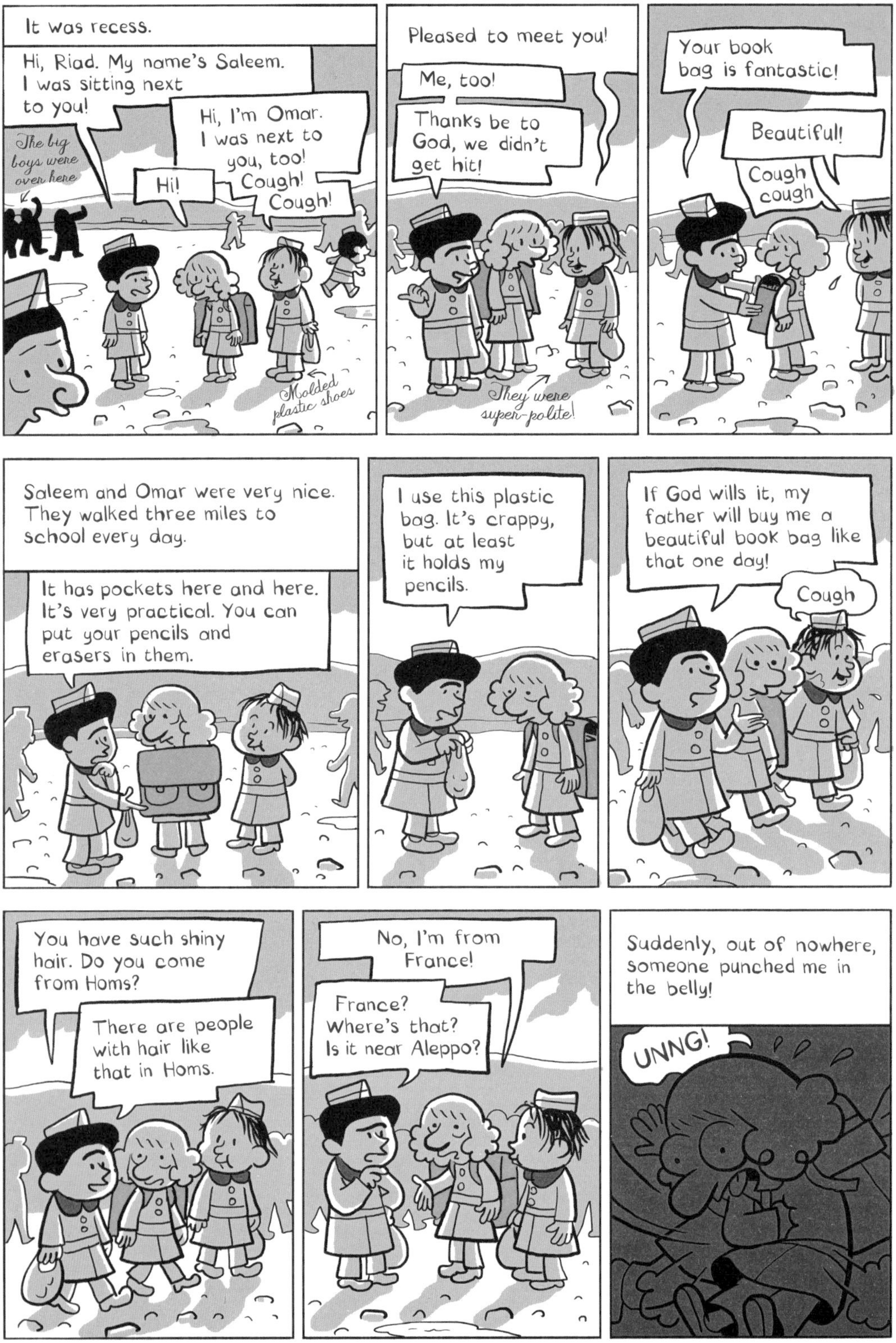
It was recess.
Hi, Riad. My name's Saleem. I was sitting next to you!
The big boys were over here
Hi!
Hi, I'm Omar. I was next to you, too! Cough! Cough!
Molded plastic shoes
Pleased to meet you!
Me, too!
Thanks be to God, we didn't get hit!
They were super-polite!
Your book bag is fantastic!
Beautiful!
Cough cough
Saleem and Omar were very nice. They walked three miles to school every day.
It has pockets here and here. It's very practical. You can put your pencils and erasers in them.
I use this plastic bag. It's crappy, but at least it holds my pencils.
If God wills it, my father will buy me a beautiful book bag like that one day!
Cough
You have such shiny hair. Do you come from Homs?
There are people with hair like that in Homs.
No, I'm from France!
France? Where's that? Is it near Aleppo?
Suddenly, out of nowhere, someone punched me in the belly!
UNNG!

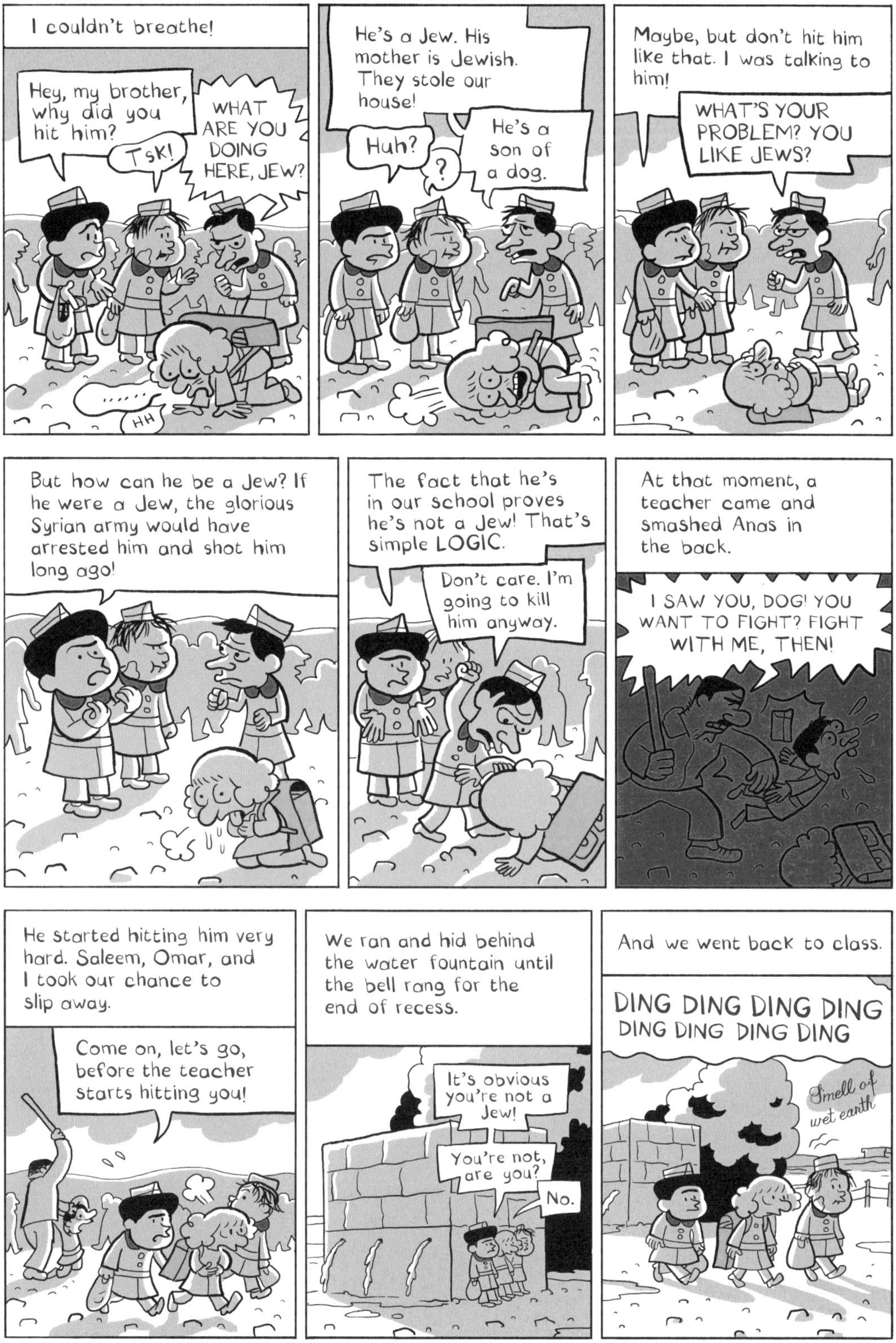
I couldn't breathe!
Hey, my brother, why did you hit him?
Tsk!
WHAT ARE YOU DOING HERE, JEW?
......
HH
He's a Jew. His mother is Jewish. They stole our house!
Huh?
?
He's a son of a dog.
Maybe, but don't hit him like that. I was talking to him!
WHAT'S YOUR PROBLEM? YOU LIKE JEWS?
But how can he be a Jew? If he were a Jew, the glorious Syrian army would have arrested him and shot him long ago!
The fact that he's in our school proves he's not a Jew! That's simple LOGIC.
Don't care. I'm going to kill him anyway.
At that moment, a teacher came and smashed Anas in the back.
I SAW YOU, DOG! YOU WANT TO FIGHT? FIGHT WITH ME, THEN!
He started hitting him very hard. Saleem, Omar, and I took our chance to slip away.
Come on, let's go, before the teacher starts hitting you!
We ran and hid behind the water fountain until the bell rang for the end of recess.
It's obvious you're not a Jew!
You're not, are you?
No.
And we went back to class.
DING DING DING DING
DING DING DING DING
Smell of wet earth

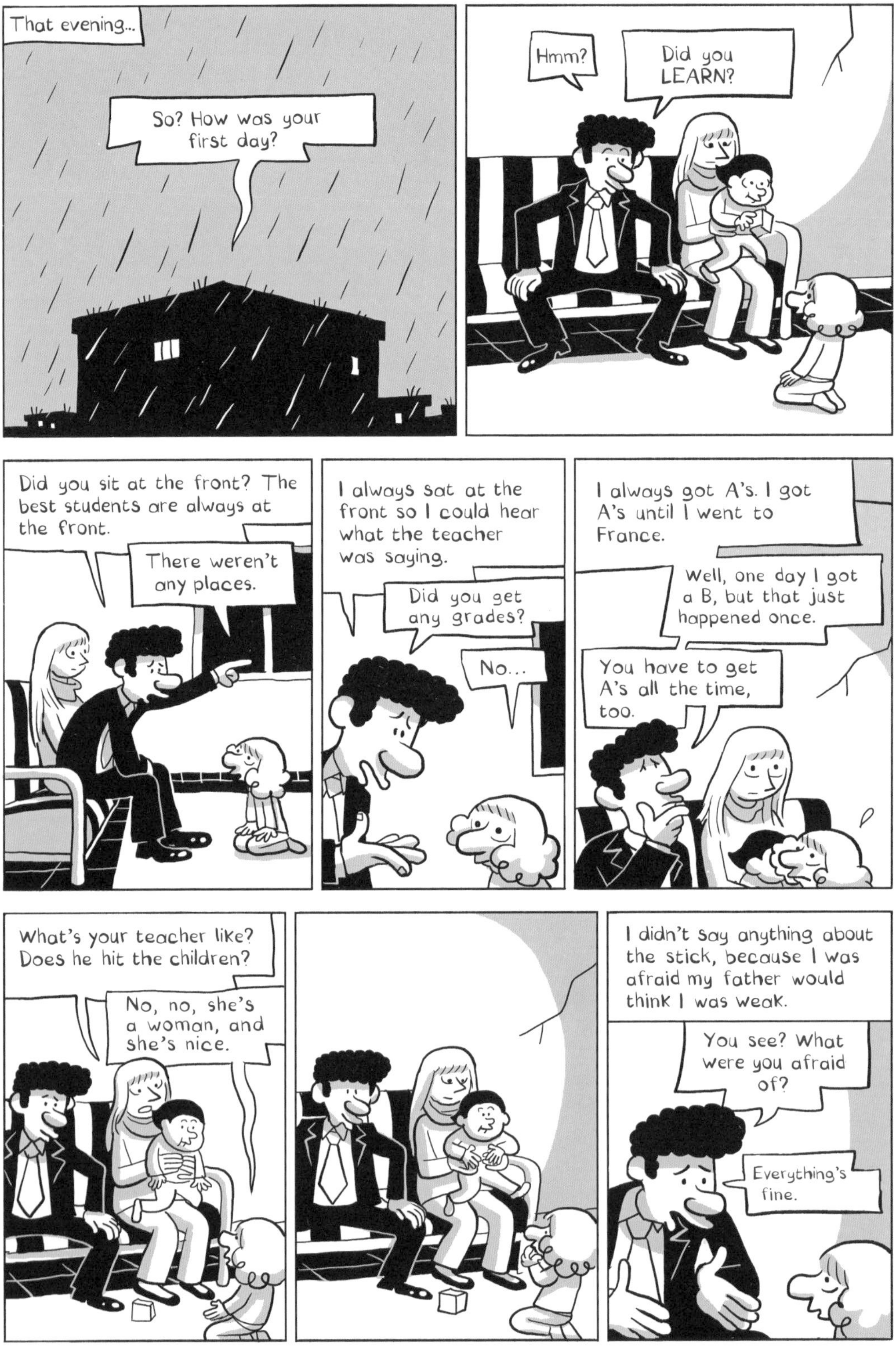
That evening...
So? How was your first day?
Hmm?
Did you LEARN?
Did you sit at the front? The best students are always at the front.
There weren't any places.
I always sat at the front so I could hear what the teacher was saying.
Did you get any grades?
No...
I always got A's. I got A's until I went to France.
Well, one day I got a B, but that just happened once.
You have to get A's all the time, too.
What's your teacher like? Does he hit the children?
No, no, she's a woman, and she's nice.
I didn't say anything about the stick, because I was afraid my father would think I was weak.
You see? What were you afraid of?
Everything's fine.

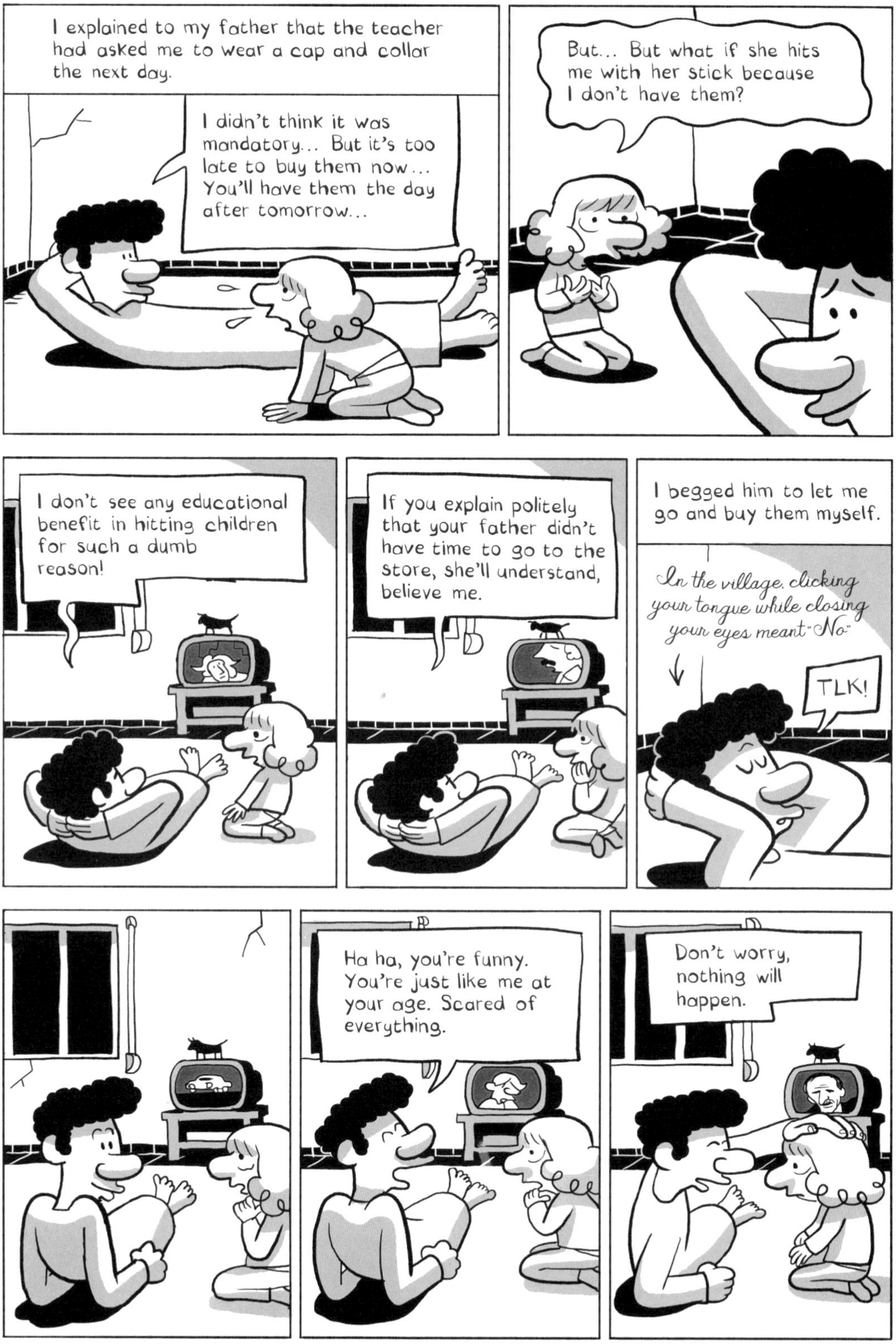
I explained to my father that the teacher had asked me to wear a cap and collar the next day.
I didn't think it was mandatory... But it's too late to buy them now... You'll have them the day after tomorrow...
But... But what if she hits me with her stick because I don't have them?
I don't see any educational benefit in hitting children for such a dumb reason!
If you explain politely that your father didn't have time to go to the store, she'll understand, believe me.
I begged him to let me go and buy them myself.
In the village, clicking your tongue while closing your eyes meant "No"
TLK!
Ha ha, you're funny. You're just like me at your age. Scared of everything.
Don't worry, nothing will happen.

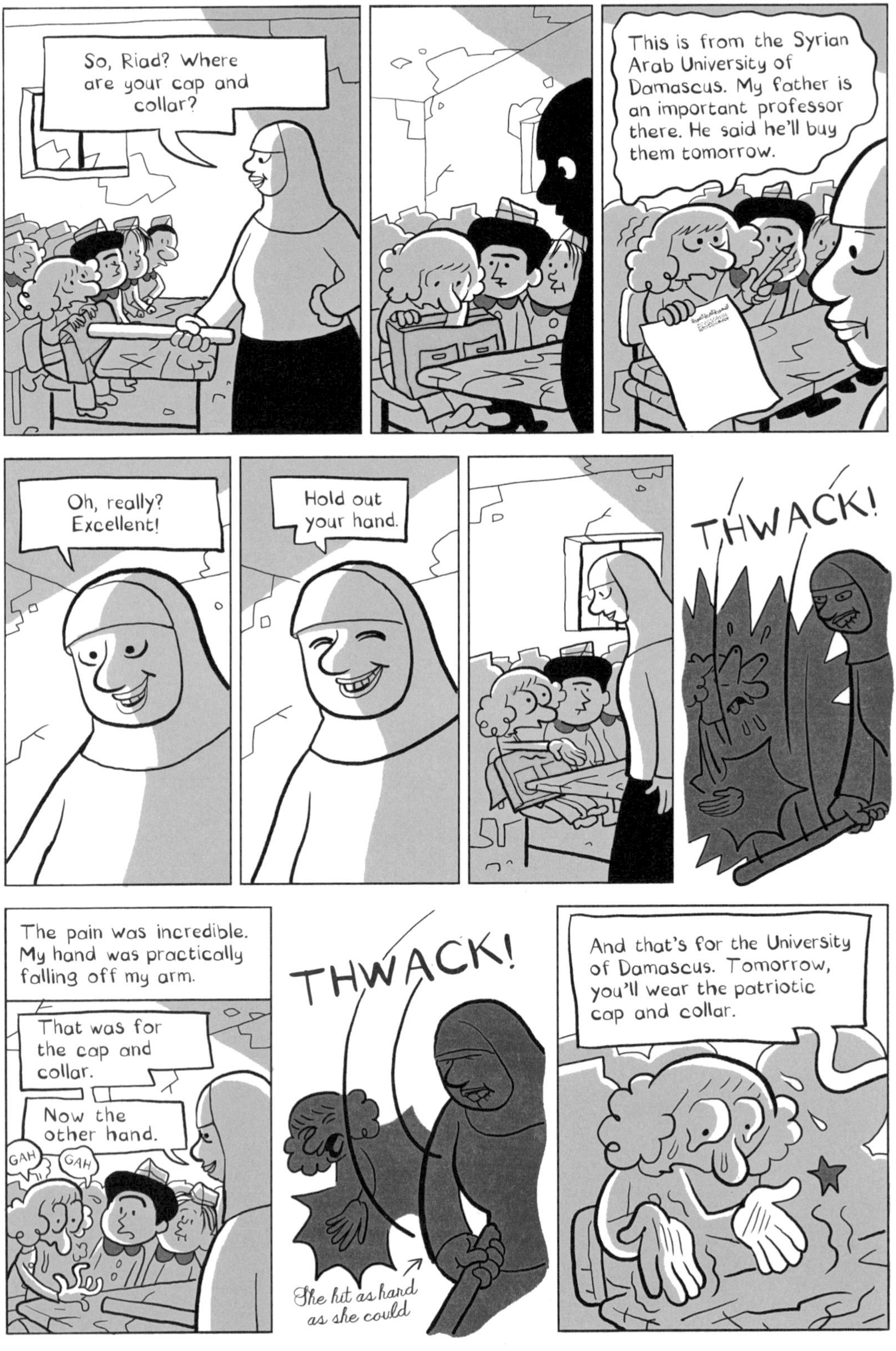
So, Riad? Where are your cap and collar?
This is from the Syrian Arab University of Damascus. My father is an important professor there. He said he'll buy them tomorrow.
Oh, really? Excellent!
Hold out your hand.
THWACK!
The pain was incredible. My hand was practically falling off my arm.
That was for the cap and collar.
Now the other hand.
GAH
GAH
THWACK!
She hit as hard as she could
And that's for the University of Damascus. Tomorrow, you'll wear the patriotic cap and collar.

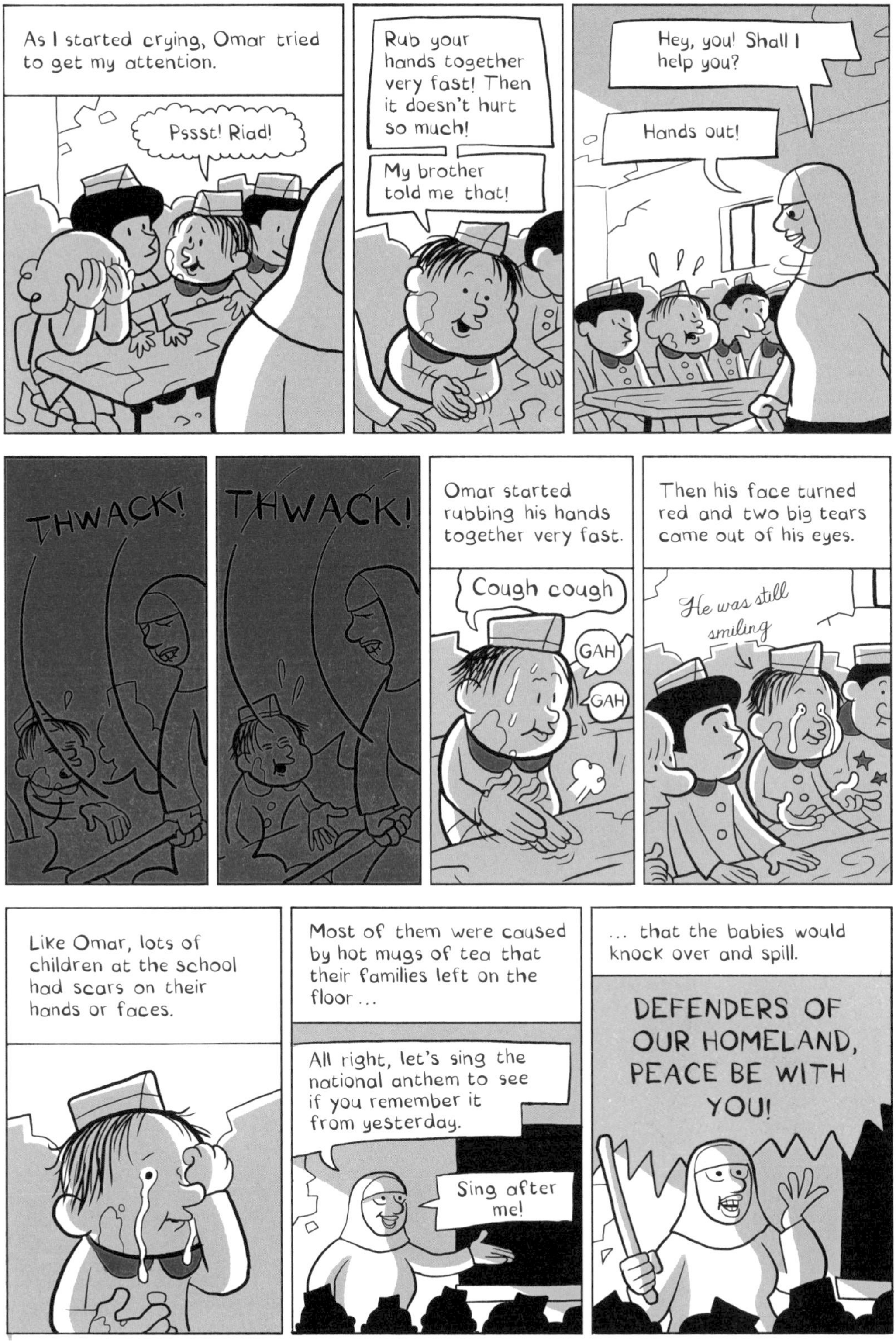
As I started crying, Omar tried to get my attention.
Pssst! Riad!
Rub your hands together very fast! Then it doesn't hurt so much!
My brother told me that!
Hey, you! Shall I help you?
Hands out!
THWACK!
THWACK!
Omar started rubbing his hands together very fast.
Cough cough
GAH
GAH
Then his face turned red and two big tears came out of his eyes.
He was still smiling
Like Omar, lots of children at the school had scars on their hands or faces.
Most of them were caused by hot mugs of tea that their families left on the floor ...
All right, let's sing the national anthem to see if you remember it from yesterday.
Sing after me!
... that the babies would knock over and spill.
DEFENDERS OF OUR HOMELAND, PEACE BE WITH YOU!

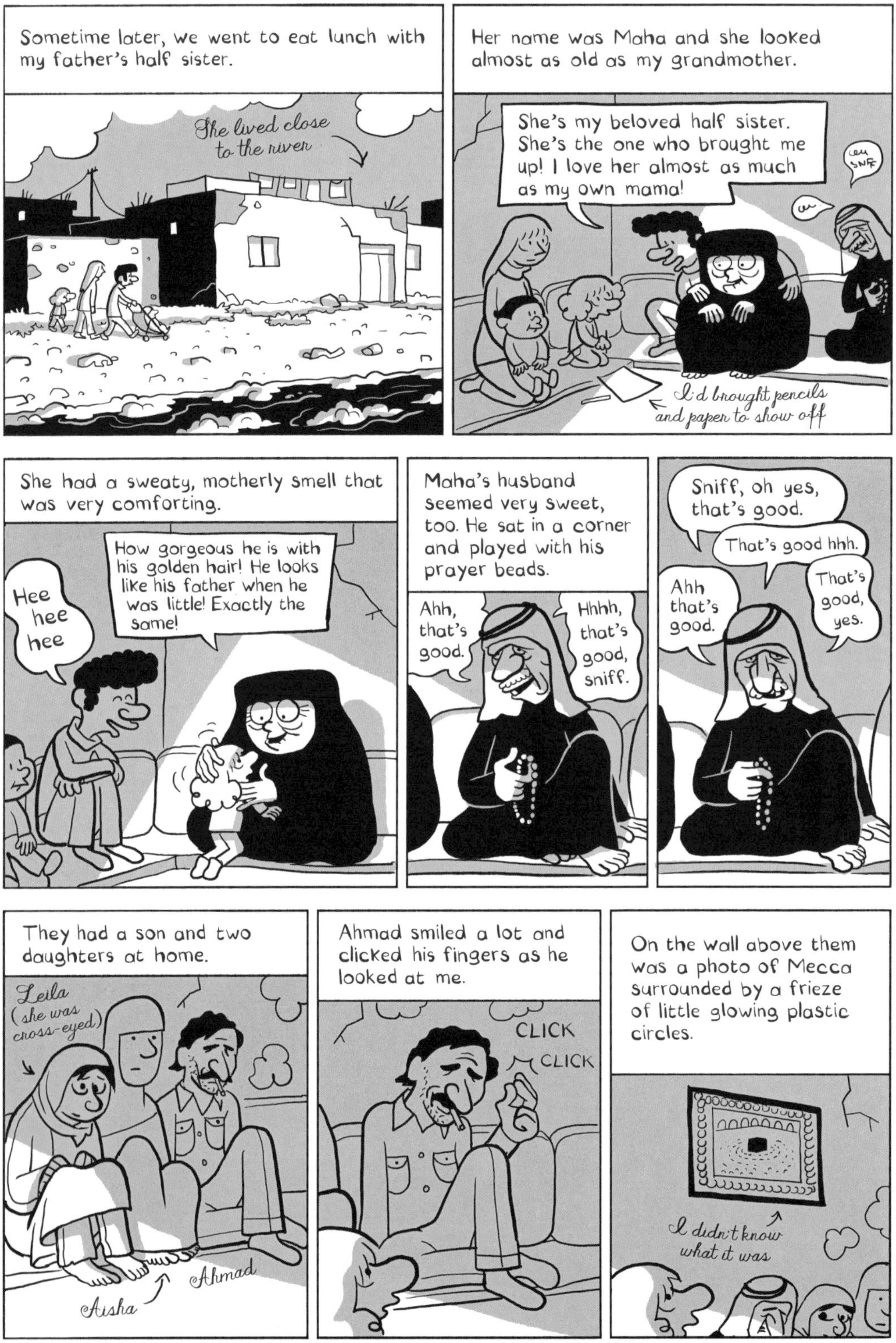
Sometime later, we went to eat lunch with my father's half sister.
She lived close to the river
Her name was Maha and she looked almost as old as my grandmother.
She's my beloved half sister. She's the one who brought me up! I love her almost as much as my own mama!
I'd brought pencils and paper to show off
She had a sweaty, motherly smell that was very comforting.
Hee hee hee
How gorgeous he is with his golden hair! He looks like his father when he was little! Exactly the same!
Maha's husband seemed very sweet, too. He sat in a corner and played with his prayer beads.
Ahh, that's good.
Hhhh, that's good, sniff.
Sniff, oh yes, that's good.
That's good hhh.
Ahh that's good.
That's good, yes.
They had a son and two daughters at home.
Leila (she was cross-eyed)
Aisha
Ahmad
Ahmad smiled a lot and clicked his fingers as he looked at me.
CLICK
CLICK
On the wall above them was a photo of Mecca surrounded by a frieze of little glowing plastic circles.
I didn't know what it was

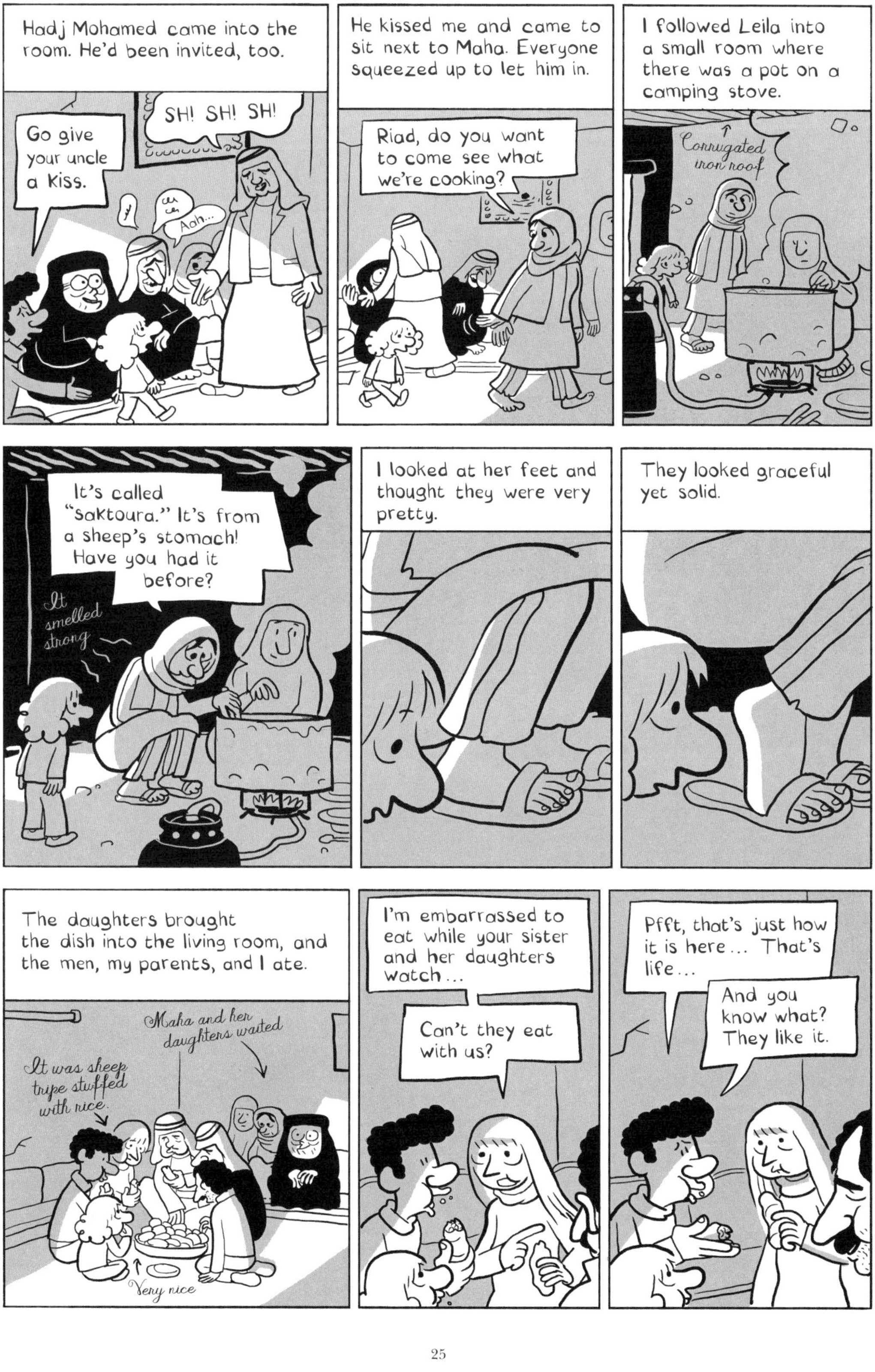
Hadj Mohamed came into the room. He'd been invited, too.
Go give your uncle a kiss.
SH! SH! SH!
Aah...
He kissed me and came to sit next to Maha. Everyone squeezed up to let him in.
Riad, do you want to come see what we're cooking?
I followed Leila into a small room where there was a pot on a camping stove.
Corrugated iron roof
It's called "saktoura." It's from a sheep's stomach! Have you had it before?
It smelled strong
I looked at her feet and thought they were very pretty.
They looked graceful yet solid.
The daughters brought the dish into the living room, and the men, my parents, and I ate.
Maha and her daughters waited
It was sheep tripe stuffed with rice.
Very nice
I'm embarrassed to eat while your sister and her daughters watch...
Can't they eat with us?
Pfft, that's just how it is here... That's life...
And you know what? They like it.

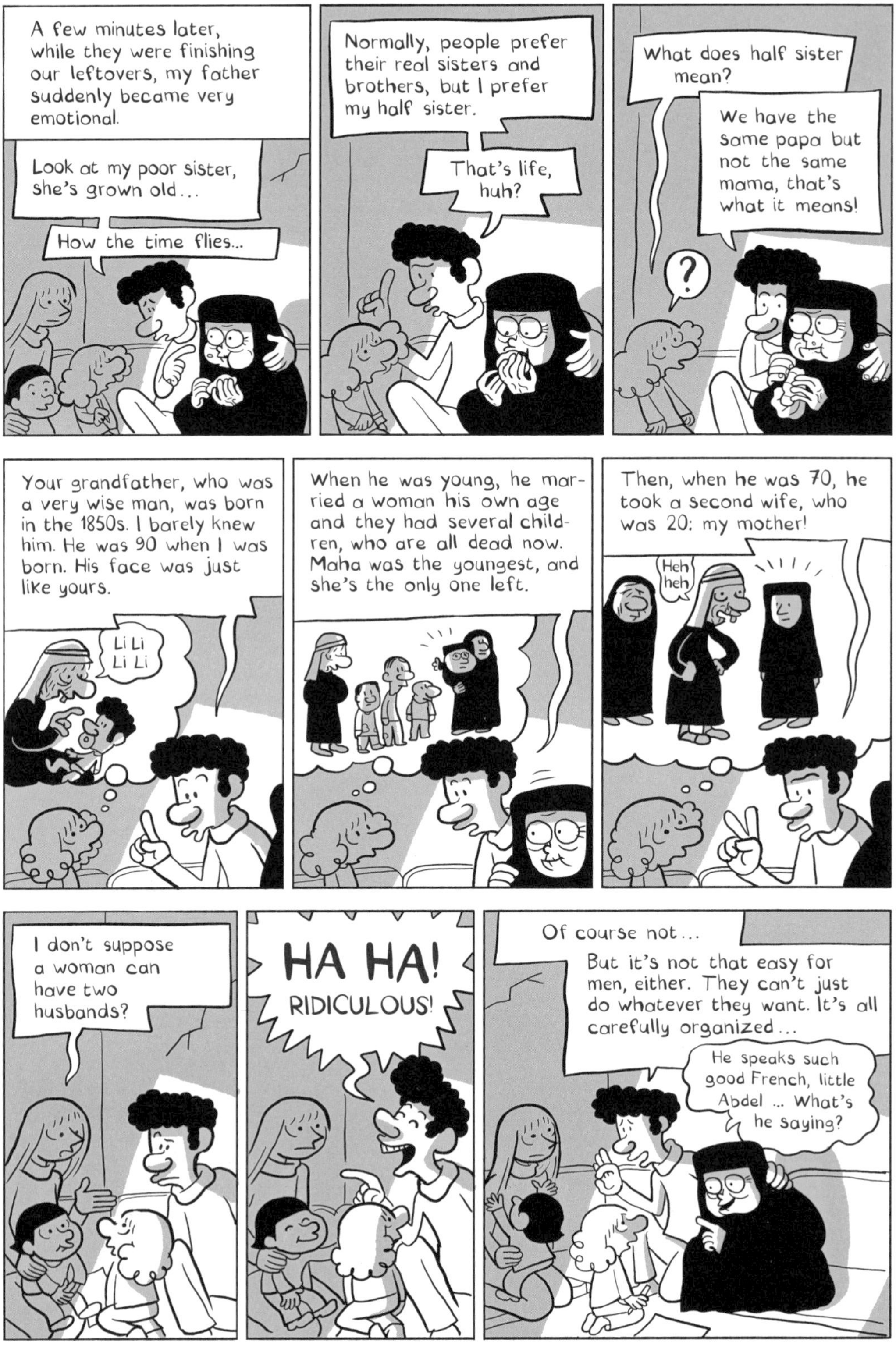
A few minutes later, while they were finishing our leftovers, my father suddenly became very emotional.
Look at my poor sister, she's grown old...
How the time flies...
Normally, people prefer their real sisters and brothers, but I prefer my half sister.
That's life, huh?
What does half sister mean?
?
We have the same papa but not the same mama, that's what it means!
Your grandfather, who was a very wise man, was born in the 1850s. I barely knew him. He was 90 when I was born. His face was just like yours.
Li Li Li Li
When he was young, he married a woman his own age and they had several children, who are all dead now. Maha was the youngest, and she's the only one left.
Then, when he was 70, he took a second wife, who was 20: my mother!
Heh heh
I don't suppose a woman can have two husbands?
HA HA!
RIDICULOUS!
Of course not...
But it's not that easy for men, either. They can't just do whatever they want. It's all carefully organized...
He speaks such good French, little Abdel ... What's he saying?

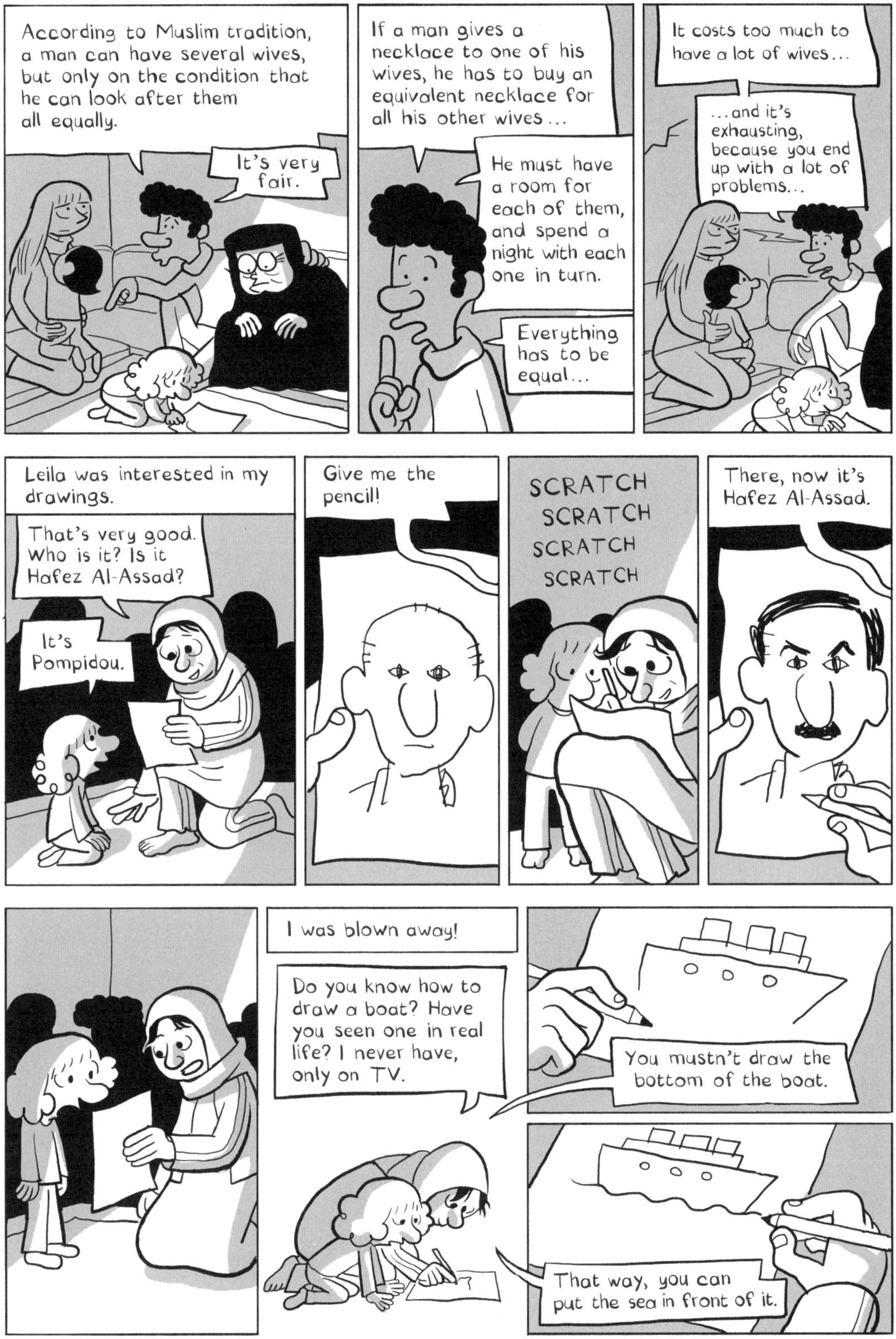
According to Muslim tradition, a man can have several wives, but only on the condition that he can look after them all equally.
It's very fair.
If a man gives a necklace to one of his wives, he has to buy an equivalent necklace for all his other wives...
He must have a room for each of them, and spend a night with each one in turn.
Everything has to be equal...
It costs too much to have a lot of wives...
...and it's exhausting, because you end up with a lot of problems...
Leila was interested in my drawings.
That's very good. Who is it? Is it Hafez Al-Assad?
It's Pompidou.
Give me the pencil!
SCRATCH
SCRATCH
SCRATCH
SCRATCH
There, now it's Hafez Al-Assad.
I was blown away!
Do you know how to draw a boat? Have you seen one in real life? I never have, only on TV.
You mustn't draw the bottom of the boat.
That way, you can put the sea in front of it.

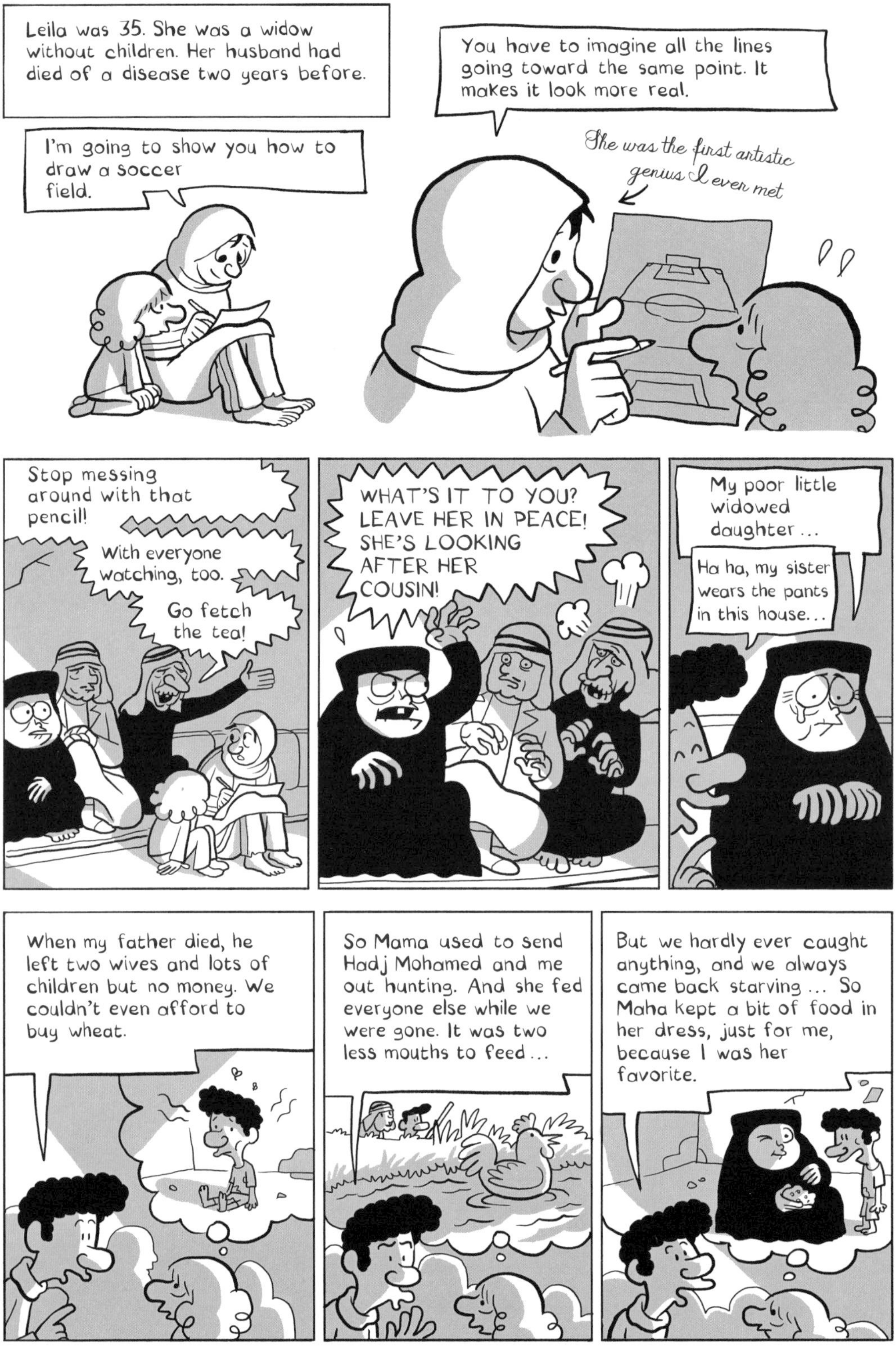
Leila was 35. She was a widow without children. Her husband had died of a disease two years before.
I'm going to show you how to draw a soccer field.
You have to imagine all the lines going toward the same point. It makes it look more real.
She was the first artistic genius I ever met
Stop messing around with that pencil!
With everyone watching, too.
Go fetch the tea!
WHAT'S IT TO YOU? LEAVE HER IN PEACE! SHE'S LOOKING AFTER HER COUSIN!
My poor little widowed daughter...
Ha ha, my sister wears the pants in this house...
When my father died, he left two wives and lots of children but no money. We couldn't even afford to buy wheat.
So Mama used to send Hadj Mohamed and me out hunting. And she fed everyone else while we were gone. It was two less mouths to feed...
But we hardly ever caught anything, and we always came back starving... So Maha kept a bit of food in her dress, just for me, because I was her favorite.

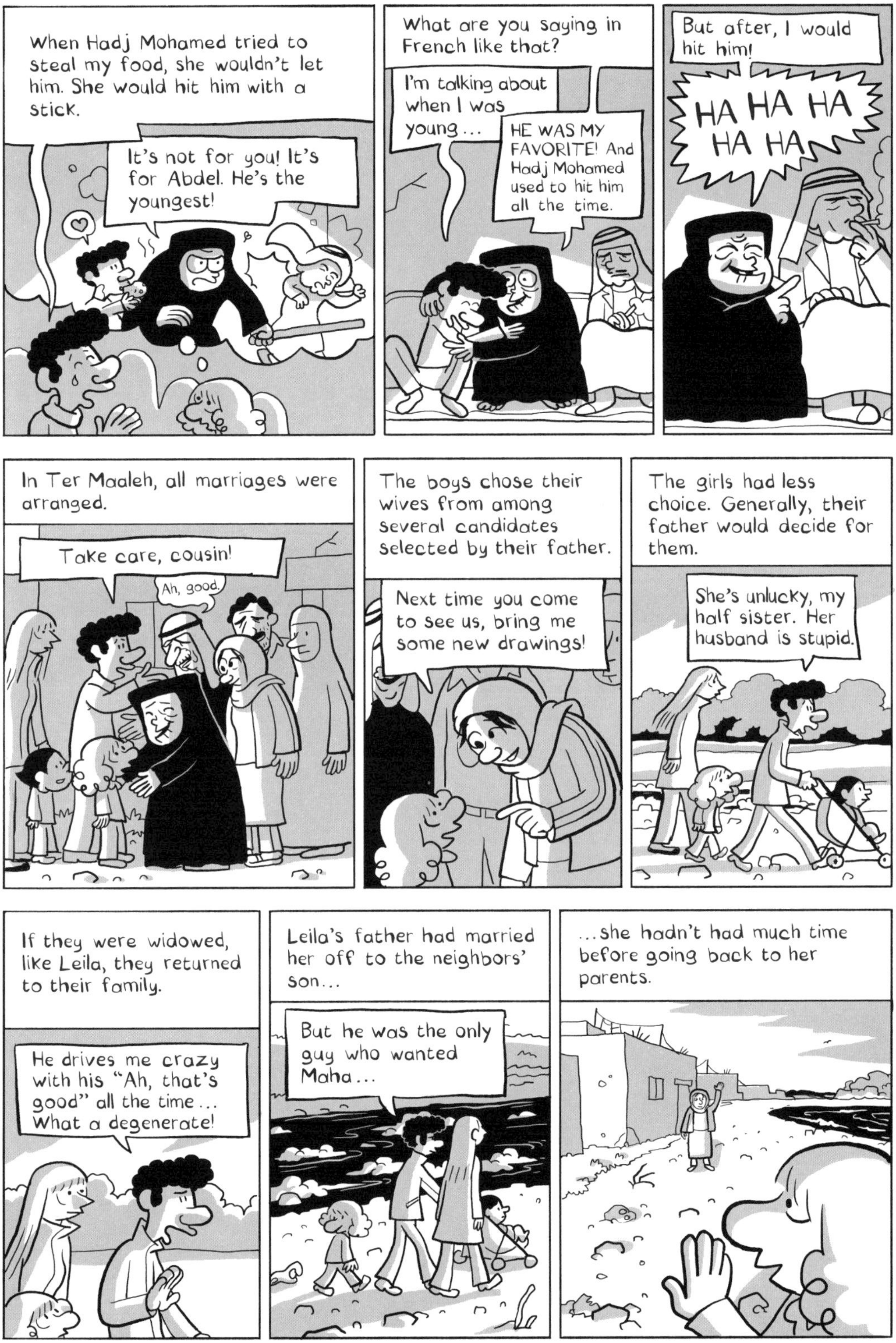
When Hadj Mohamed tried to steal my food, she wouldn't let him. She would hit him with a stick.
It's not for you! It's for Abdel. He's the youngest!
What are you saying in French like that?
I'm talking about when I was young...
HE WAS MY FAVORITE! And Hadj Mohamed used to hit him all the time.
But after, I would hit him!
HA HA HA HA HA
In Ter Maaleh, all marriages were arranged.
Take care, cousin!
Ah, good.
The boys chose their wives from among several candidates selected by their father.
Next time you come to see us, bring me some new drawings!
The girls had less choice. Generally, their father would decide for them.
She's unlucky, my half sister. Her husband is stupid.
If they were widowed, like Leila, they returned to their family.
He drives me crazy with his "Ah, that's good" all the time... What a degenerate!
Leila's father had married her off to the neighbors' son...
But he was the only guy who wanted Maha...
...she hadn't had much time before going back to her parents.

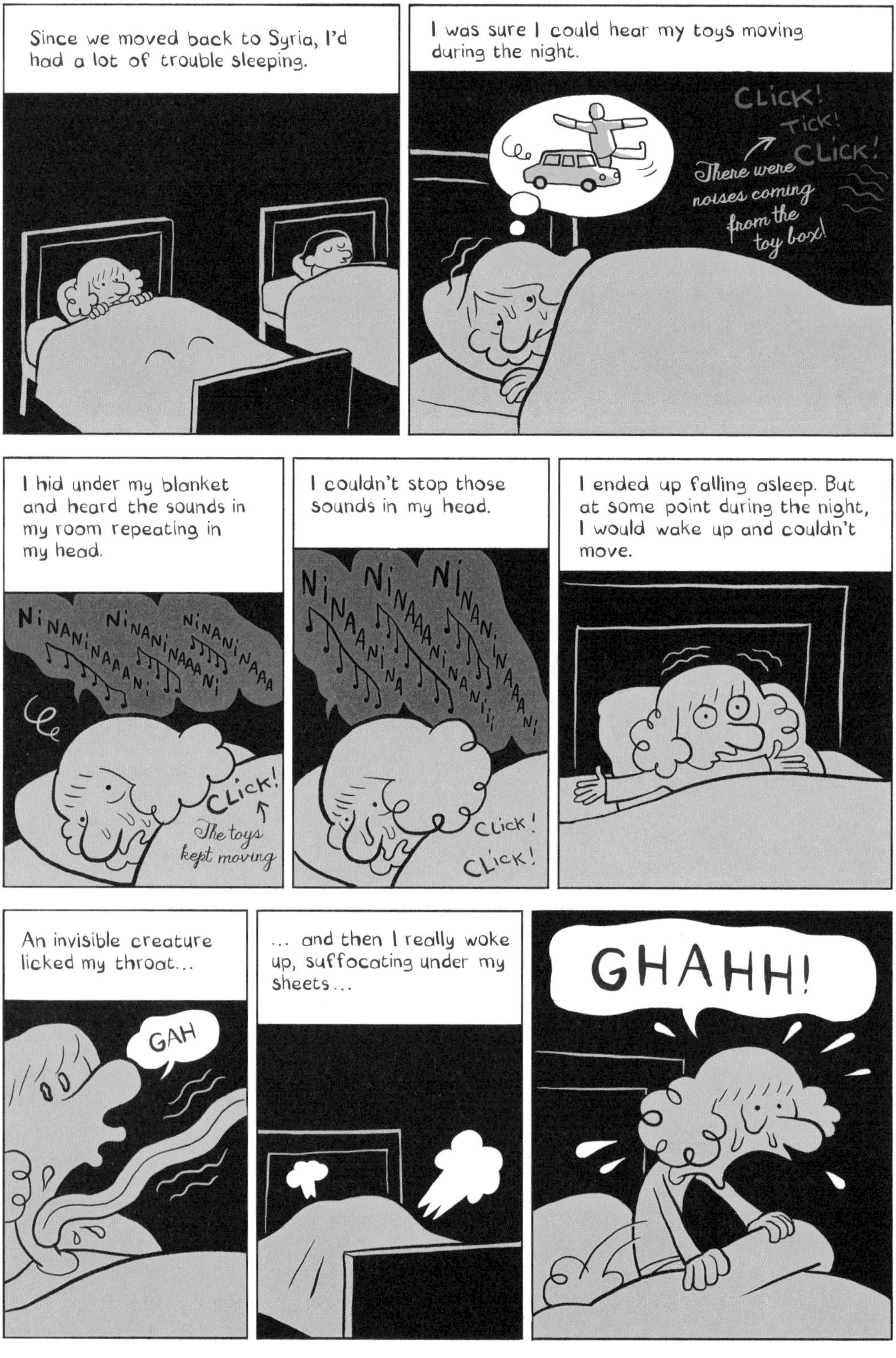

Since we moved back to Syria, I'd had a lot of trouble sleeping.
I was sure I could hear my toys moving during the night.
CLICK! TICK! CLICK!
There were noises coming from the toy box!
I hid under my blanket and heard the sounds in my room repeating in my head.
NiNANiNAAANi NiNANiNAAANi NiNANiNAAA
CLICK!
The toys kept moving
I couldn't stop those sounds in my head.
NiNAANiNA NiNAAANiNANiii NiNANiNAAANi
CLICK! CLICK!
I ended up falling asleep. But at some point during the night, I would wake up and couldn't move.
An invisible creature licked my throat...
GAH
... and then I really woke up, suffocating under my sheets...
GHAHH!

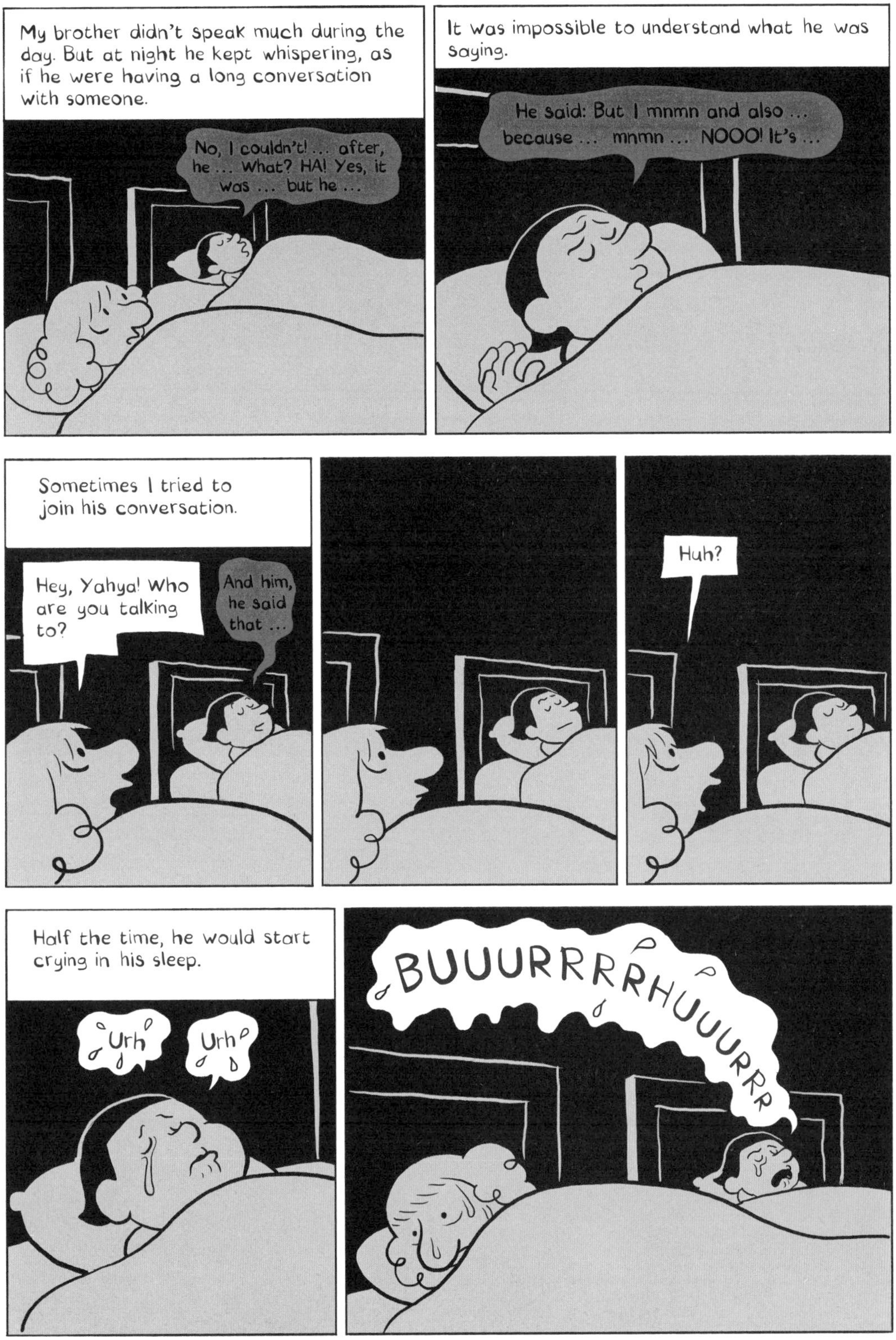
My brother didn't speak much during the day. But at night he kept whispering, as if he were having a long conversation with someone.
No, I couldn't! ... after, he ... What? HA! Yes, it was ... but he ...
It was impossible to understand what he was saying.
He said: But I mnmn and also ... because ... mnmn ... NOOO! It's ...
Sometimes I tried to join his conversation.
Hey, Yahya! Who are you talking to?
And him, he said that ...
Huh?
Half the time, he would start crying in his sleep.
Urh
Urh
BUUURRRRHUUURRR

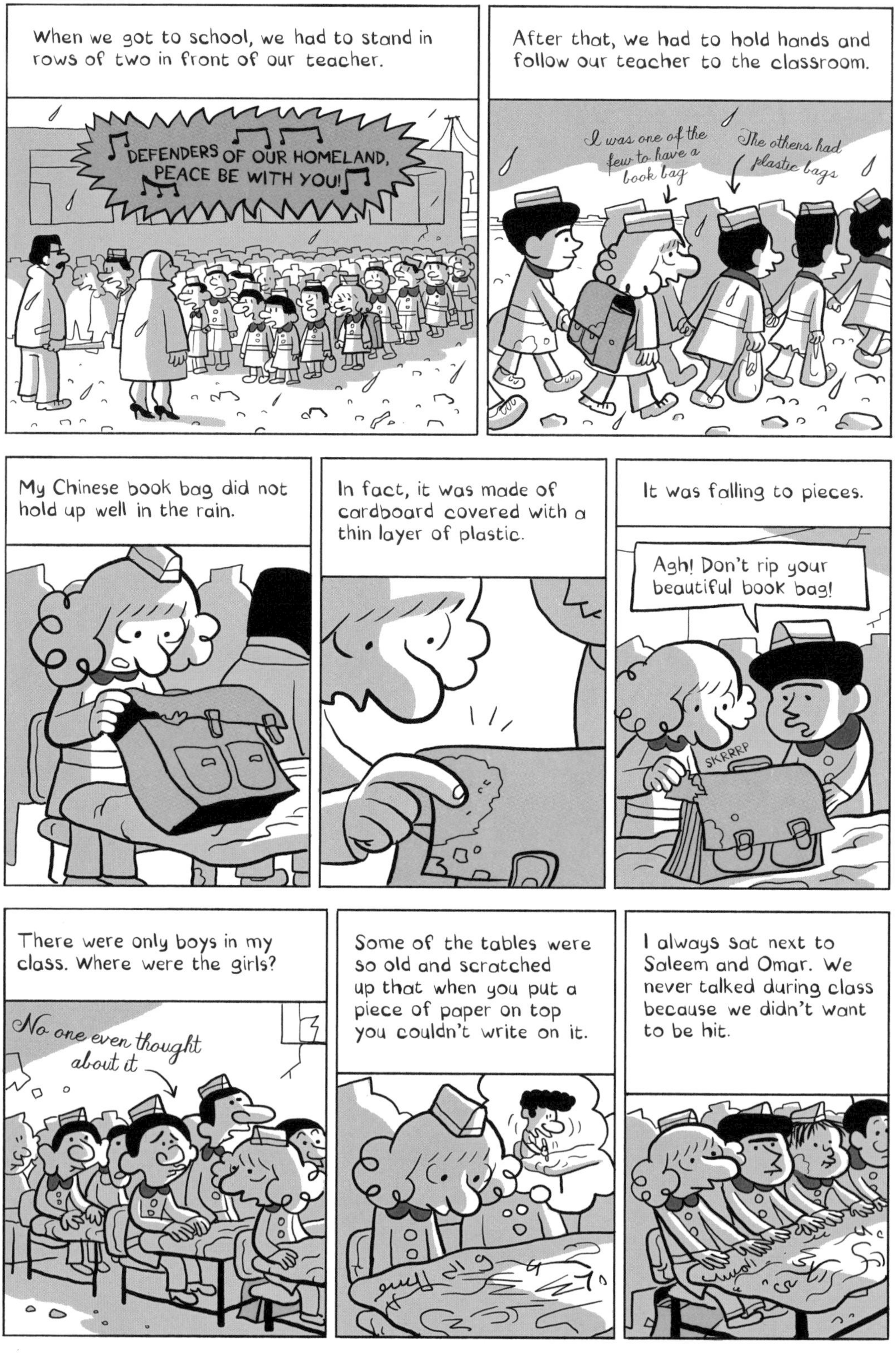
When we got to school, we had to stand in rows of two in front of our teacher.
DEFENDERS OF OUR HOMELAND, PEACE BE WITH YOU!
After that, we had to hold hands and follow our teacher to the classroom.
I was one of the few to have a book bag
The others had plastic bags
My Chinese book bag did not hold up well in the rain.
In fact, it was made of cardboard covered with a thin layer of plastic.
It was falling to pieces.
Agh! Don't rip your beautiful book bag!
SKRRRP
There were only boys in my class. Where were the girls?
No one even thought about it
Some of the tables were so old and scratched up that when you put a piece of paper on top you couldn't write on it.
I always sat next to Saleem and Omar. We never talked during class because we didn't want to be hit.

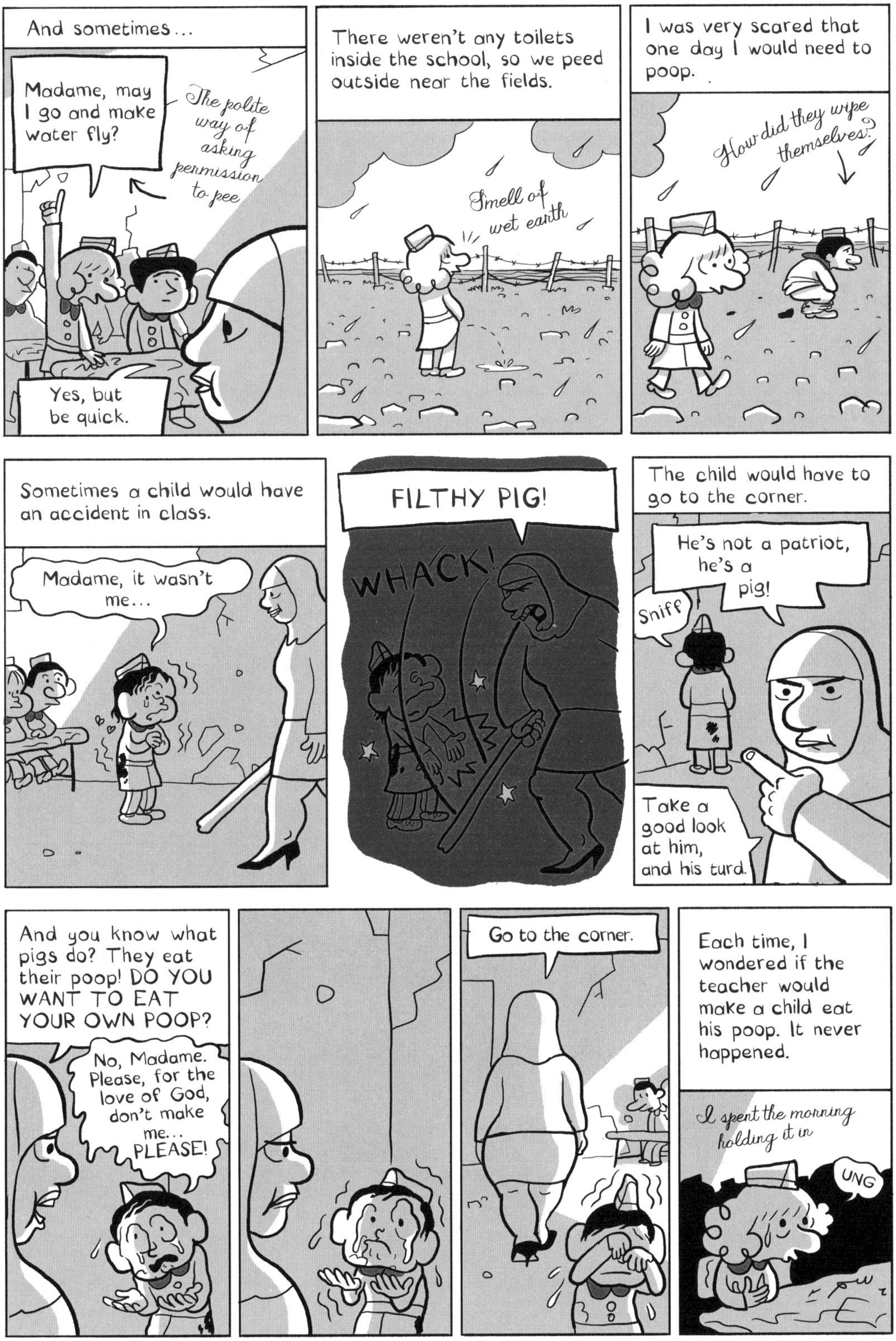

And sometimes...
Madame, may I go and make water fly?
The polite way of asking permission to pee
Yes, but be quick.
There weren't any toilets inside the school, so we peed outside near the fields.
Smell of wet earth
I was very scared that one day I would need to poop.
How did they wipe themselves?
Sometimes a child would have an accident in class.
Madame, it wasn't me...
FILTHY PIG!
WHACK!
The child would have to go to the corner.
He's not a patriot, he's a pig!
Sniff
Take a good look at him, and his turd.
And you know what pigs do? They eat their poop! DO YOU WANT TO EAT YOUR OWN POOP?
No, Madame. Please, for the love of God, don't make me... PLEASE!
Go to the corner.
Each time, I wondered if the teacher would make a child eat his poop. It never happened.
I spent the morning holding it in
UNG

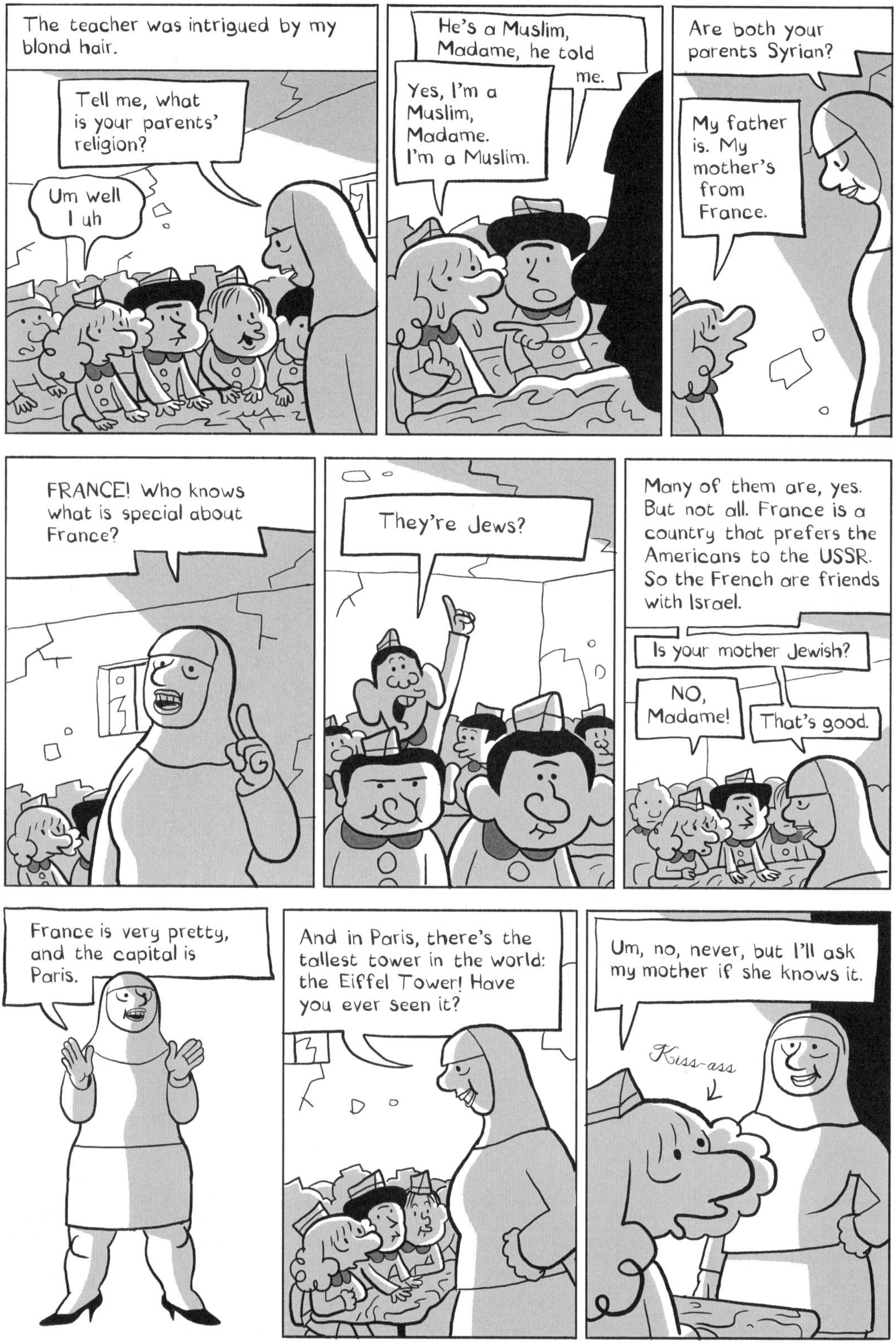

The teacher was intrigued by my blond hair.
Tell me, what is your parents' religion?
Um well I uh
He's a Muslim, Madame, he told me.
Yes, I'm a Muslim, Madame. I'm a Muslim.
Are both your parents Syrian?
My father is. My mother's from France.
FRANCE! Who knows what is special about France?
They're Jews?
Many of them are, yes. But not all. France is a country that prefers the Americans to the USSR. So the French are friends with Israel.
Is your mother Jewish?
NO, Madame!
That's good.
France is very pretty, and the capital is Paris.
And in Paris, there's the tallest tower in the world: the Eiffel Tower! Have you ever seen it?
Um, no, never, but I'll ask my mother if she knows it.
Kiss-ass

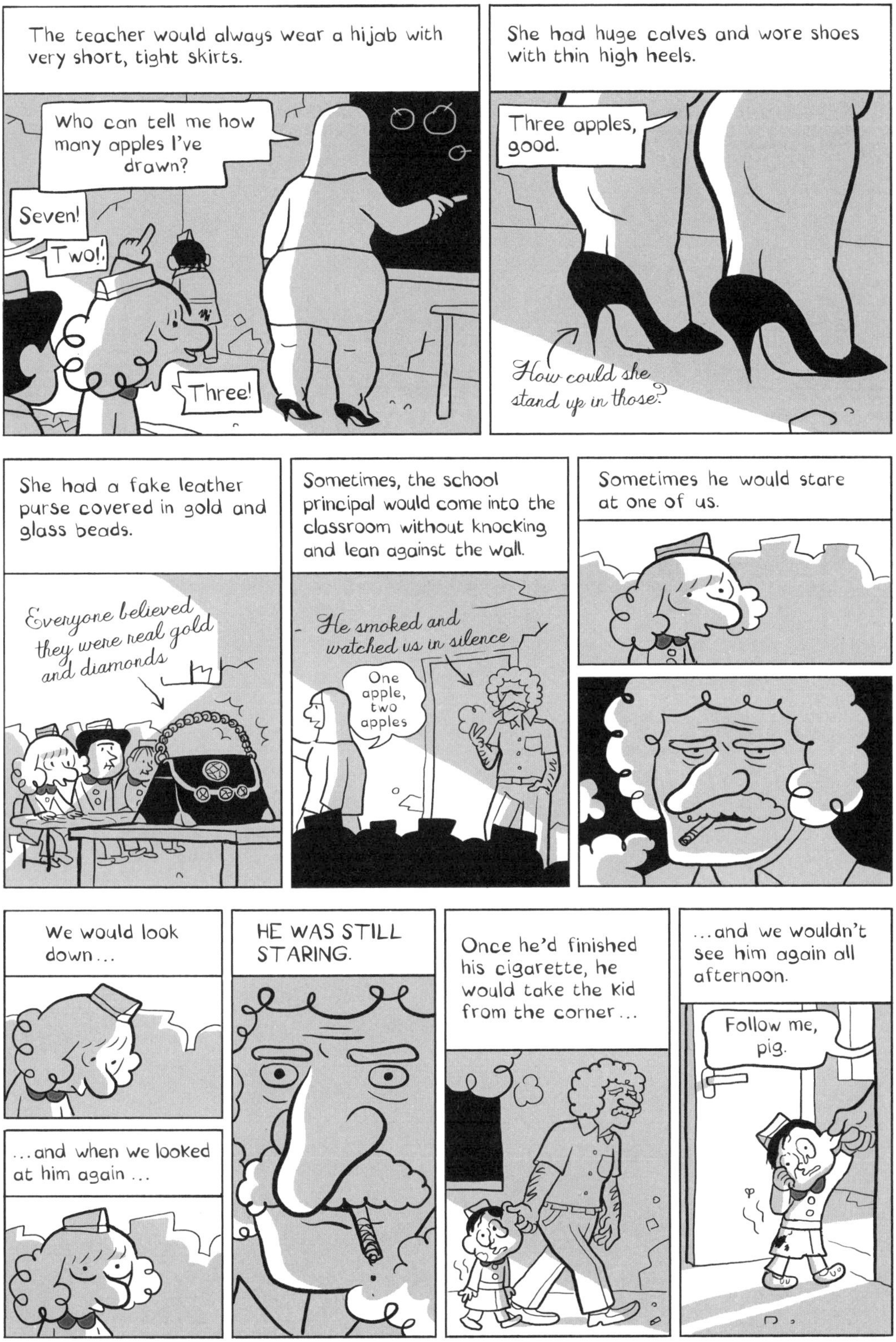
The teacher would always wear a hijab with very short, tight skirts.
Who can tell me how many apples I've drawn?
Seven!
Two!
Three!
She had huge calves and wore shoes with thin high heels.
Three apples, good.
How could she stand up in those?
She had a fake leather purse covered in gold and glass beads.
Everyone believed they were real gold and diamonds
Sometimes, the school principal would come into the classroom without knocking and lean against the wall.
He smoked and watched us in silence
One apple, two apples
Sometimes he would stare at one of us.
We would look down...
...and when we looked at him again...
HE WAS STILL STARING.
Once he'd finished his cigarette, he would take the kid from the corner...
...and we wouldn't see him again all afternoon.
Follow me, pig.

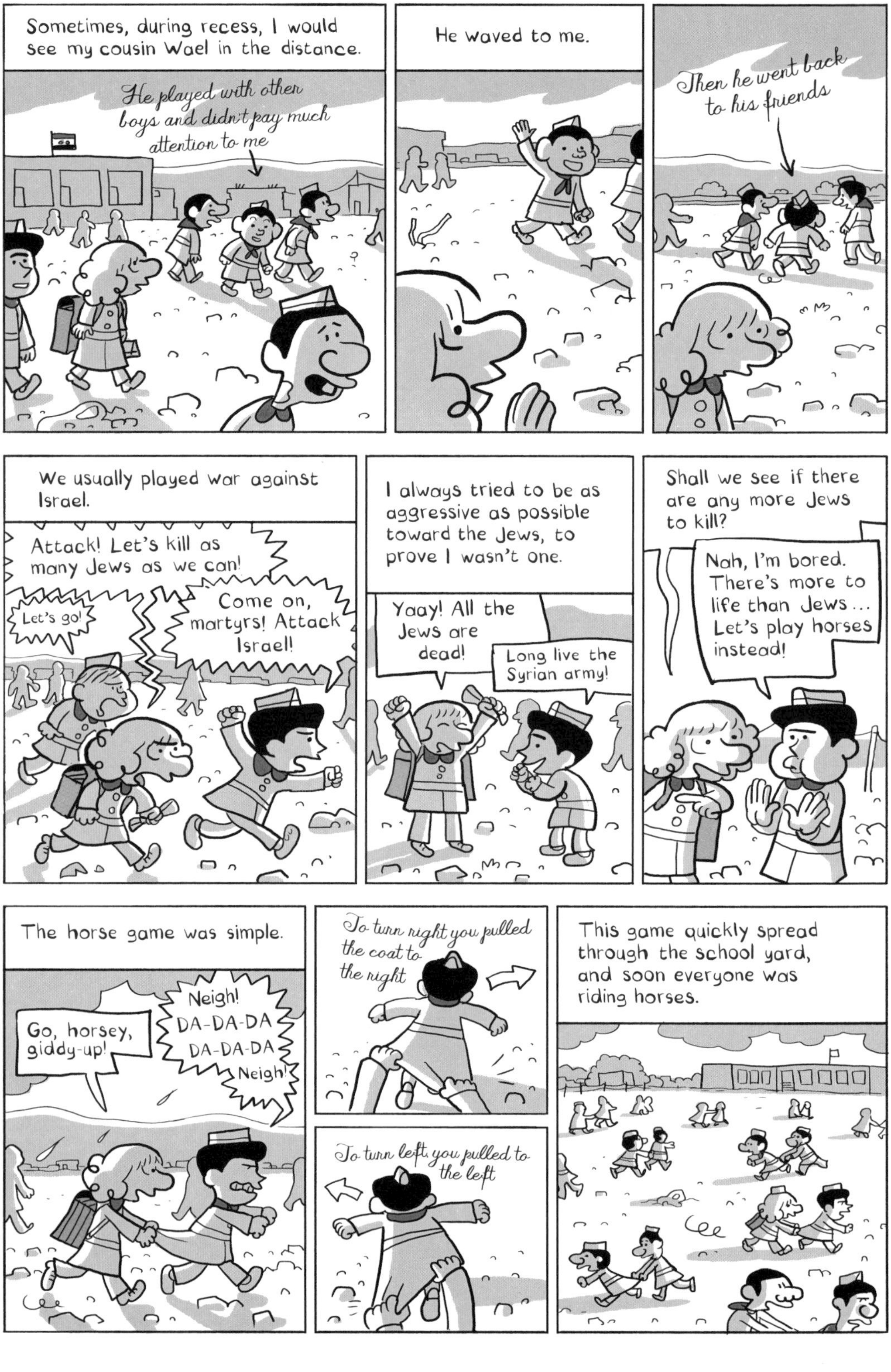
Sometimes, during recess, I would see my cousin Wael in the distance.
He played with other boys and didn't pay much attention to me
He waved to me.
Then he went back to his friends
We usually played war against Israel.
Attack! Let's kill as many Jews as we can!
Let's go!
Come on, martyrs! Attack Israel!
I always tried to be as aggressive as possible toward the Jews, to prove I wasn't one.
Yaay! All the Jews are dead!
Long live the Syrian army!
Shall we see if there are any more Jews to kill?
Nah, I'm bored. There's more to life than Jews... Let's play horses instead!
The horse game was simple.
Go, horsey, giddy-up!
Neigh! DA-DA-DA DA-DA-DA Neigh!
To turn right you pulled the coat to the right
To turn left, you pulled to the left
This game quickly spread through the school yard, and soon everyone was riding horses.

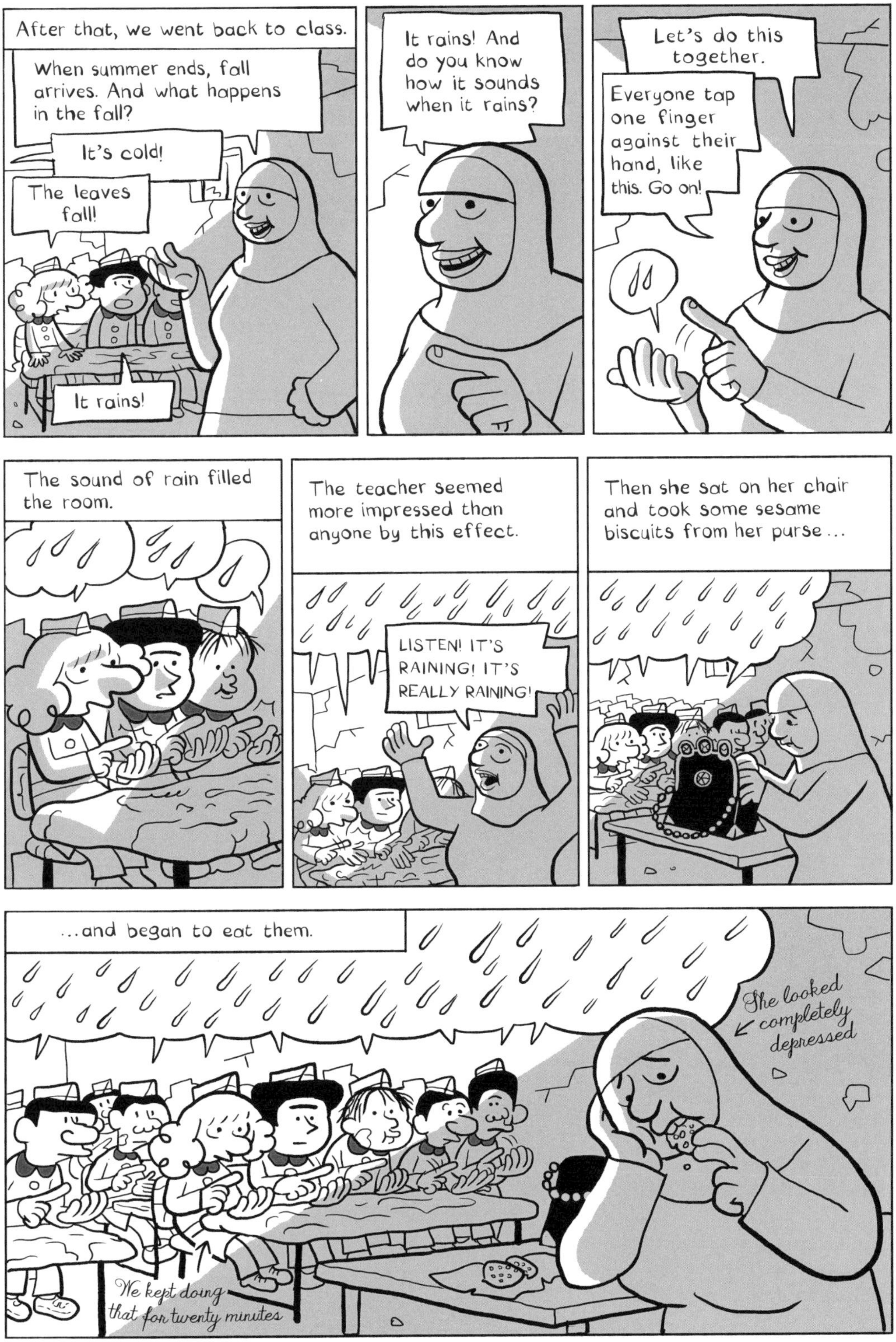

After that, we went back to class.
When summer ends, fall arrives. And what happens in the fall?
It's cold!
The leaves fall!
It rains!
It rains! And do you know how it sounds when it rains?
Let's do this together.
Everyone tap one finger against their hand, like this. Go on!
The sound of rain filled the room.
The teacher seemed more impressed than anyone by this effect.
LISTEN! IT'S RAINING! IT'S REALLY RAINING!
Then she sat on her chair and took some sesame biscuits from her purse...
...and began to eat them.
She looked completely depressed
We kept doing that for twenty minutes

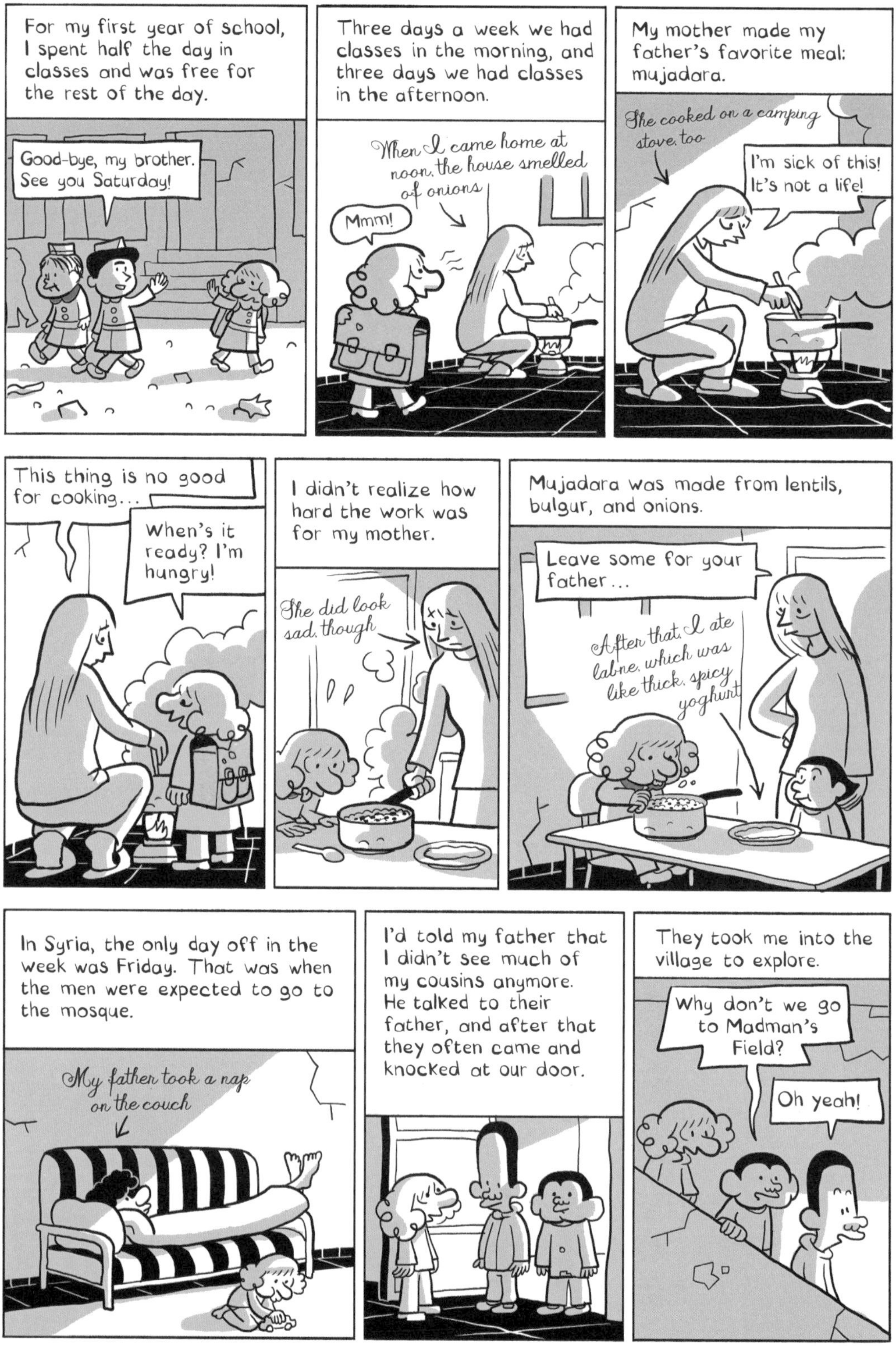
For my first year of school, I spent half the day in classes and was free for the rest of the day.
Good-bye, my brother. See you Saturday!
Three days a week we had classes in the morning, and three days we had classes in the afternoon.
When I came home at noon, the house smelled of onions
Mmm!
My mother made my father's favorite meal: mujadara.
She cooked on a camping stove, too
I'm sick of this! It's not a life!
This thing is no good for cooking...
When's it ready? I'm hungry!
I didn't realize how hard the work was for my mother.
She did look sad, though
Mujadara was made from lentils, bulgur, and onions.
Leave some for your father...
After that, I ate labne, which was like thick, spicy yoghurt
In Syria, the only day off in the week was Friday. That was when the men were expected to go to the mosque.
My father took a nap on the couch
I'd told my father that I didn't see much of my cousins anymore. He talked to their father, and after that they often came and knocked at our door.
They took me into the village to explore.
Why don't we go to Madman's Field?
Oh yeah!

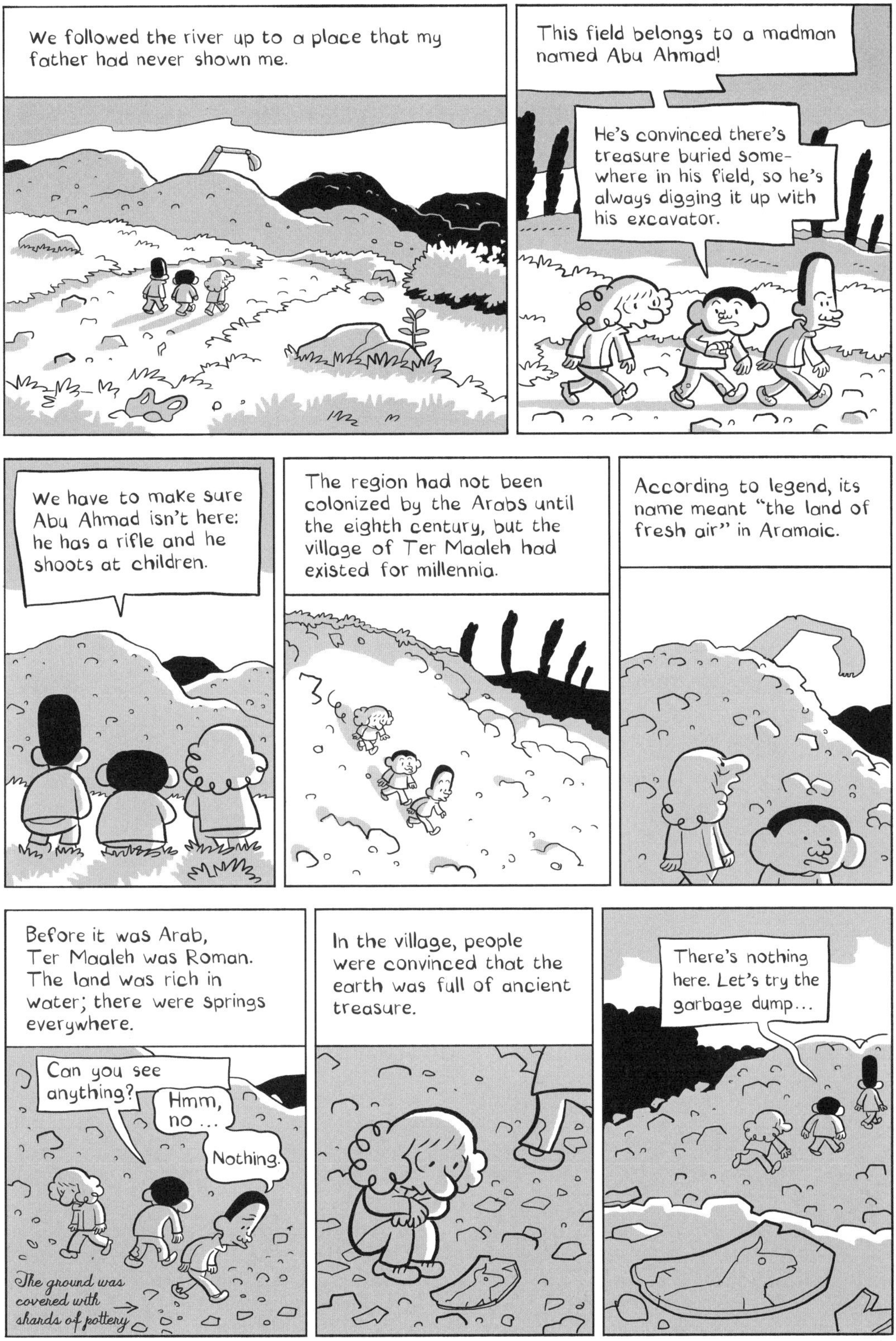
We followed the river up to a place that my father had never shown me.
This field belongs to a madman named Abu Ahmad!
He's convinced there's treasure buried somewhere in his field, so he's always digging it up with his excavator.
We have to make sure Abu Ahmad isn't here: he has a rifle and he shoots at children.
The region had not been colonized by the Arabs until the eighth century, but the village of Ter Maaleh had existed for millennia.
According to legend, its name meant "the land of fresh air" in Aramaic.
Before it was Arab, Ter Maaleh was Roman. The land was rich in water; there were springs everywhere.
Can you see anything?
Hmm, no...
Nothing.
The ground was covered with shards of pottery
In the village, people were convinced that the earth was full of ancient treasure.
There's nothing here. Let's try the garbage dump...

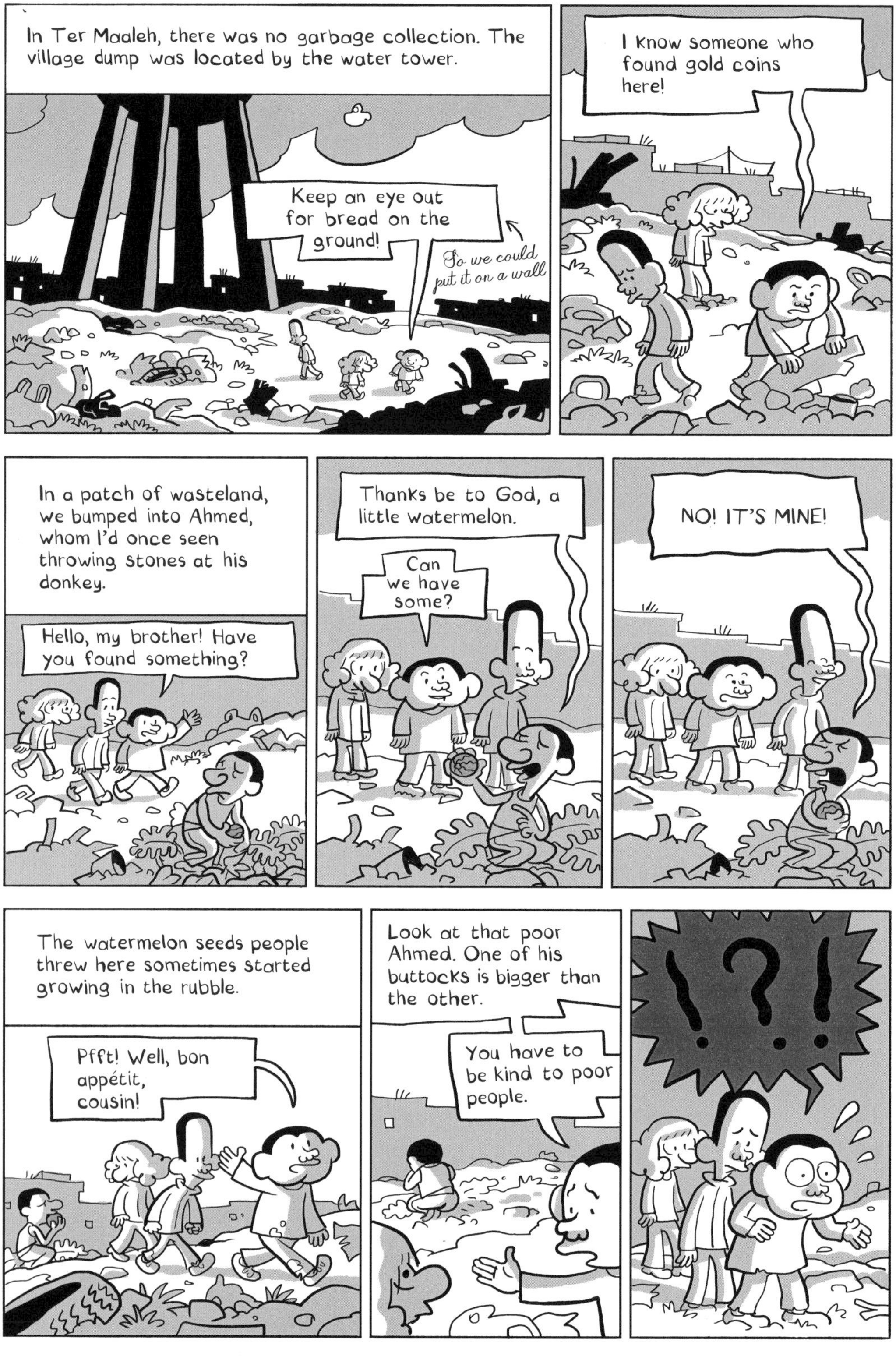
In Ter Maaleh, there was no garbage collection. The village dump was located by the water tower.
Keep an eye out for bread on the ground!
So we could put it on a wall
I know someone who found gold coins here!
In a patch of wasteland, we bumped into Ahmed, whom I'd once seen throwing stones at his donkey.
Hello, my brother! Have you found something?
Thanks be to God, a little watermelon.
Can we have some?
NO! IT'S MINE!
The watermelon seeds people threw here sometimes started growing in the rubble.
Pfft! Well, bon appétit, cousin!
Look at that poor Ahmed. One of his buttocks is bigger than the other.
You have to be kind to poor people.
!?!

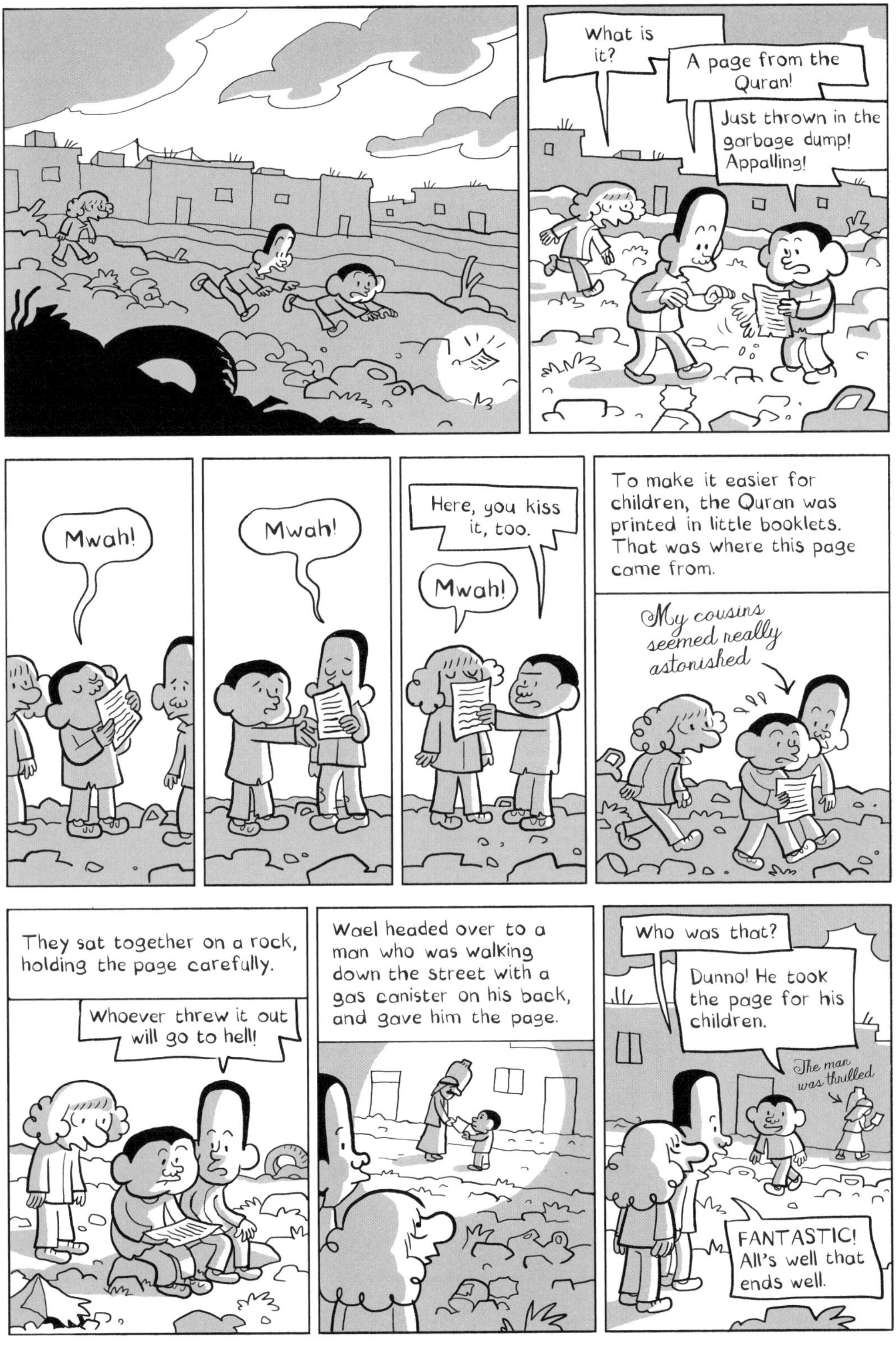
What is it?
A page from the Quran!
Just thrown in the garbage dump! Appalling!
Mwah!
Mwah!
Here, you kiss it, too.
Mwah!
To make it easier for children, the Quran was printed in little booklets. That was where this page came from.
My cousins seemed really astonished
They sat together on a rock, holding the page carefully.
Whoever threw it out will go to hell!
Wael headed over to a man who was walking down the street with a gas canister on his back, and gave him the page.
Who was that?
Dunno! He took the page for his children.
The man was thrilled
FANTASTIC! All's well that ends well.

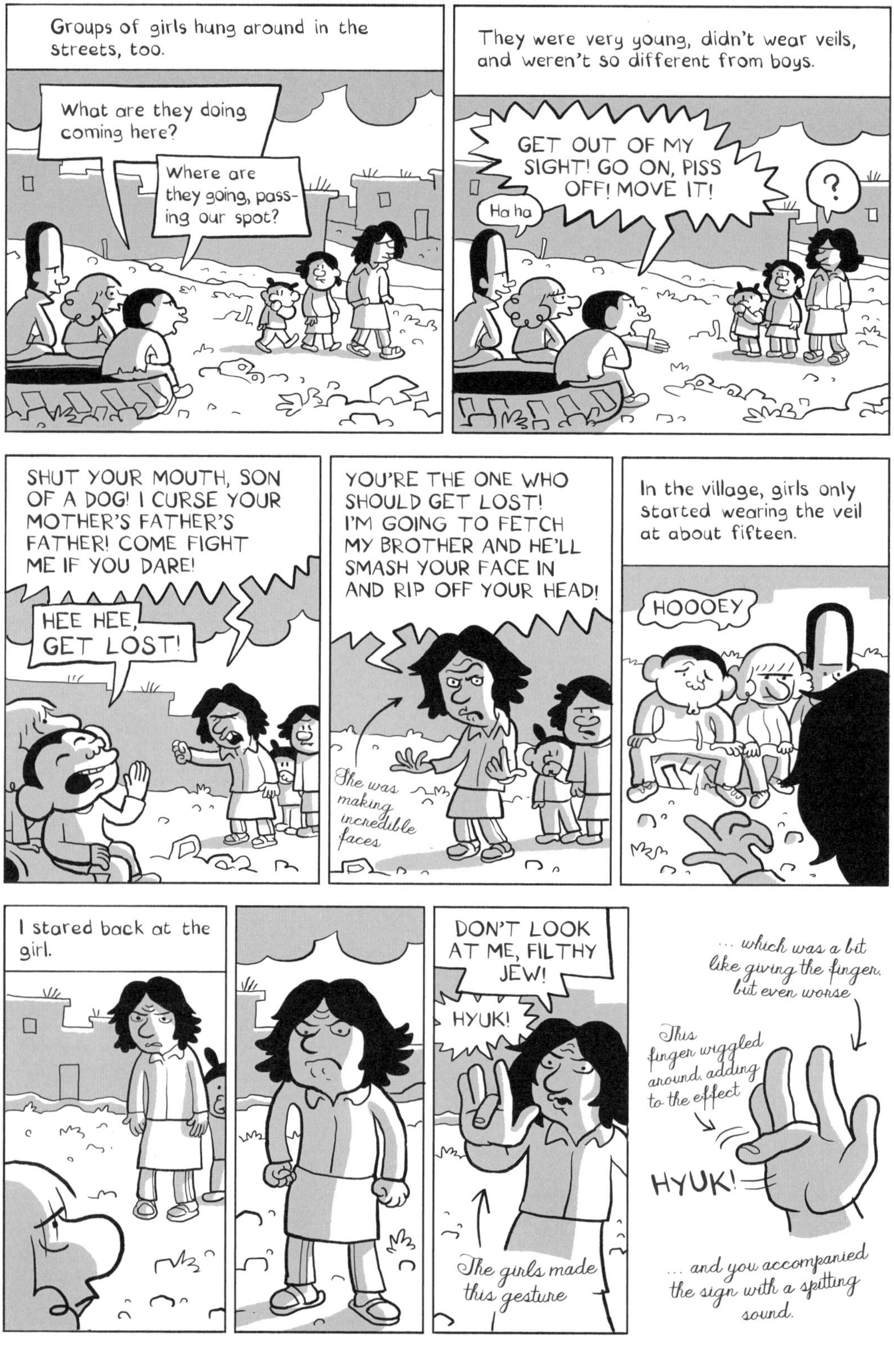

Groups of girls hung around in the streets, too.
What are they doing coming here?
Where are they going, passing our spot?
They were very young, didn't wear veils, and weren't so different from boys.
GET OUT OF MY SIGHT! GO ON, PISS OFF! MOVE IT!
Ha ha
?
SHUT YOUR MOUTH, SON OF A DOG! I CURSE YOUR MOTHER'S FATHER'S FATHER! COME FIGHT ME IF YOU DARE!
HEE HEE, GET LOST!
YOU'RE THE ONE WHO SHOULD GET LOST! I'M GOING TO FETCH MY BROTHER AND HE'LL SMASH YOUR FACE IN AND RIP OFF YOUR HEAD!
She was making incredible faces
In the village, girls only started wearing the veil at about fifteen.
HOOOEY
I stared back at the girl.
DON'T LOOK AT ME, FILTHY JEW!
HYUK!
The girls made this gesture
... which was a bit like giving the finger, but even worse
This finger wiggled around, adding to the effect
HYUK!
... and you accompanied the sign with a spitting sound.

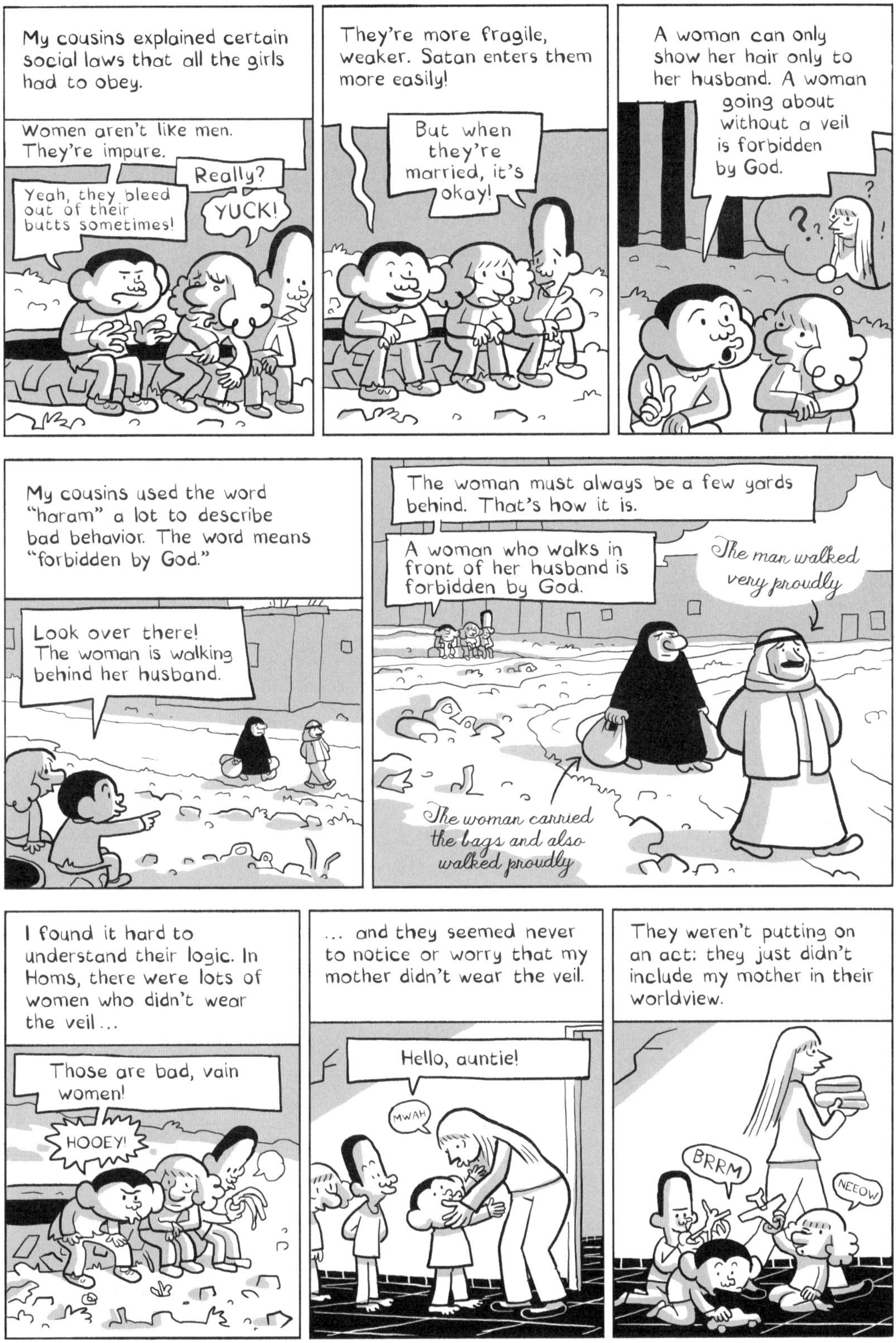
My cousins explained certain social laws that all the girls had to obey.
Women aren't like men. They're impure.
Yeah, they bleed out of their butts sometimes!
Really?
YUCK!
They're more fragile, weaker. Satan enters them more easily!
But when they're married, it's okay!
A woman can only show her hair only to her husband. A woman going about without a veil is forbidden by God.
?
??
!
My cousins used the word "haram" a lot to describe bad behavior. The word means "forbidden by God."
Look over there! The woman is walking behind her husband.
The woman must always be a few yards behind. That's how it is.
A woman who walks in front of her husband is forbidden by God.
The man walked very proudly
The woman carried the bags and also walked proudly
I found it hard to understand their logic. In Homs, there were lots of women who didn't wear the veil...
Those are bad, vain women!
HOOEY!
... and they seemed never to notice or worry that my mother didn't wear the veil.
Hello, auntie!
MWAH
They weren't putting on an act: they just didn't include my mother in their worldview.
BRRM
NEEOW

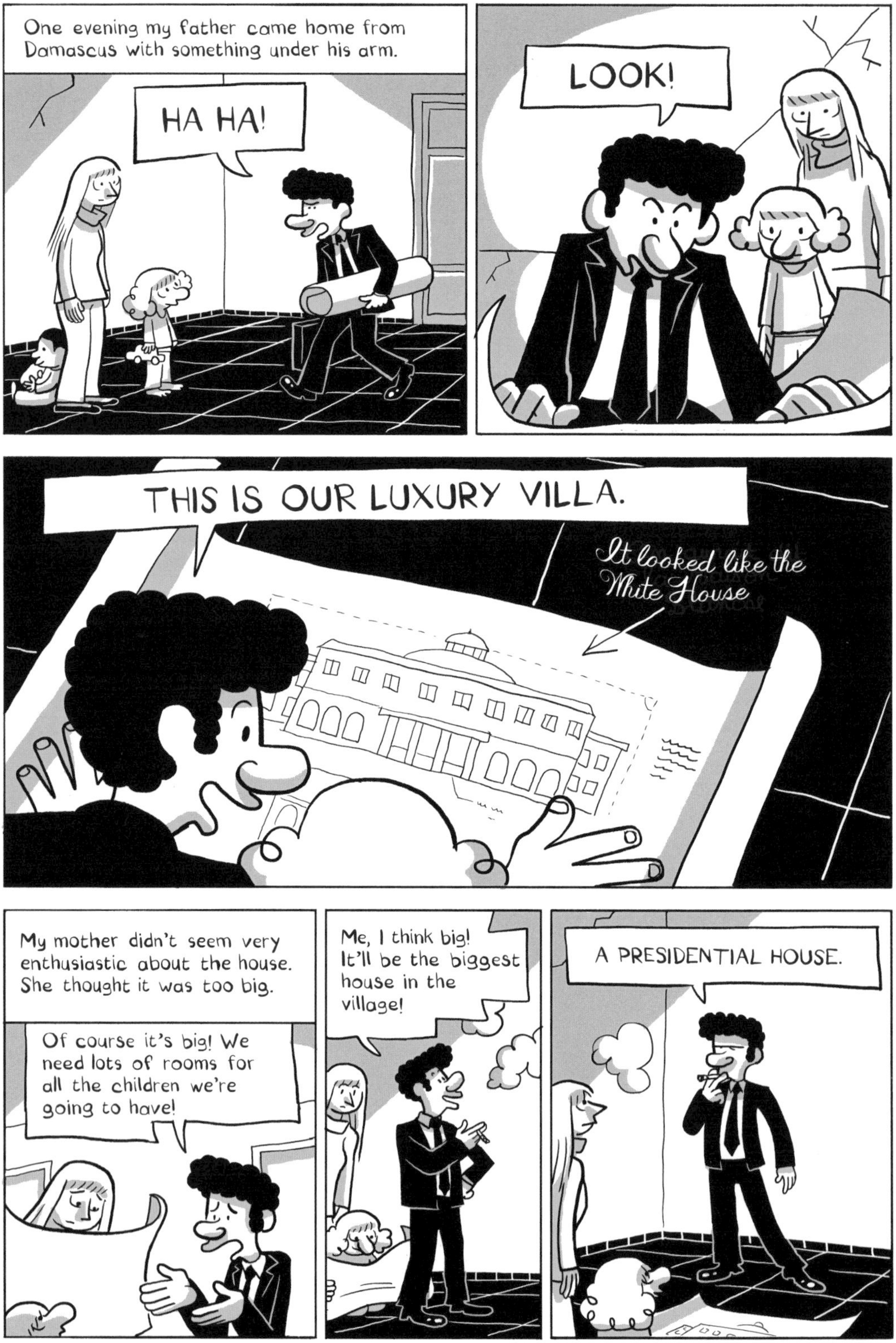
One evening my father came home from Damascus with something under his arm.
HA HA!
LOOK!
THIS IS OUR LUXURY VILLA.
It looked like the White House
My mother didn't seem very enthusiastic about the house. She thought it was too big.
Of course it's big! We need lots of rooms for all the children we're going to have!
Me, I think big! It'll be the biggest house in the village!
A PRESIDENTIAL HOUSE.

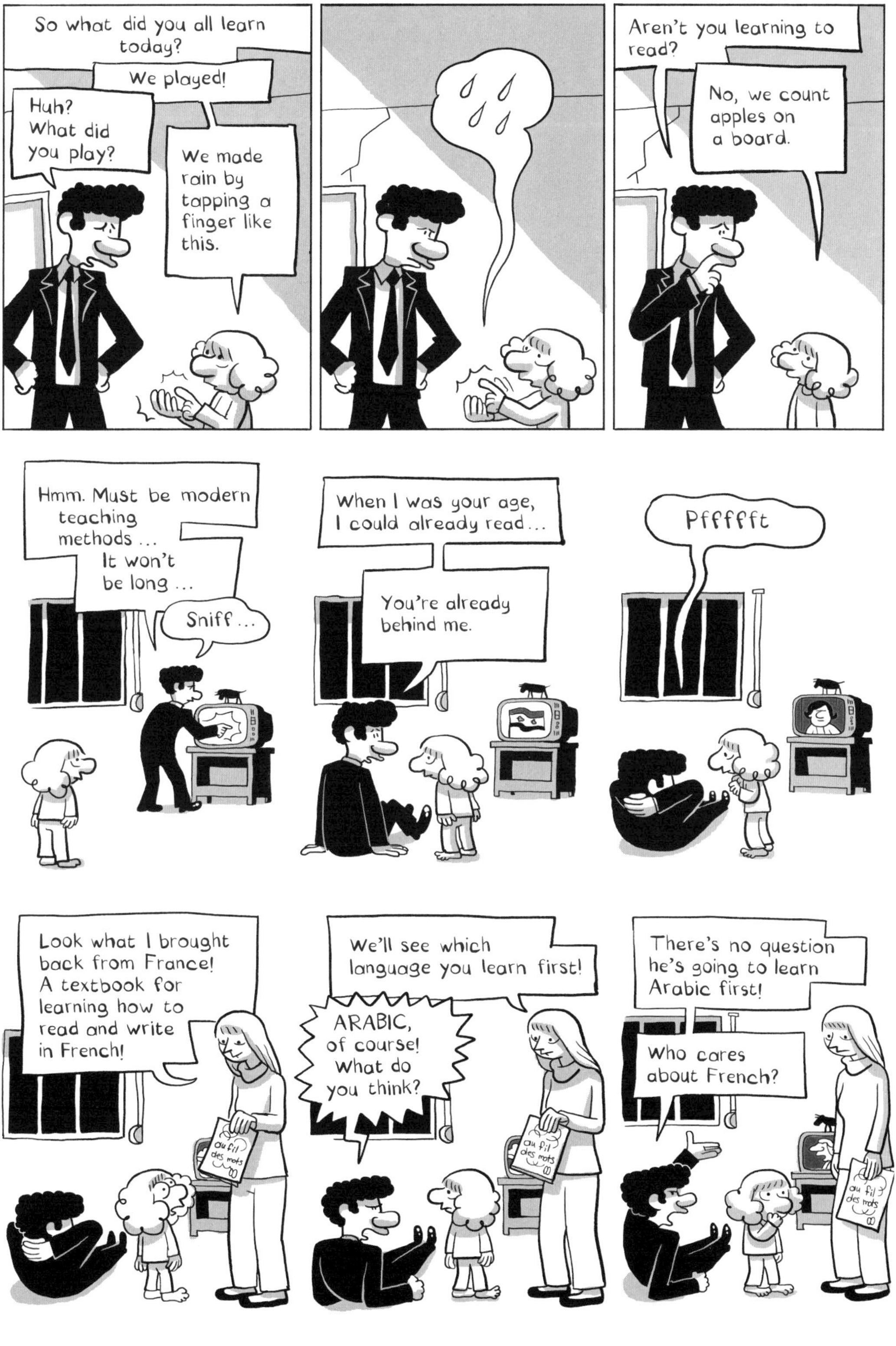
So what did you all learn today?
We played!
Huh? What did you play?
We made rain by tapping a finger like this.
Aren't you learning to read?
No, we count apples on a board.
Hmm. Must be modern teaching methods ... It won't be long ...
Sniff ...
When I was your age, I could already read ...
You're already behind me.
Pffffft
Look what I brought back from France! A textbook for learning how to read and write in French!
au fil des mots
We'll see which language you learn first!
ARABIC, of course! What do you think?
au fil des mots
There's no question he's going to learn Arabic first!
Who cares about French?
au fil des mots

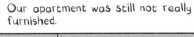
Our apartment was still not really furnished.

There was nothing in the gigantic entrance hall but a few cushions, which I used to make forts...

The only room that seemed finished was my parents' bedroom.

Bed made of expensive-looking wood

Vanity table

I was quite awed when I went in that room

There were many photos under the glass top of the vanity table.

In one of them, my father looked very young.

Oversize suit

Ha ha! That picture was taken in Damascus, when I was a student!

It was just before I left for France.

I got it taken for my mother, so she'd have something to remember me by.

When she saw it, she fainted.

Ha ha

She didn't understand how I could be all flat, and why the photo didn't reply when she talked to it.

She still doesn't really understand what photos are.

She's from another age.

I'm not smiling in this photo because I was frightened of leaving Syria and going to France.

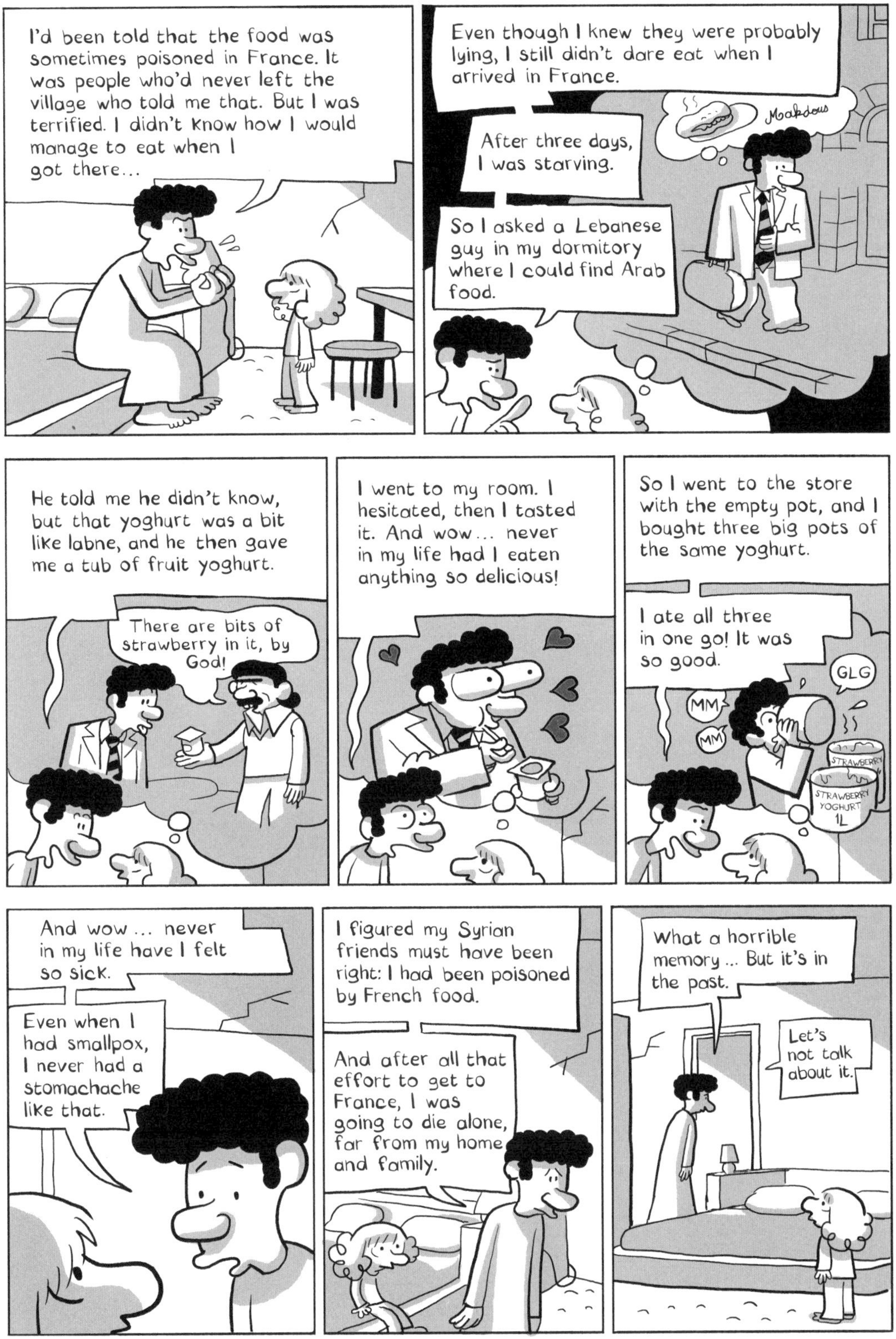
I'd been told that the food was sometimes poisoned in France. It was people who'd never left the village who told me that. But I was terrified. I didn't know how I would manage to eat when I got there...
Even though I knew they were probably lying, I still didn't dare eat when I arrived in France.
After three days, I was starving.
Makdous
So I asked a Lebanese guy in my dormitory where I could find Arab food.
He told me he didn't know, but that yoghurt was a bit like labne, and he then gave me a tub of fruit yoghurt.
There are bits of strawberry in it, by God!
I went to my room. I hesitated, then I tasted it. And wow... never in my life had I eaten anything so delicious!
So I went to the store with the empty pot, and I bought three big pots of the same yoghurt.
I ate all three in one go! It was so good.
MM
MM
GLG
STRAWBERRY
STRAWBERRY YOGHURT 1L
And wow... never in my life have I felt so sick.
Even when I had smallpox, I never had a stomachache like that.
I figured my Syrian friends must have been right: I had been poisoned by French food.
And after all that effort to get to France, I was going to die alone, far from my home and family.
What a horrible memory... But it's in the past.
Let's not talk about it.

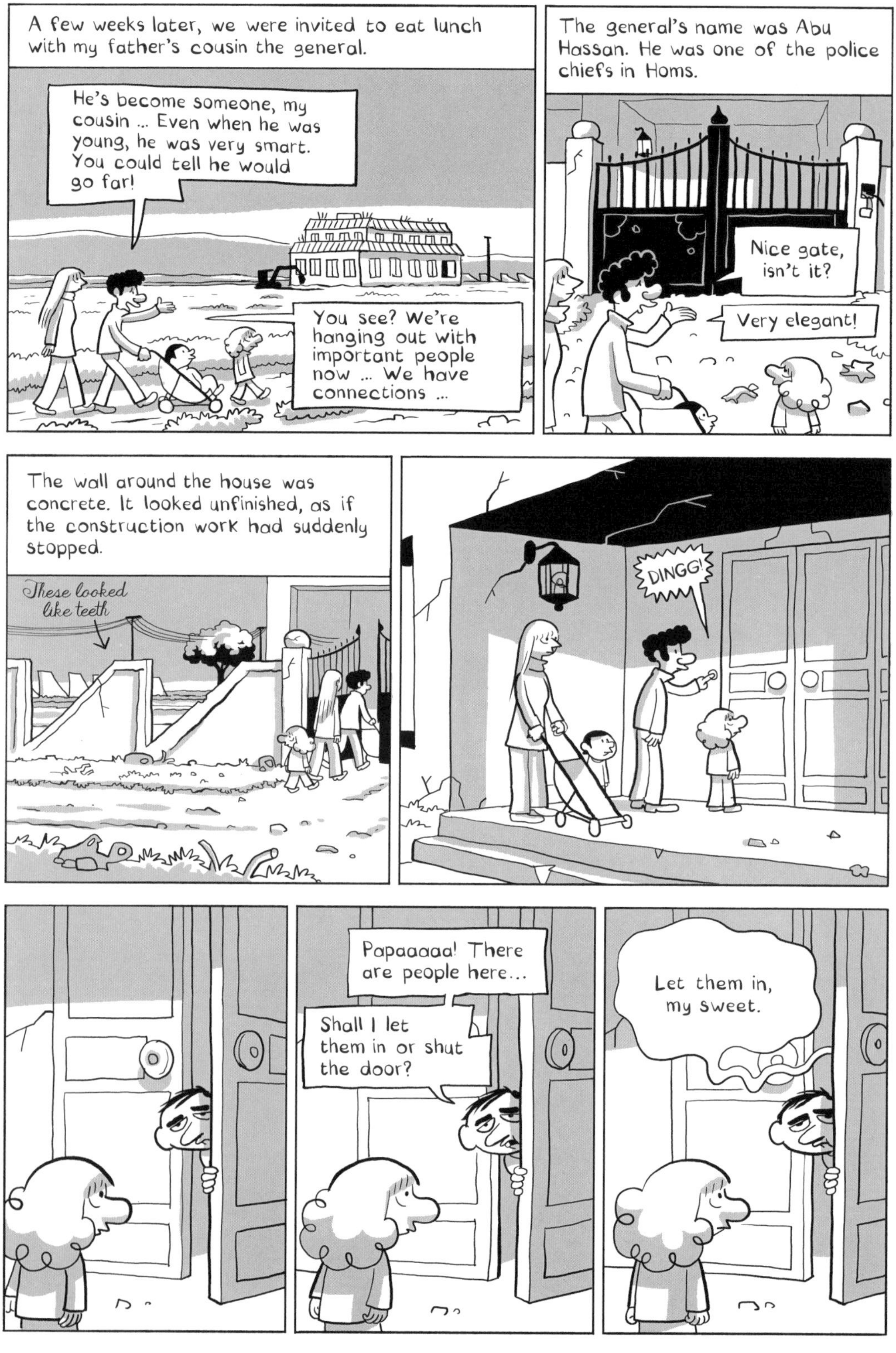
A few weeks later, we were invited to eat lunch with my father's cousin the general.
He's become someone, my cousin ... Even when he was young, he was very smart. You could tell he would go far!
You see? We're hanging out with important people now ... We have connections ...
The general's name was Abu Hassan. He was one of the police chiefs in Homs.
Nice gate, isn't it?
Very elegant!
The wall around the house was concrete. It looked unfinished, as if the construction work had suddenly stopped.
These looked like teeth
DINGG!
Papaaaaa! There are people here...
Shall I let them in or shut the door?
Let them in, my sweet.

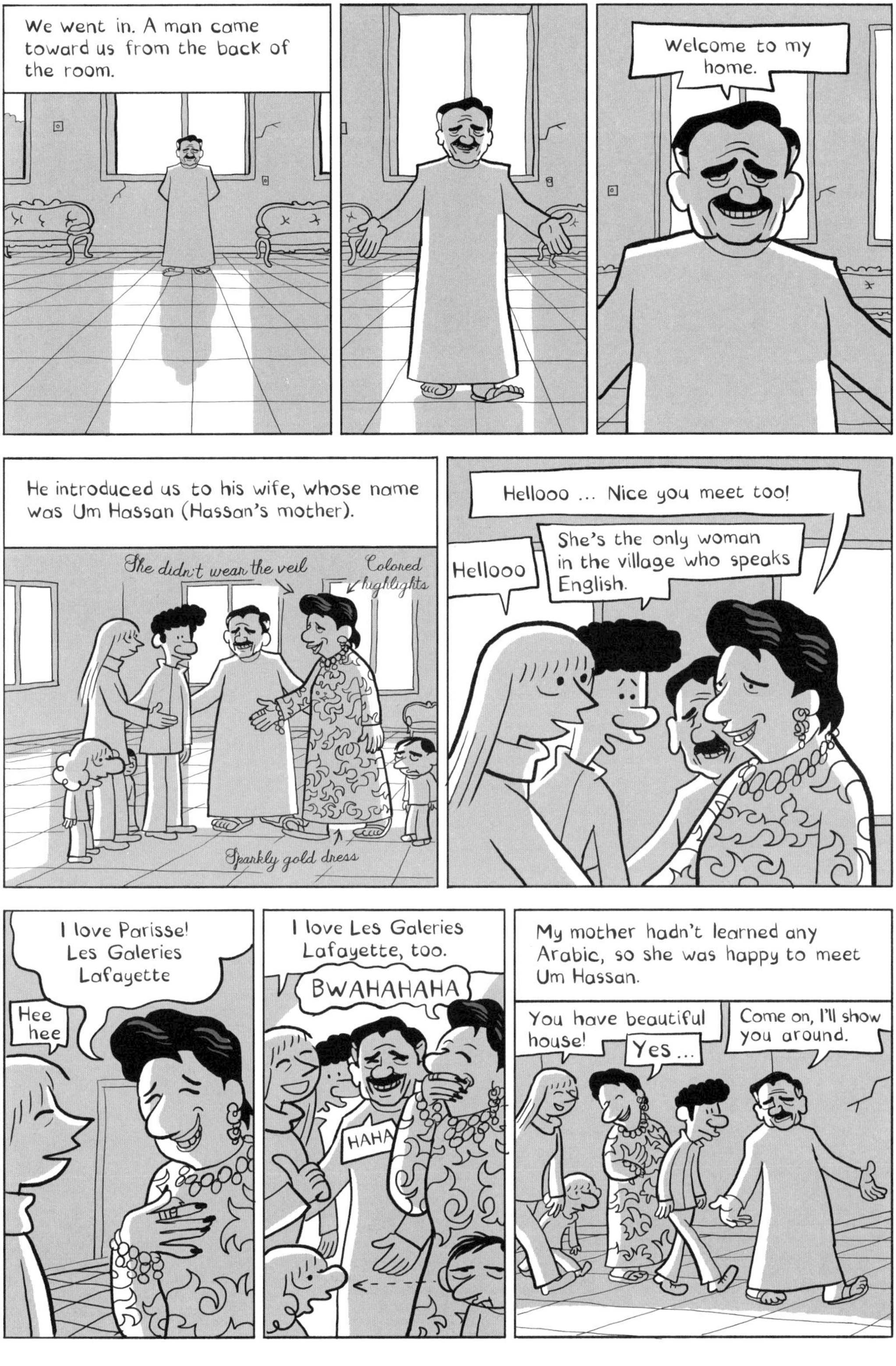
We went in. A man came toward us from the back of the room.
Welcome to my home.
He introduced us to his wife, whose name was Um Hassan (Hassan's mother).
She didn't wear the veil
Colored highlights
Sparkly gold dress
Hellooo ... Nice you meet too!
Hellooo
She's the only woman in the village who speaks English.
I love Parisse! Les Galeries Lafayette
Hee hee
I love Les Galeries Lafayette, too.
BWAHAHAHA
HAHA
My mother hadn't learned any Arabic, so she was happy to meet Um Hassan.
You have beautiful house!
Yes ...
Come on, I'll show you around.

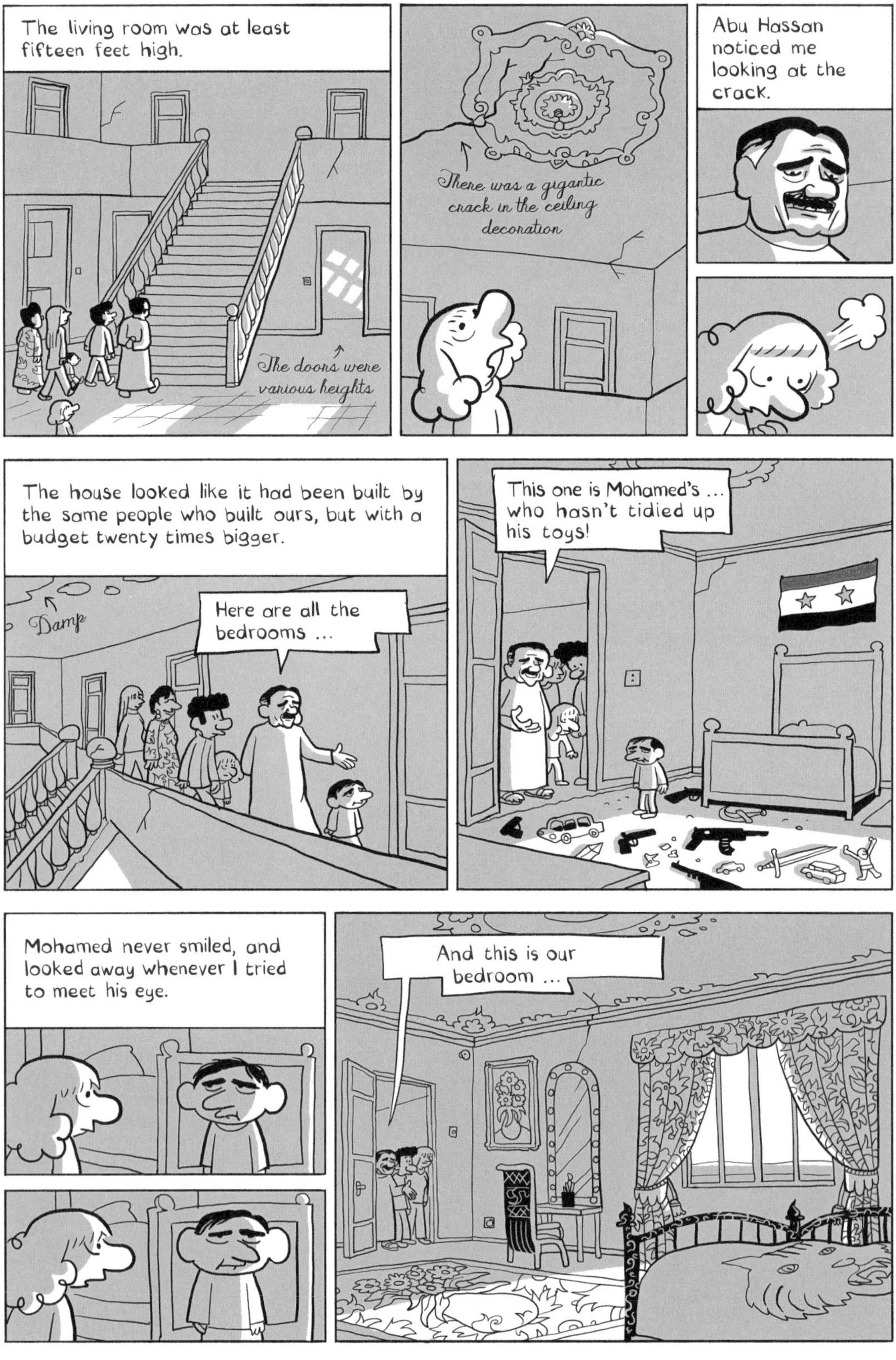
The living room was at least fifteen feet high.
The doors were various heights
There was a gigantic crack in the ceiling decoration
Abu Hassan noticed me looking at the crack.
The house looked like it had been built by the same people who built ours, but with a budget twenty times bigger.
Damp
Here are all the bedrooms ...
This one is Mohamed's ... who hasn't tidied up his toys!
Mohamed never smiled, and looked away whenever I tried to meet his eye.
And this is our bedroom ...

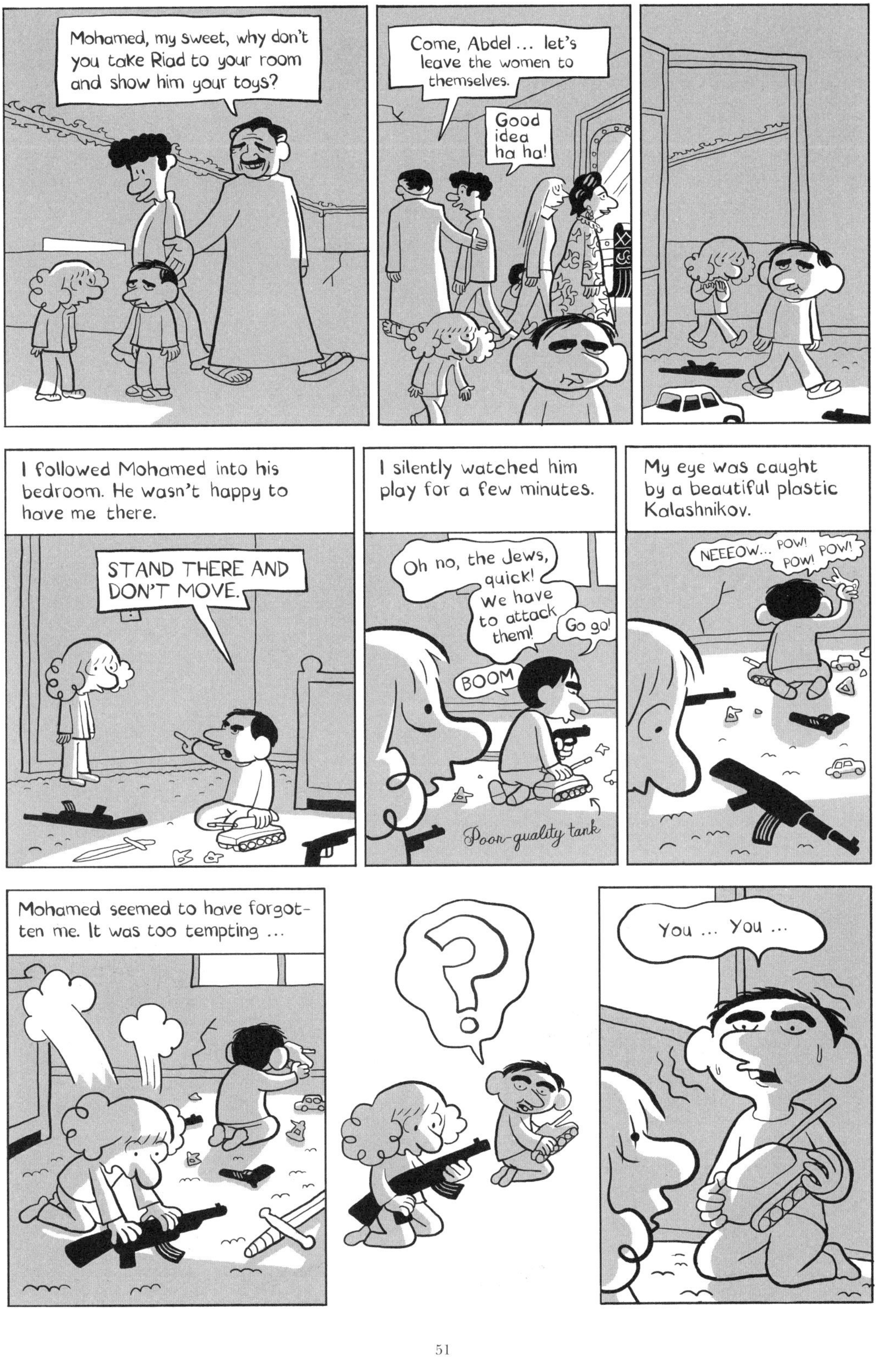
Mohamed, my sweet, why don't you take Riad to your room and show him your toys?
Come, Abdel ... let's leave the women to themselves.
Good idea ha ha!
I followed Mohamed into his bedroom. He wasn't happy to have me there.
STAND THERE AND DON'T MOVE.
I silently watched him play for a few minutes.
Oh no, the Jews, quick! We have to attack them!
Go go!
BOOM
Poor-quality tank
My eye was caught by a beautiful plastic Kalashnikov.
NEEEOW... POW! POW! POW!
Mohamed seemed to have forgot-ten me. It was too tempting ...
?
You ... You ...

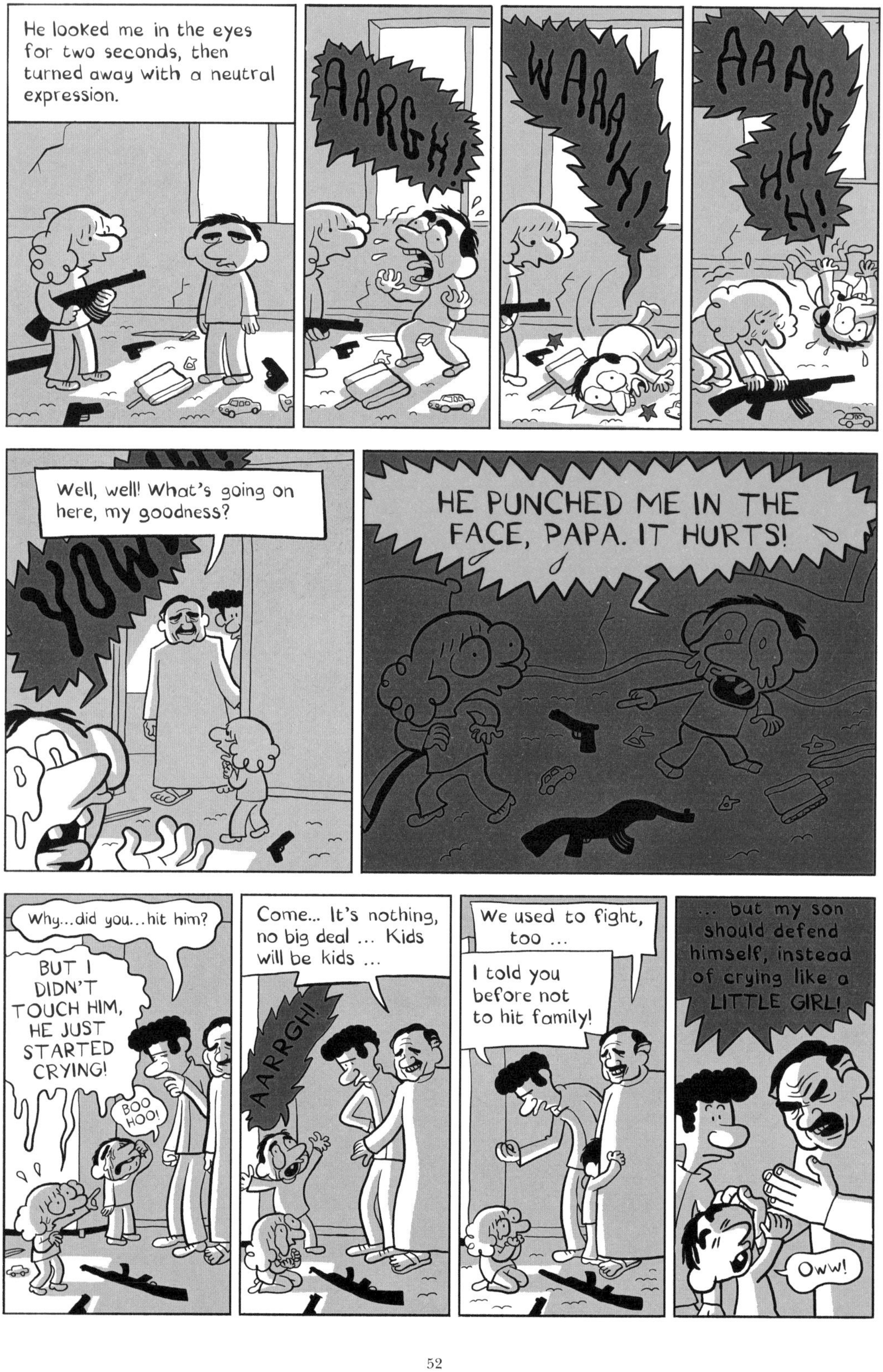
He looked me in the eyes for two seconds, then turned away with a neutral expression.
AARGH!
WAAAAK!
AAAGHHH!
Well, well! What's going on here, my goodness?
YOW
HE PUNCHED ME IN THE FACE, PAPA. IT HURTS!
Why...did you...hit him?
BUT I DIDN'T TOUCH HIM, HE JUST STARTED CRYING!
BOO HOO!
Come... It's nothing, no big deal ... Kids will be kids ...
AARRGH!
We used to fight, too ...
I told you before not to hit family!
... but my son should defend himself, instead of crying like a LITTLE GIRL!
OWW!

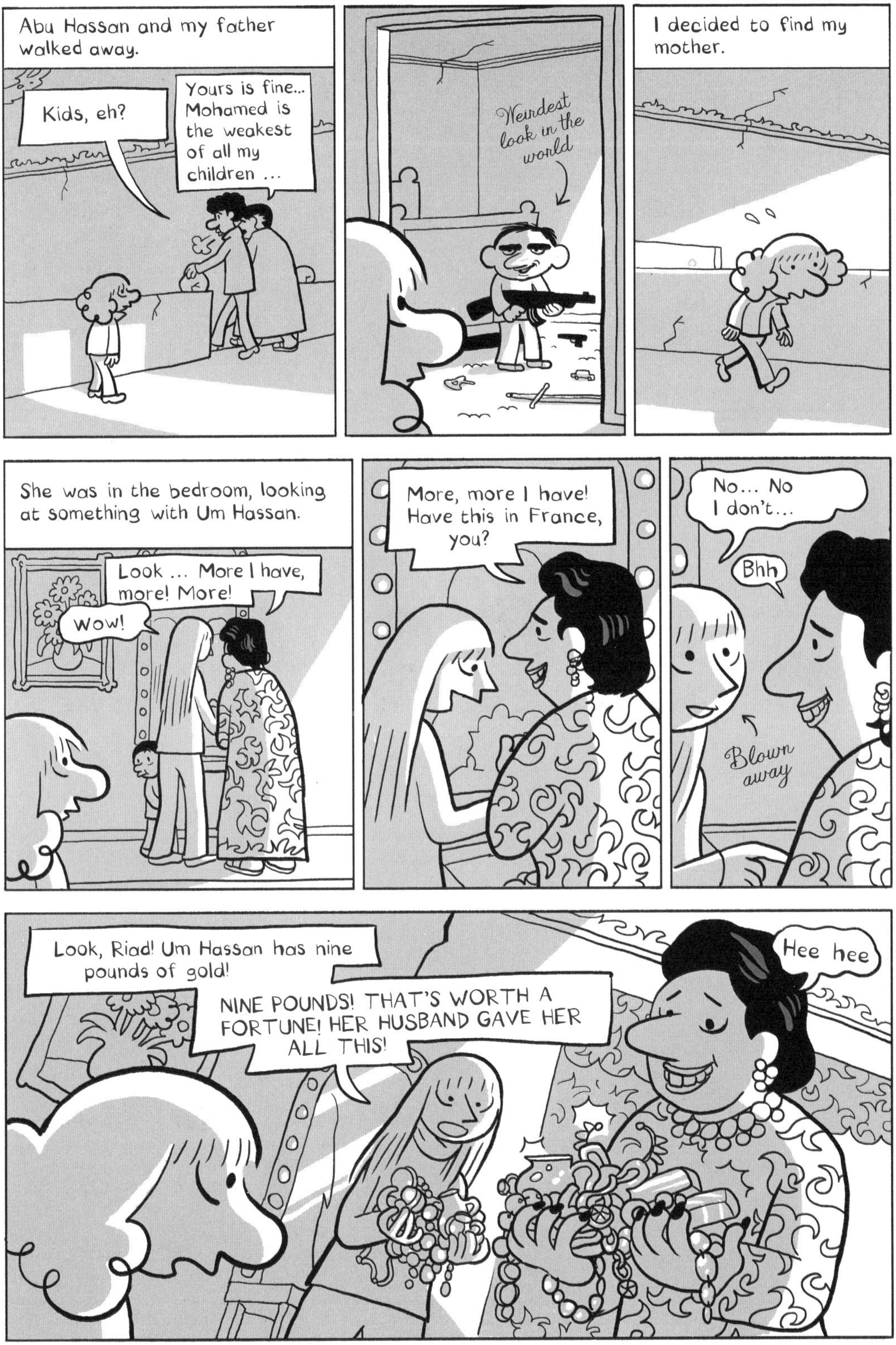
Abu Hassan and my father walked away.
Kids, eh?
Yours is fine... Mohamed is the weakest of all my children ...
Weirdest look in the world
I decided to find my mother.
She was in the bedroom, looking at something with Um Hassan.
Look ... More I have, more! More!
Wow!
More, more I have! Have this in France, you?
No... No I don't...
Bhh
Blown away
Look, Riad! Um Hassan has nine pounds of gold!
NINE POUNDS! THAT'S WORTH A FORTUNE! HER HUSBAND GAVE HER ALL THIS!
Hee hee

We sat down to eat. My father was trying to flatter his cousin, but the general seemed more interested in the potential for friendship between his wife and my mother.

Wonderful meal!

So, did you speak English?

Yes...

Thank God

The kept bringing over delicious smelling dishes

A draft of air blew through a huge crack in the wall.

WHOOOOO

My father seemed nervous. He laughed every time the general spoke.

Abu Riad. Drink with me! I'm opening a bottle of Jack Daniel's to toast your return!

Ha ha

You're not going to let me drink alone, are you?

Abu Hassan poured himself a generous amount.

Let me taste it first.

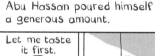

GLUG

Burp

Let's drink to seeing each other again

AH, IT TASTES GOOD, THIS AMERICAN ALCOHOL!

The consumption of alcohol is strictly forbidden by Islam. My father seemed a little embarrassed at breaking this law in front of his cousin.

OUR WIVES ARE GETTING ALONG WELL! THEY'RE MODERN! LIKE US!

CLINK

CHIN CHIN!

54

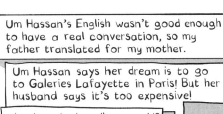

Um Hassan's English wasn't good enough to have a real conversation, so my father translated for my mother.

Um Hassan says her dream is to go to Galeries Lafayette in Paris! But her husband says it's too expensive!

Why doesn't she sell some gold? She'd be rich in France!

What is she saying?

She says that if God wills it, one day they will both go shopping in Galeries Lafayette!

That's good, if God wills it ...

Ha ha!

Yes, if God wills it ...

And what about you? I've heard you're going to build a house on your land?

Soon, if God wills it. A big villa.

GLUG

Empty →

I hope it will be beautiful! Because I'll see it every day from my window!

If God wills it, it will be very beautiful.

But tell me, cousin, what are you doing with that excavator? Looking for treasure?

HA HA HA HA! No, not at all ...

I'm building a swimming pool thirty feet deep so my children can dive off the roof.

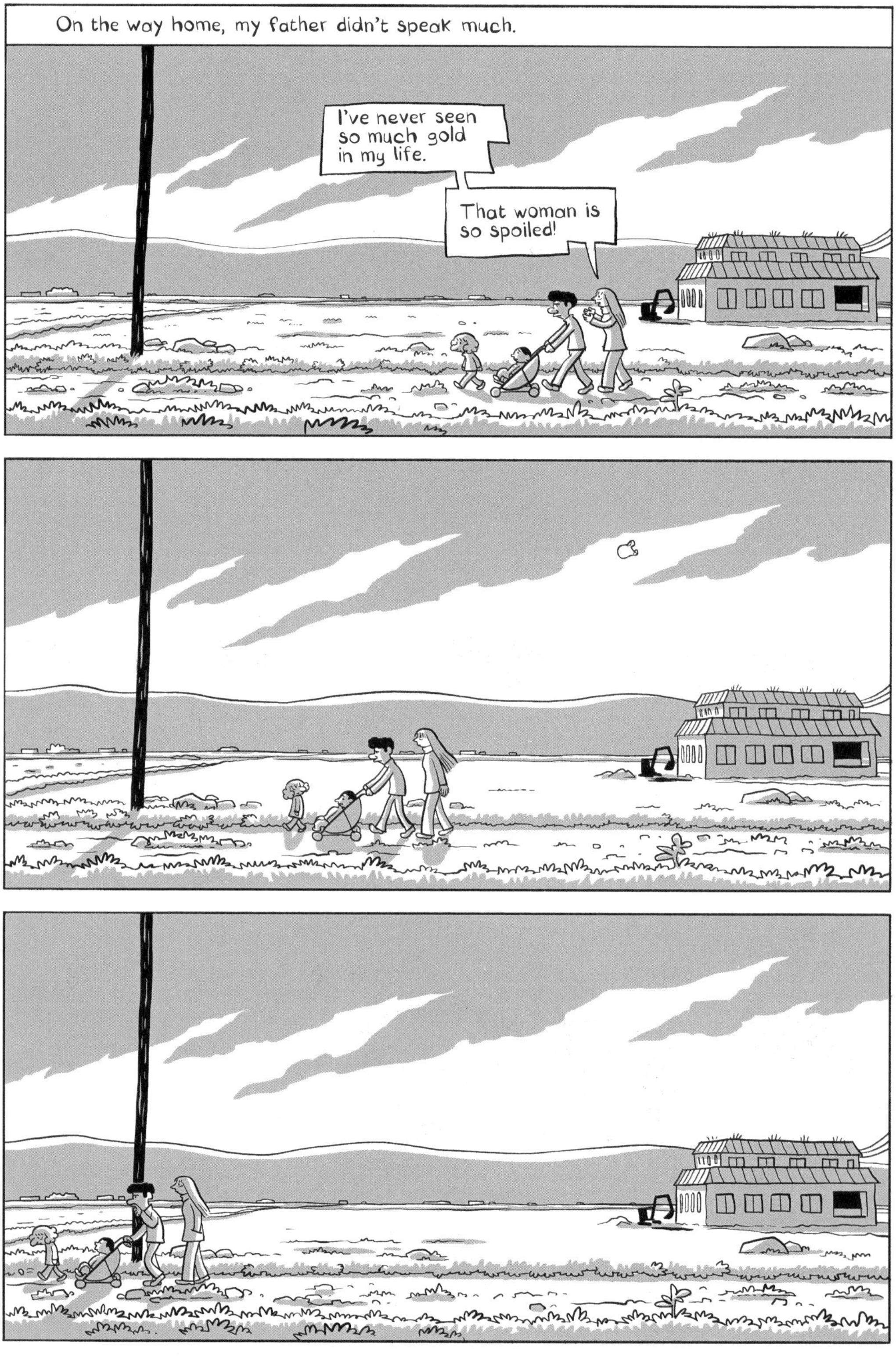
On the way home, my father didn't speak much.
I've never seen so much gold in my life.
That woman is so spoiled!

CHAPTER 2

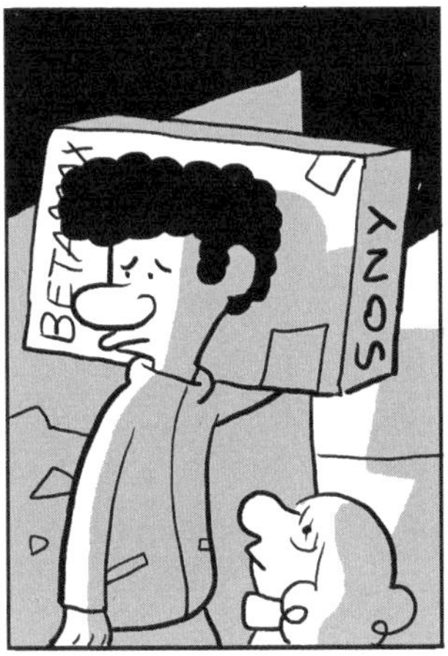
SONY

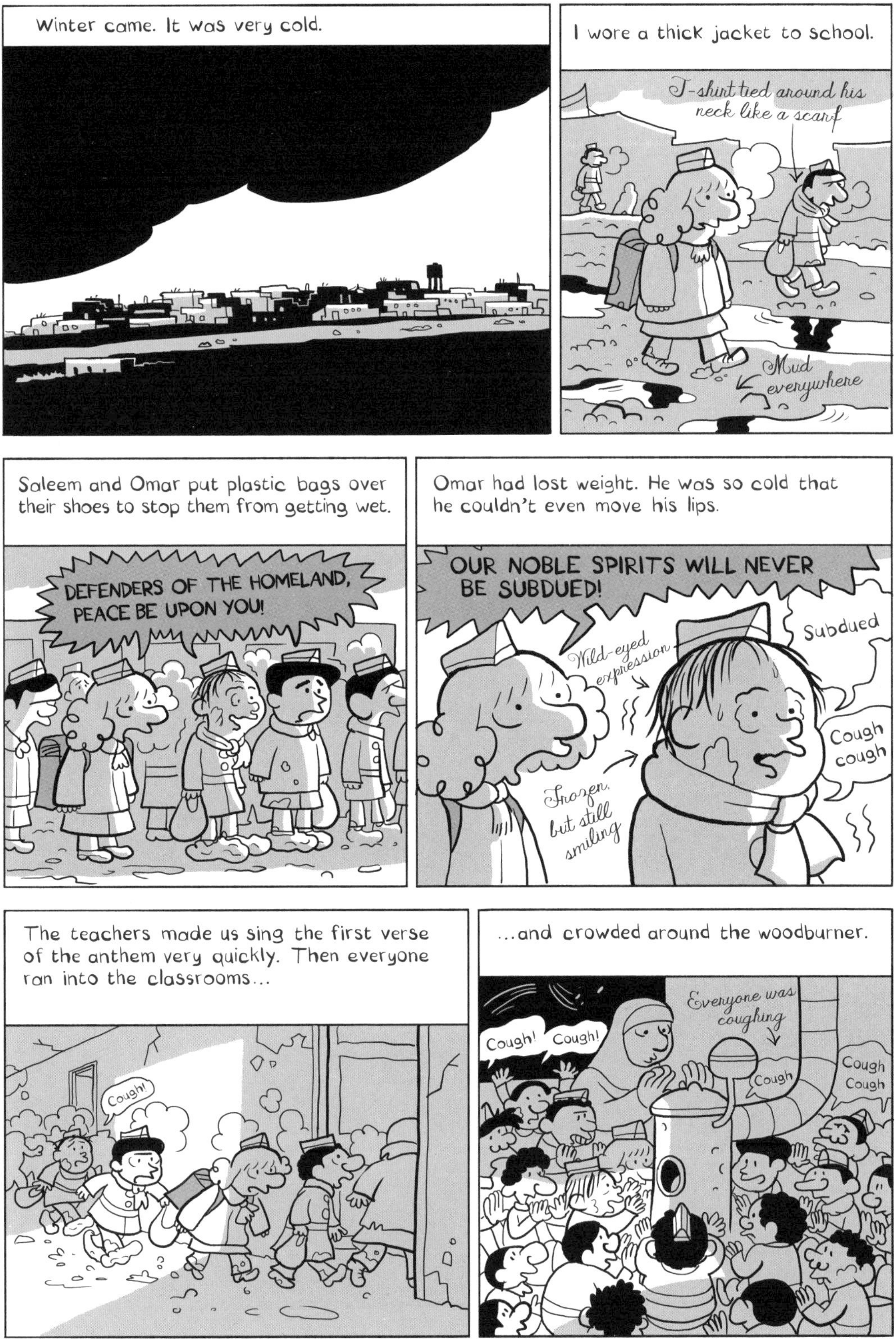
Winter came. It was very cold.
I wore a thick jacket to school.
T-shirt tied around his neck like a scarf
Mud everywhere
Saleem and Omar put plastic bags over their shoes to stop them from getting wet.
DEFENDERS OF THE HOMELAND, PEACE BE UPON YOU!
Omar had lost weight. He was so cold that he couldn't even move his lips.
OUR NOBLE SPIRITS WILL NEVER BE SUBDUED!
Wild-eyed expression
Subdued
Cough cough
Frozen, but still smiling
The teachers made us sing the first verse of the anthem very quickly. Then everyone ran into the classrooms...
Cough!
...and crowded around the woodburner.
Everyone was coughing
Cough! Cough!
Cough
Cough Cough

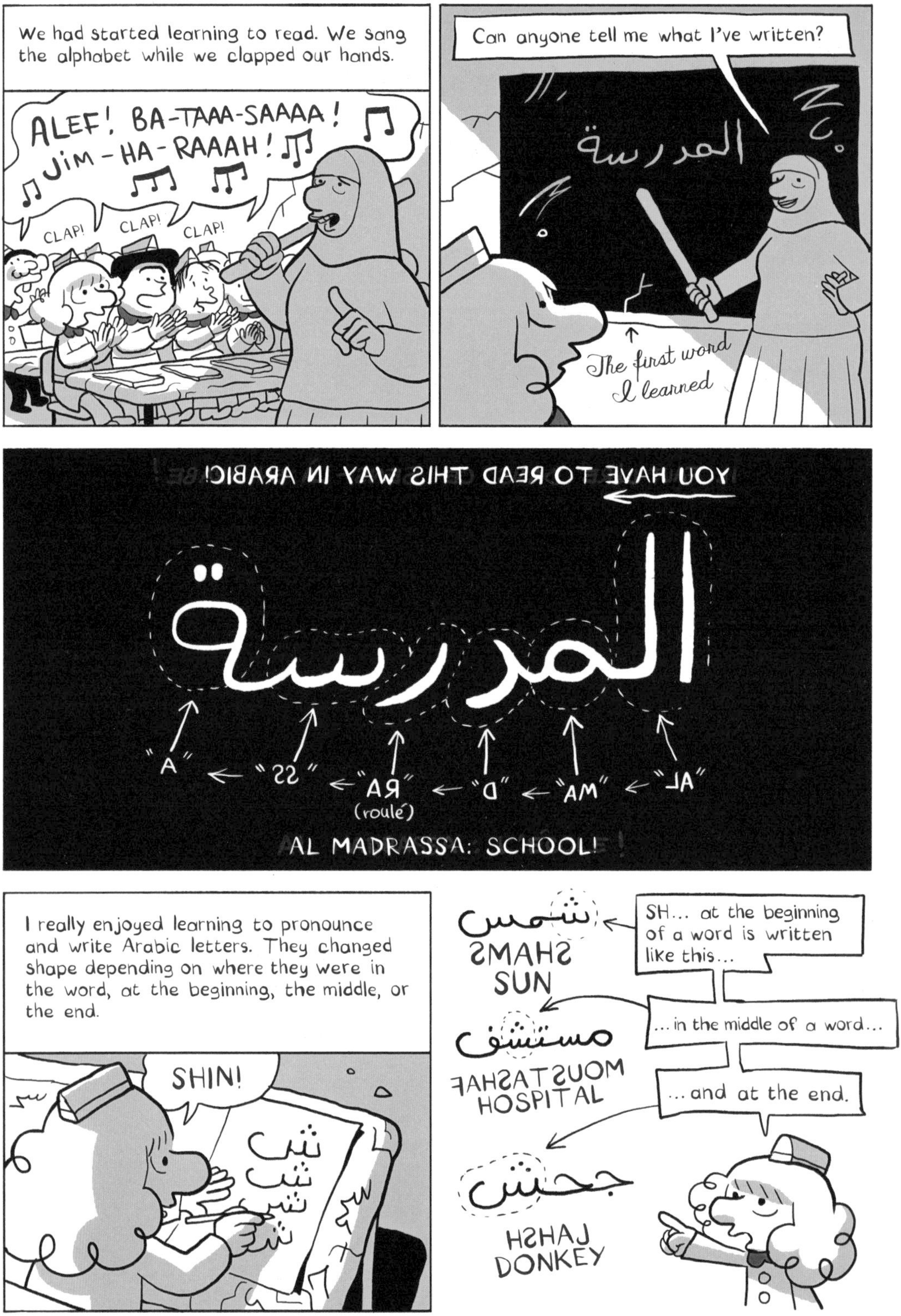
We had started learning to read. We sang the alphabet while we clapped our hands.
ALEF! BA-TAAA-SAAAA! JIM-HA-RAAAH!
CLAP! CLAP! CLAP!
Can anyone tell me what I've written?
المدرسة
The first word I learned
YOU HAVE TO READ THIS WAY IN ARABIC!
المدرسة
"AL" "AM" "D" "RA" (roulé) "SS" "A"
AL MADRASSA: SCHOOL!
I really enjoyed learning to pronounce and write Arabic letters. They changed shape depending on where they were in the word, at the beginning, the middle, or the end.
SHIN!
SH... at the beginning of a word is written like this...
شمس
SHAMS
SUN
... in the middle of a word...
MOUSTASHAF
HOSPITAL
... and at the end.
جحش
JAHSH
DONKEY

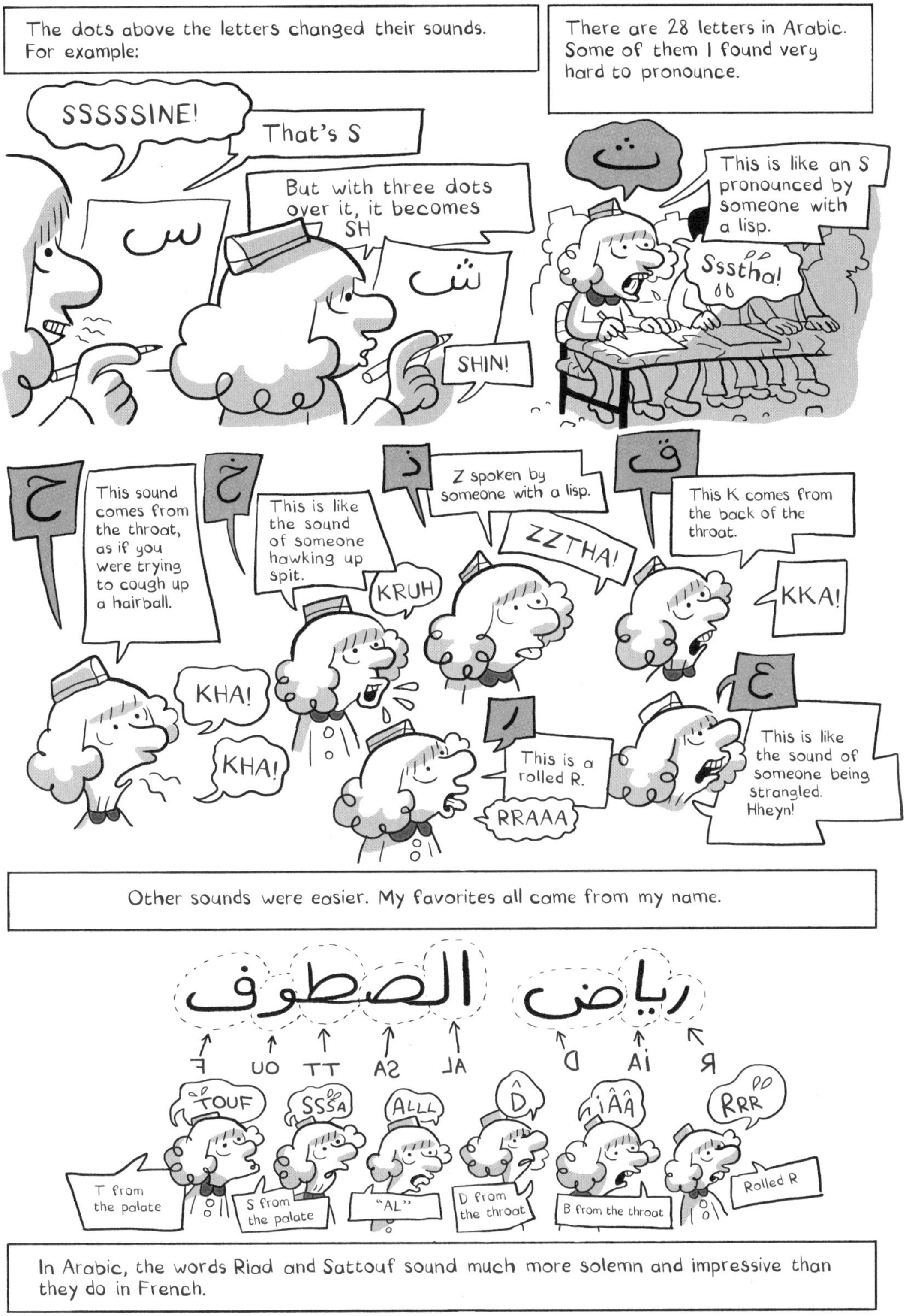
The dots above the letters changed their sounds. For example:
SSSSSINE!
That's S
س
But with three dots over it, it becomes SH
ش
SHIN!
There are 28 letters in Arabic. Some of them I found very hard to pronounce.
ث
This is like an S pronounced by someone with a lisp.
Sssthaǃ
ح
This sound comes from the throat, as if you were trying to cough up a hairball.
KHA!
KHA!
خ
This is like the sound of someone hawking up spit.
KRUH
ذ
Z spoken by someone with a lisp.
ZZTHA!
ر
This is a rolled R.
RRAAA
ق
This K comes from the back of the throat.
KKA!
ع
This is like the sound of someone being strangled. Hheyn!
Other sounds were easier. My favorites all come from my name.
رياض الصطوف
ꟻ UO TT AƧ ⅃A ᗡ Ai Я
TOUF
SSSA
ALLL
D̂
iÂÂ
RRR
T from the palate
S from the palate
"AL"
D from the throat
B from the throat
Rolled R
In Arabic, the words Riad and Sattouf sound much more solemn and impressive than they do in French.

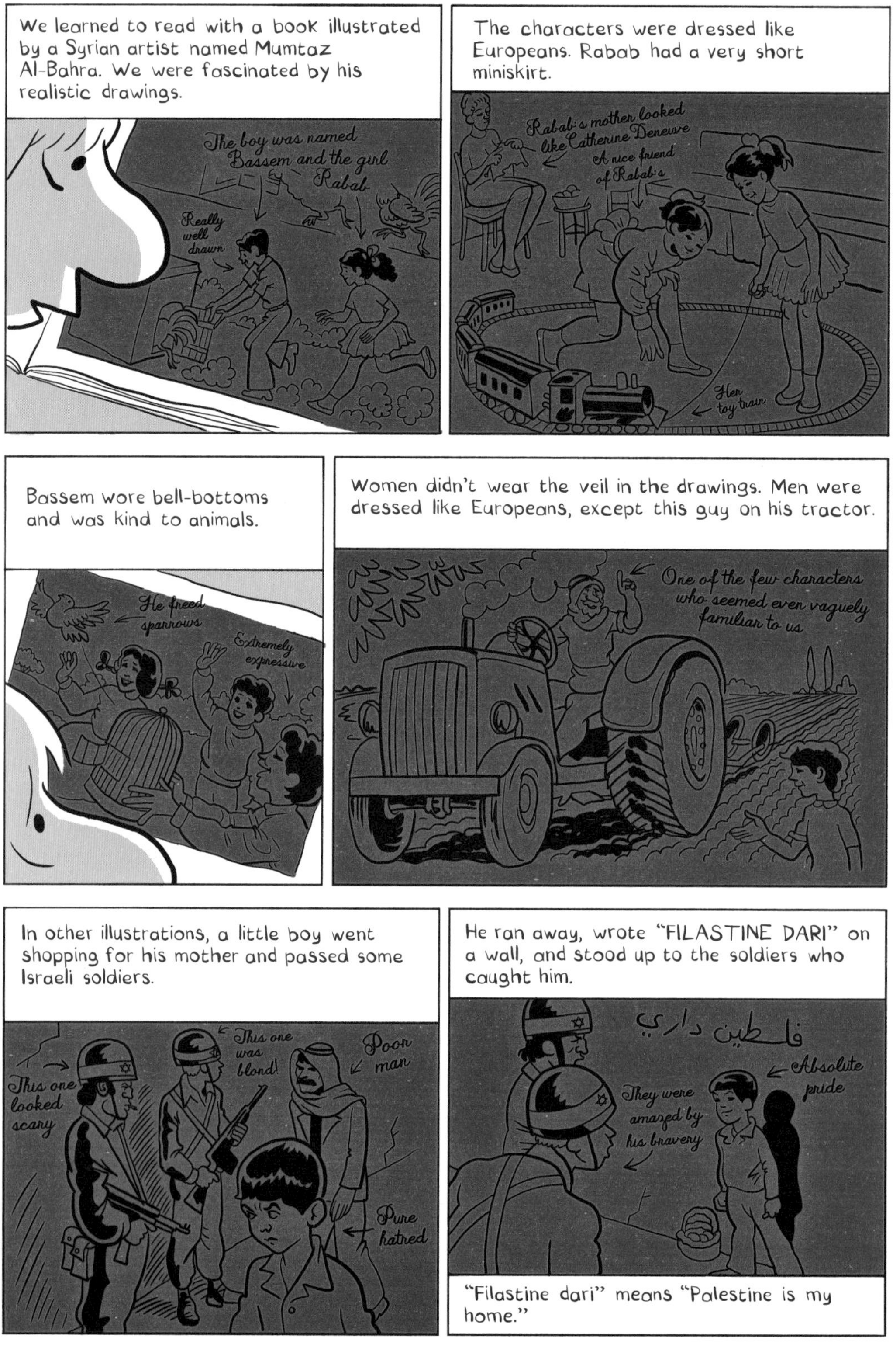
We learned to read with a book illustrated by a Syrian artist named Mumtaz Al-Bahra. We were fascinated by his realistic drawings.
The boy was named Bassem and the girl Rabab
Really well drawn
The characters were dressed like Europeans. Rabab had a very short miniskirt.
Rabab's mother looked like Catherine Deneuve
A nice friend of Rabab's
Her toy train
Bassem wore bell-bottoms and was kind to animals.
He freed sparrows
Extremely expressive
Women didn't wear the veil in the drawings. Men were dressed like Europeans, except this guy on his tractor.
One of the few characters who seemed even vaguely familiar to us
In other illustrations, a little boy went shopping for his mother and passed some Israeli soldiers.
This one looked scary
This one was blond!
Poor man
Pure hatred
He ran away, wrote "FILASTINE DARI" on a wall, and stood up to the soldiers who caught him.
فلسطين داري
They were amazed by his bravery
Absolute pride
"Filastine dari" means "Palestine is my home."

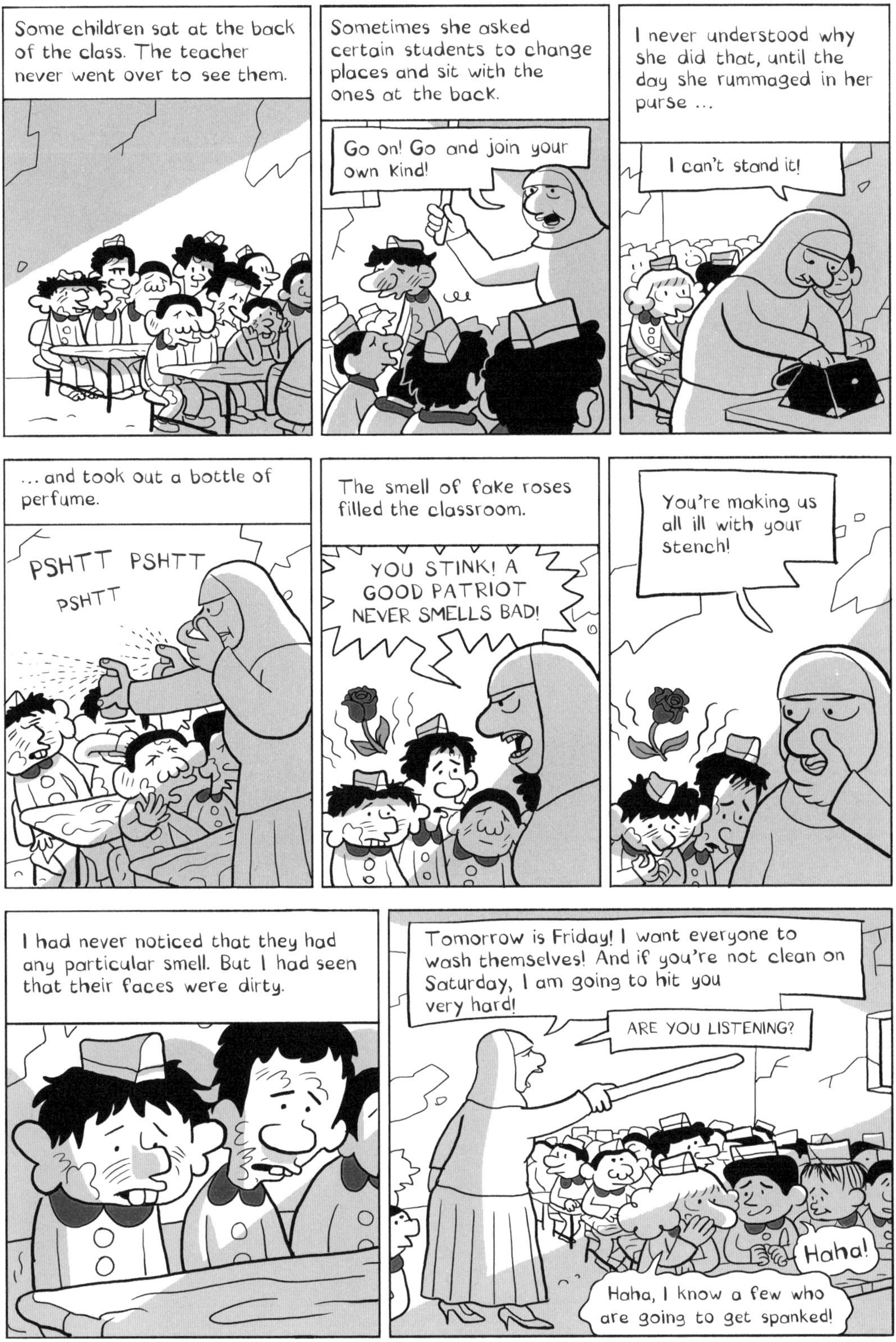
Some children sat at the back of the class. The teacher never went over to see them.
Sometimes she asked certain students to change places and sit with the ones at the back.
Go on! Go and join your own kind!
I never understood why she did that, until the day she rummaged in her purse ...
I can't stand it!
... and took out a bottle of perfume.
PSHTT PSHTT PSHTT
The smell of fake roses filled the classroom.
YOU STINK! A GOOD PATRIOT NEVER SMELLS BAD!
You're making us all ill with your stench!
I had never noticed that they had any particular smell. But I had seen that their faces were dirty.
Tomorrow is Friday! I want everyone to wash themselves! And if you're not clean on Saturday, I am going to hit you very hard!
ARE YOU LISTENING?
Haha!
Haha, I know a few who are going to get spanked!

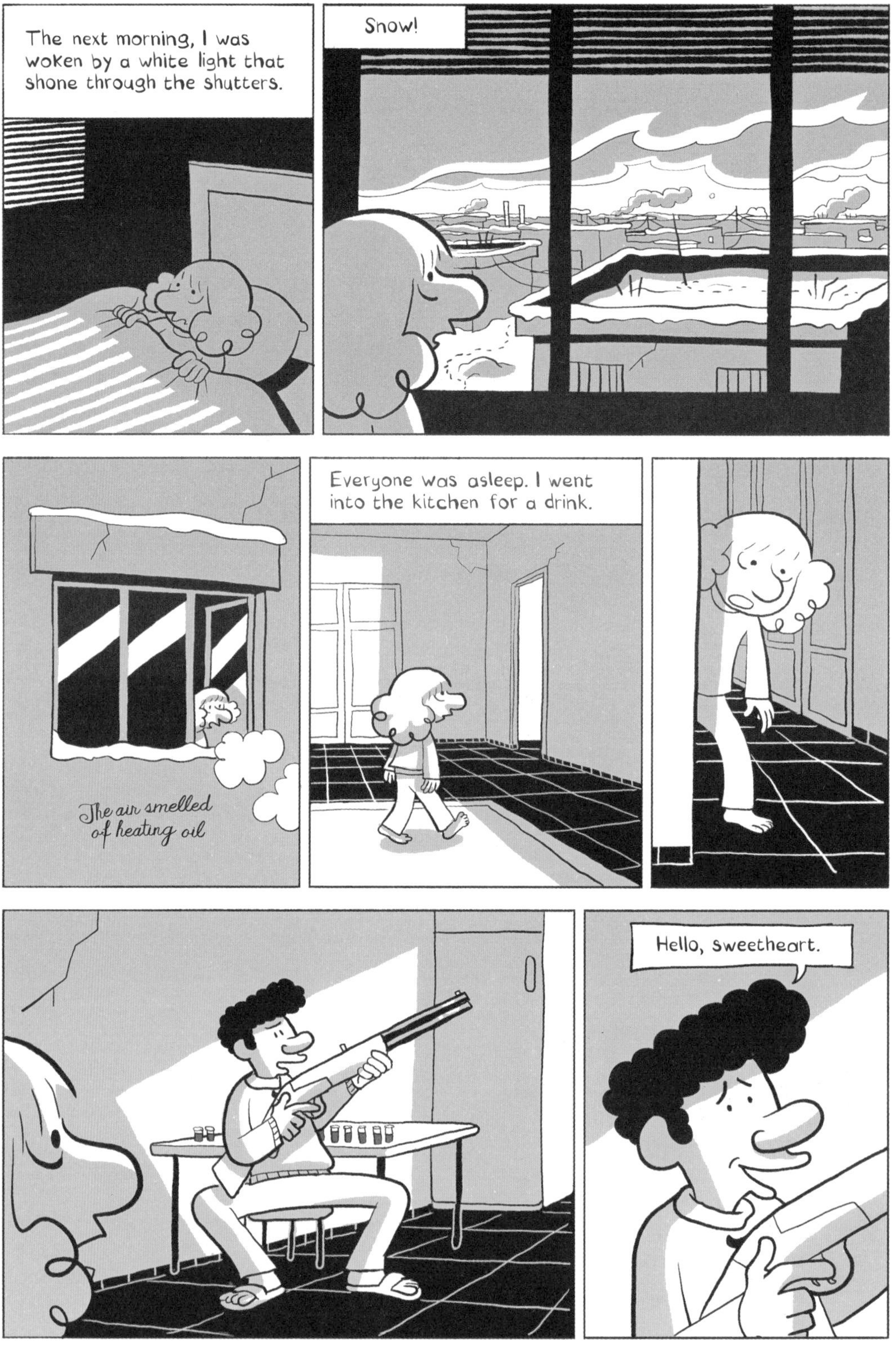
The next morning, I was woken by a white light that shone through the shutters.
Snow!
The air smelled of heating oil
Everyone was asleep. I went into the kitchen for a drink.
Hello, sweetheart.

Look at this rifle! Not bad, huh? I borrowed it from one of Hadj Mohamed's sons!

Fascinated
↓

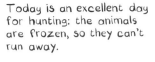

Today is an excellent day for hunting: the animals are frozen, so they can't run away.

You want to come hunting with Papa?

Yes!

Here, take this.

It's not loaded.

It was impossible to carry.

Haha, it's for men!

How could anyone do anything with such a heavy contraption?

To aim, you have to line up this metal thing with this slit.

SHOOT!

GO ON!

SHOOT!

My fingers weren't strong enough to pull the trigger

You put the lead cartridges in here ... That way, you can fire two shots.

But I don't really like barrels on top of each other. I prefer it when they're side by side ...

Come on, get dressed. We're going out to get lunch!

I feel like some nice grilled meat!

He looked so happy
↓

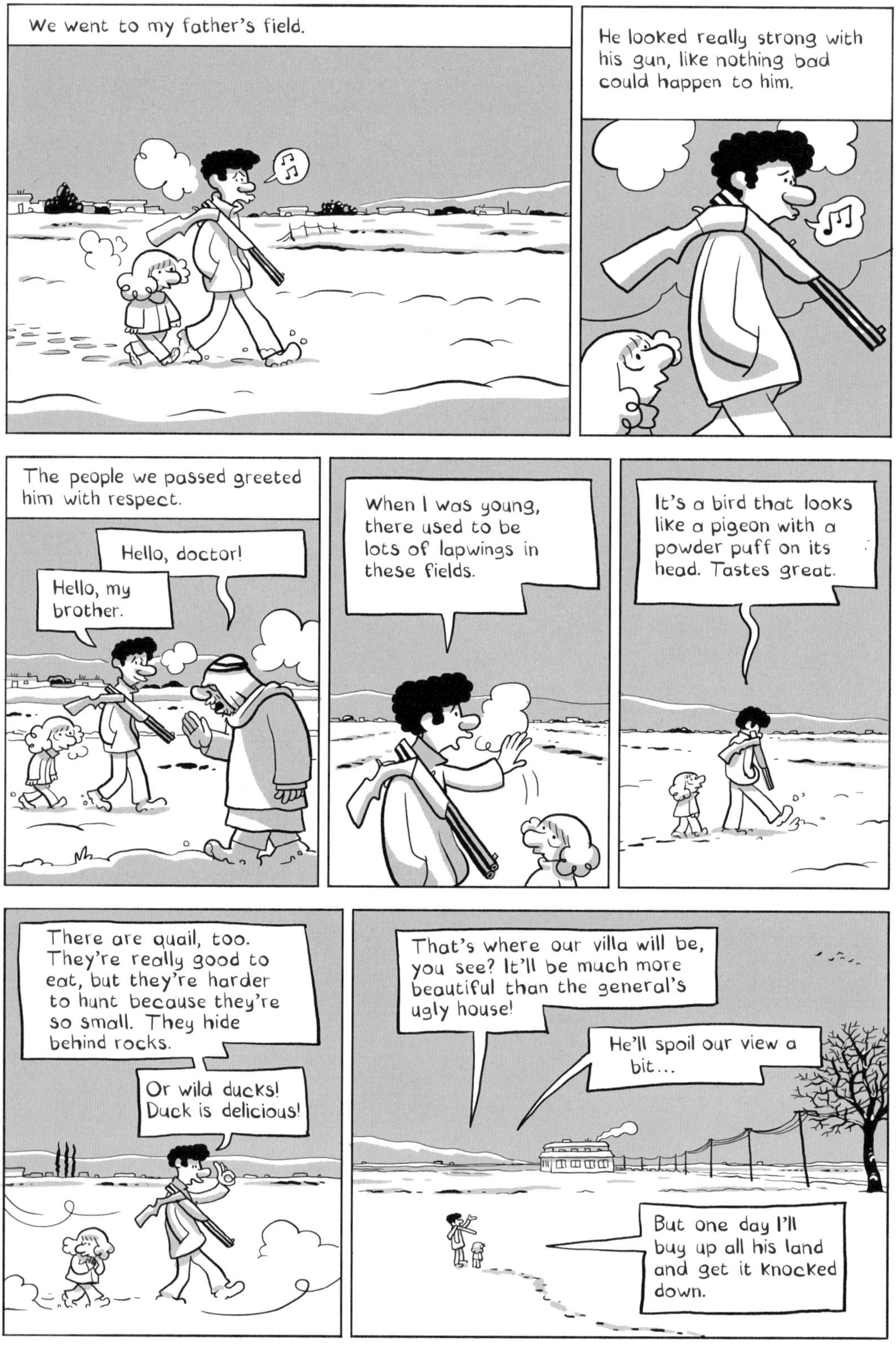
We went to my father's field.
He looked really strong with his gun, like nothing bad could happen to him.
The people we passed greeted him with respect.
Hello, doctor!
Hello, my brother.
When I was young, there used to be lots of lapwings in these fields.
It's a bird that looks like a pigeon with a powder puff on its head. Tastes great.
There are quail, too. They're really good to eat, but they're harder to hunt because they're so small. They hide behind rocks.
Or wild ducks! Duck is delicious!
That's where our villa will be, you see? It'll be much more beautiful than the general's ugly house!
He'll spoil our view a bit...
But one day I'll buy up all his land and get it knocked down.

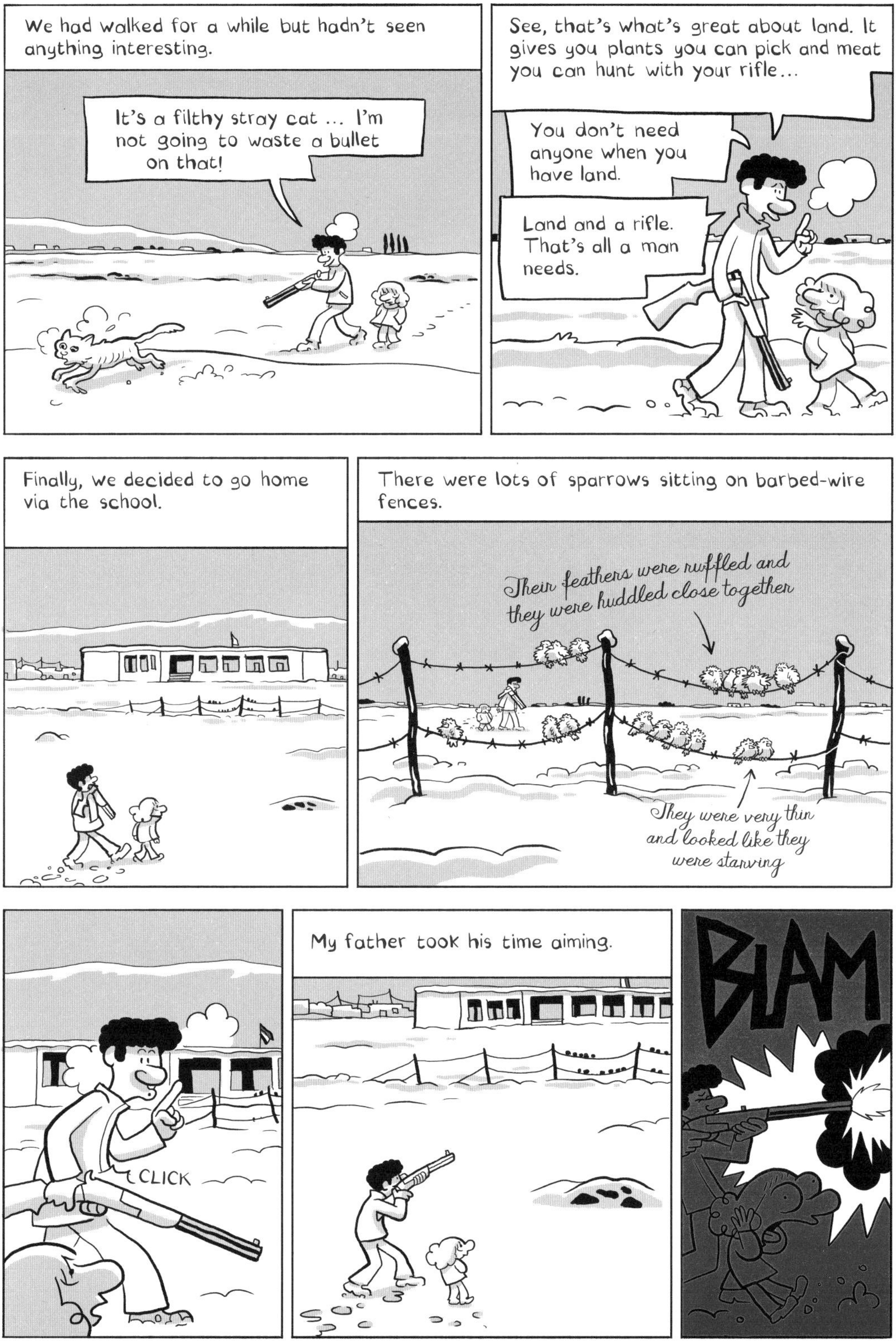
We had walked for a while but hadn't seen anything interesting.
It's a filthy stray cat ... I'm not going to waste a bullet on that!
See, that's what's great about land. It gives you plants you can pick and meat you can hunt with your rifle...
You don't need anyone when you have land.
Land and a rifle. That's all a man needs.
Finally, we decided to go home via the school.
There were lots of sparrows sitting on barbed-wire fences.
Their feathers were ruffled and they were huddled close together
They were very thin and looked like they were starving
CLICK
My father took his time aiming.
BLAM

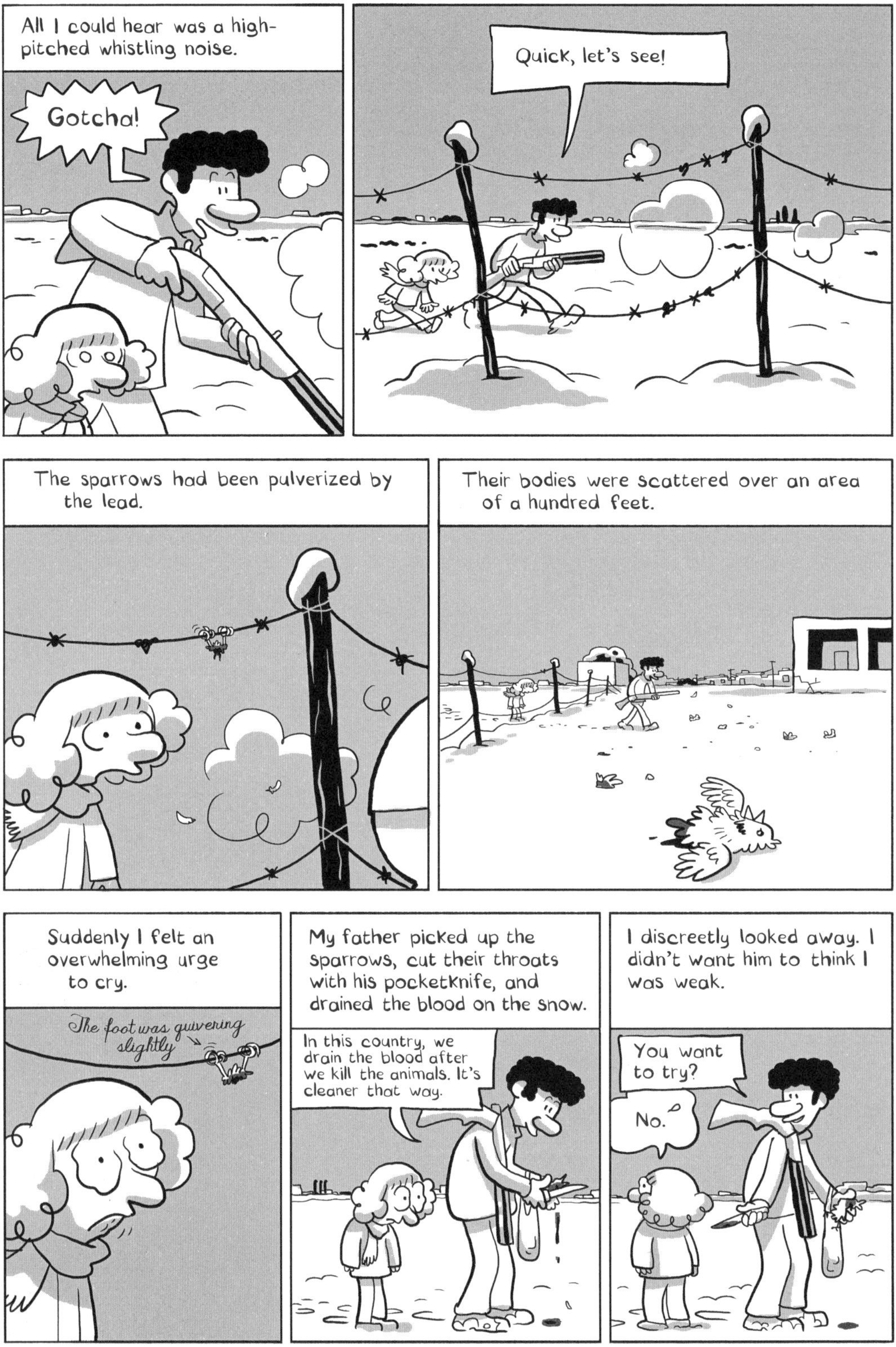
All I could hear was a high-pitched whistling noise.
Gotcha!
Quick, let's see!
The sparrows had been pulverized by the lead.
Their bodies were scattered over an area of a hundred feet.
Suddenly I felt an overwhelming urge to cry.
The foot was quivering slightly
My father picked up the sparrows, cut their throats with his pocketknife, and drained the blood on the snow.
In this country, we drain the blood after we kill the animals. It's cleaner that way.
I discreetly looked away. I didn't want him to think I was weak.
You want to try?
No.

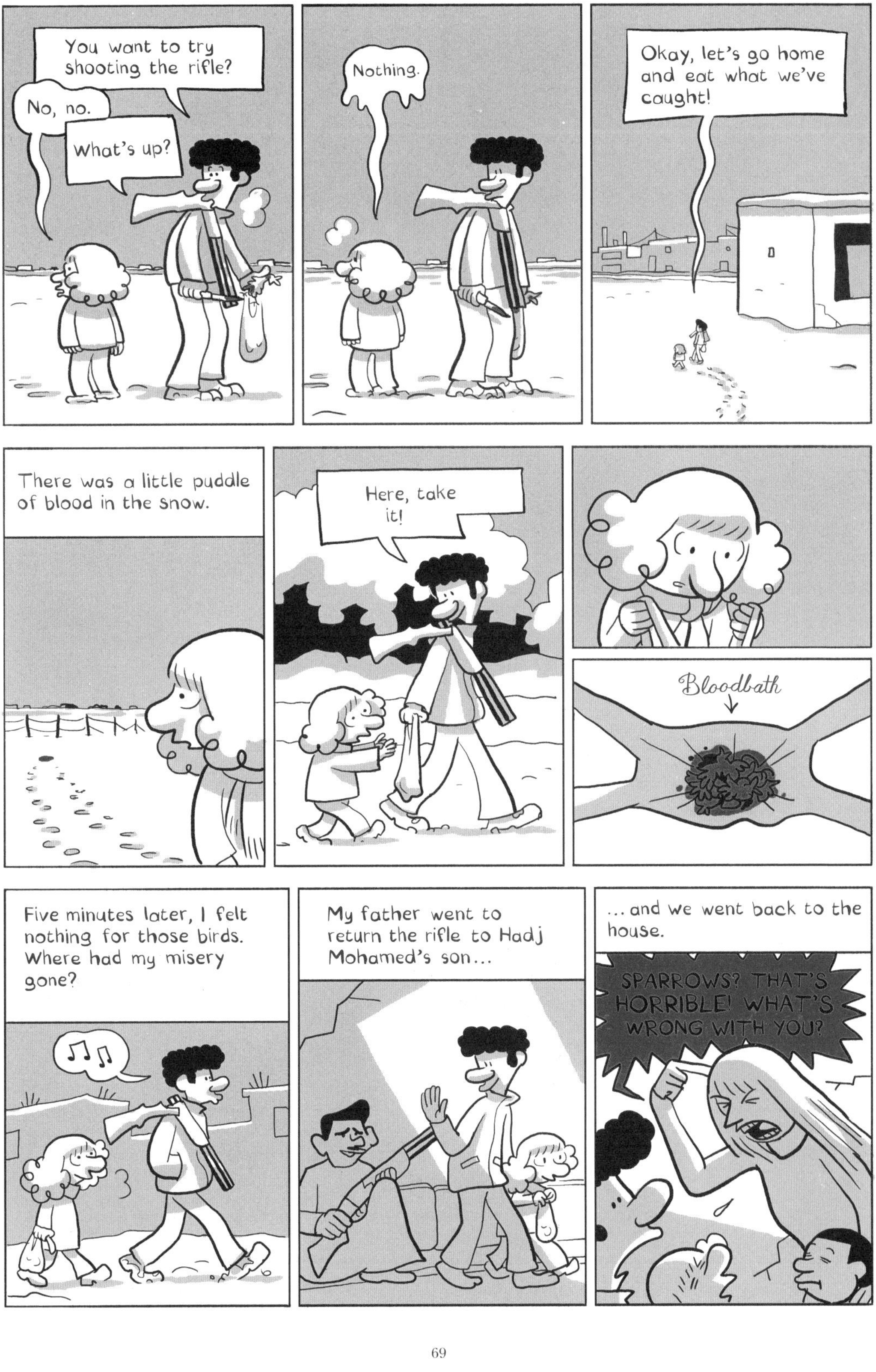
You want to try shooting the rifle?
No, no.
What's up?
Nothing.
Okay, let's go home and eat what we've caught!
There was a little puddle of blood in the snow.
Here, take it!
Bloodbath
Five minutes later, I felt nothing for those birds. Where had my misery gone?
My father went to return the rifle to Hadj Mohamed's son...
... and we went back to the house.
SPARROWS? THAT'S HORRIBLE! WHAT'S WRONG WITH YOU?

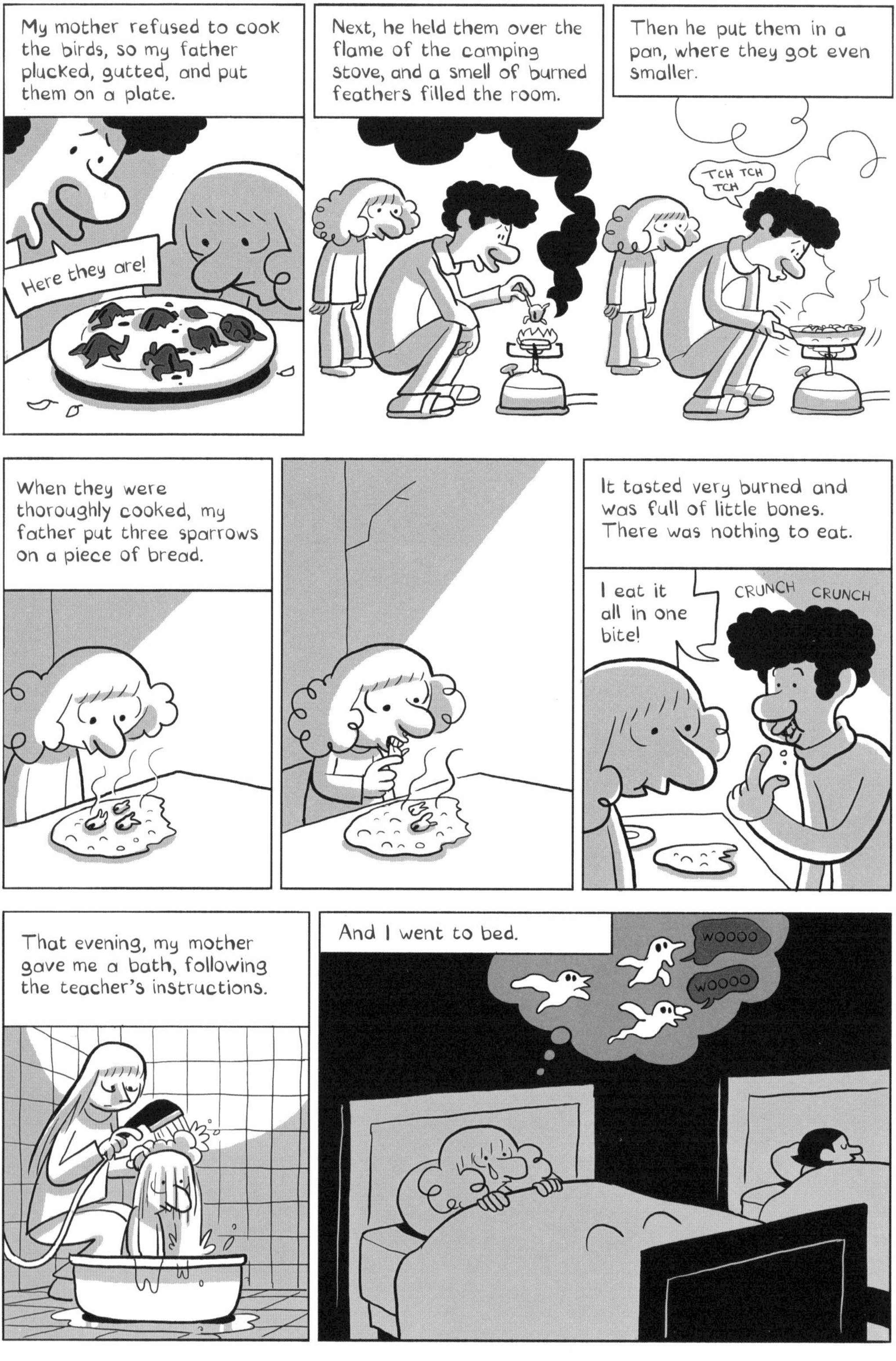
My mother refused to cook the birds, so my father plucked, gutted, and put them on a plate.
Here they are!
Next, he held them over the flame of the camping stove, and a smell of burned feathers filled the room.
Then he put them in a pan, where they got even smaller.
TCH TCH TCH
When they were thoroughly cooked, my father put three sparrows on a piece of bread.
It tasted very burned and was full of little bones. There was nothing to eat.
I eat it all in one bite!
CRUNCH CRUNCH
That evening, my mother gave me a bath, following the teacher's instructions.
And I went to bed.
WOOOO
WOOOO

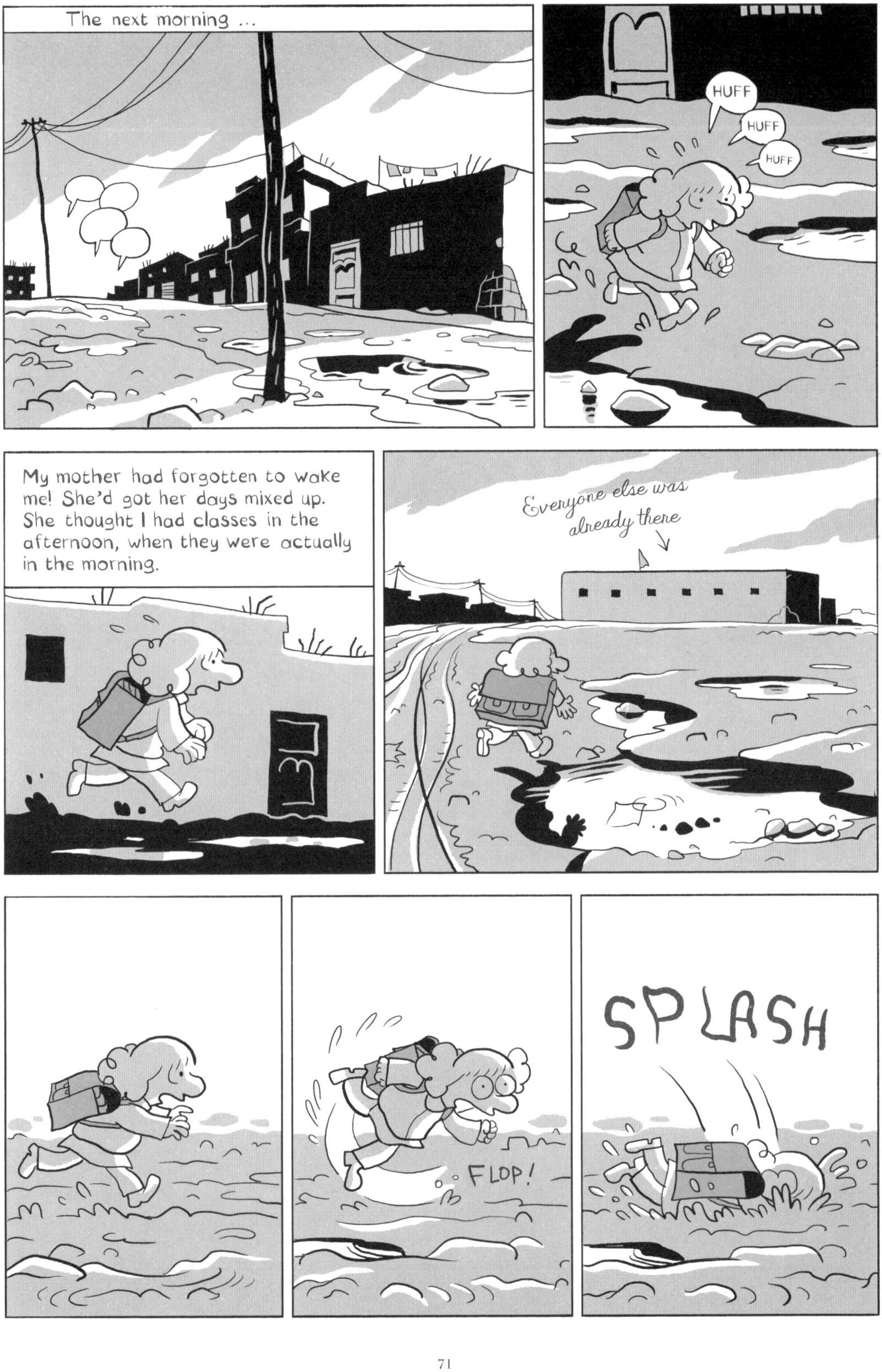

The next morning ...
HUFF
HUFF
HUFF
My mother had forgotten to wake me! She'd got her days mixed up. She thought I had classes in the afternoon, when they were actually in the morning.
Everyone else was already there
FLOP!
SPLASH

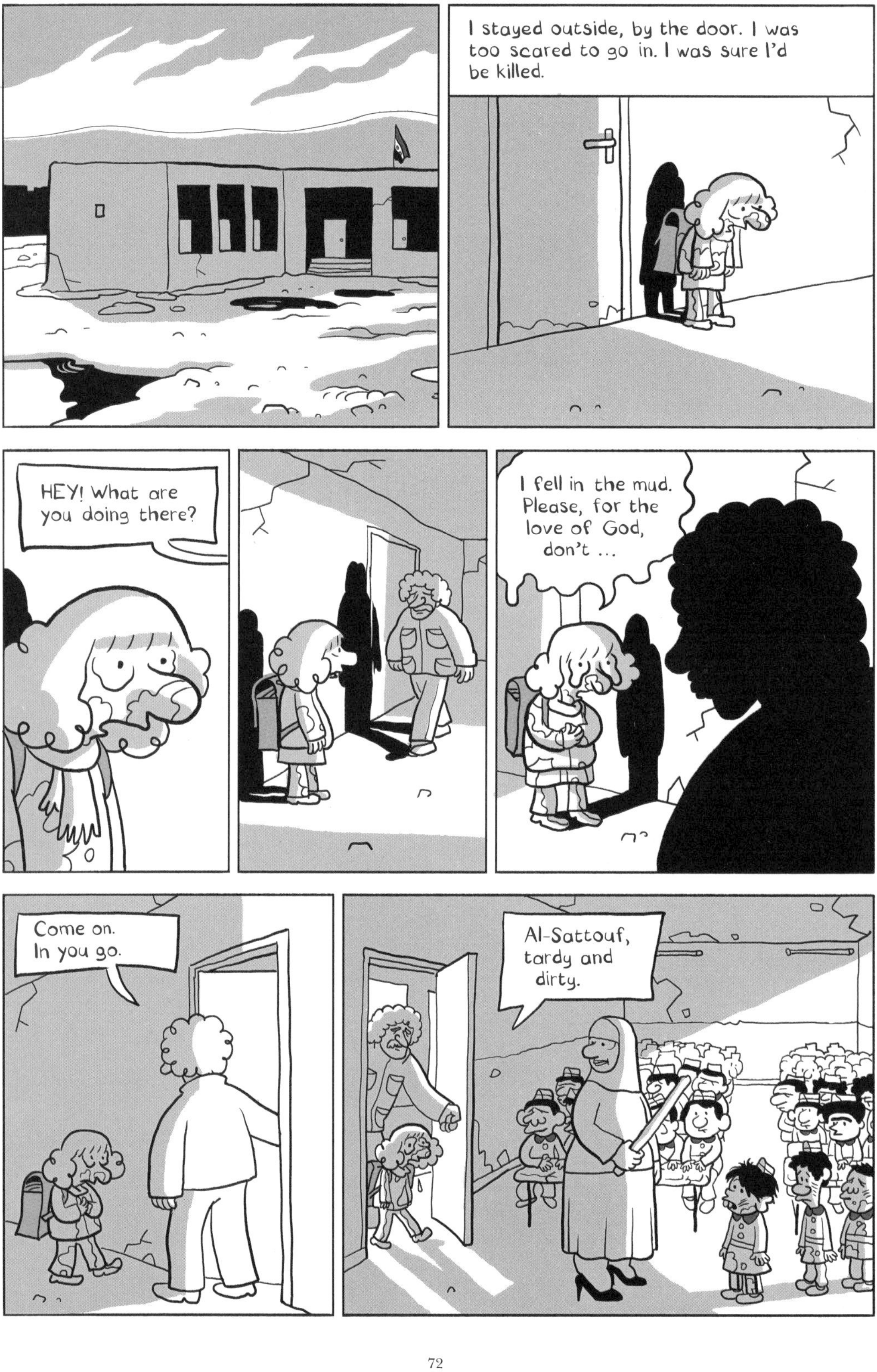
I stayed outside, by the door. I was too scared to go in. I was sure I'd be killed.
HEY! What are you doing there?
I fell in the mud. Please, for the love of God, don't ...
Come on. In you go.
Al-Sattouf, tardy and dirty.

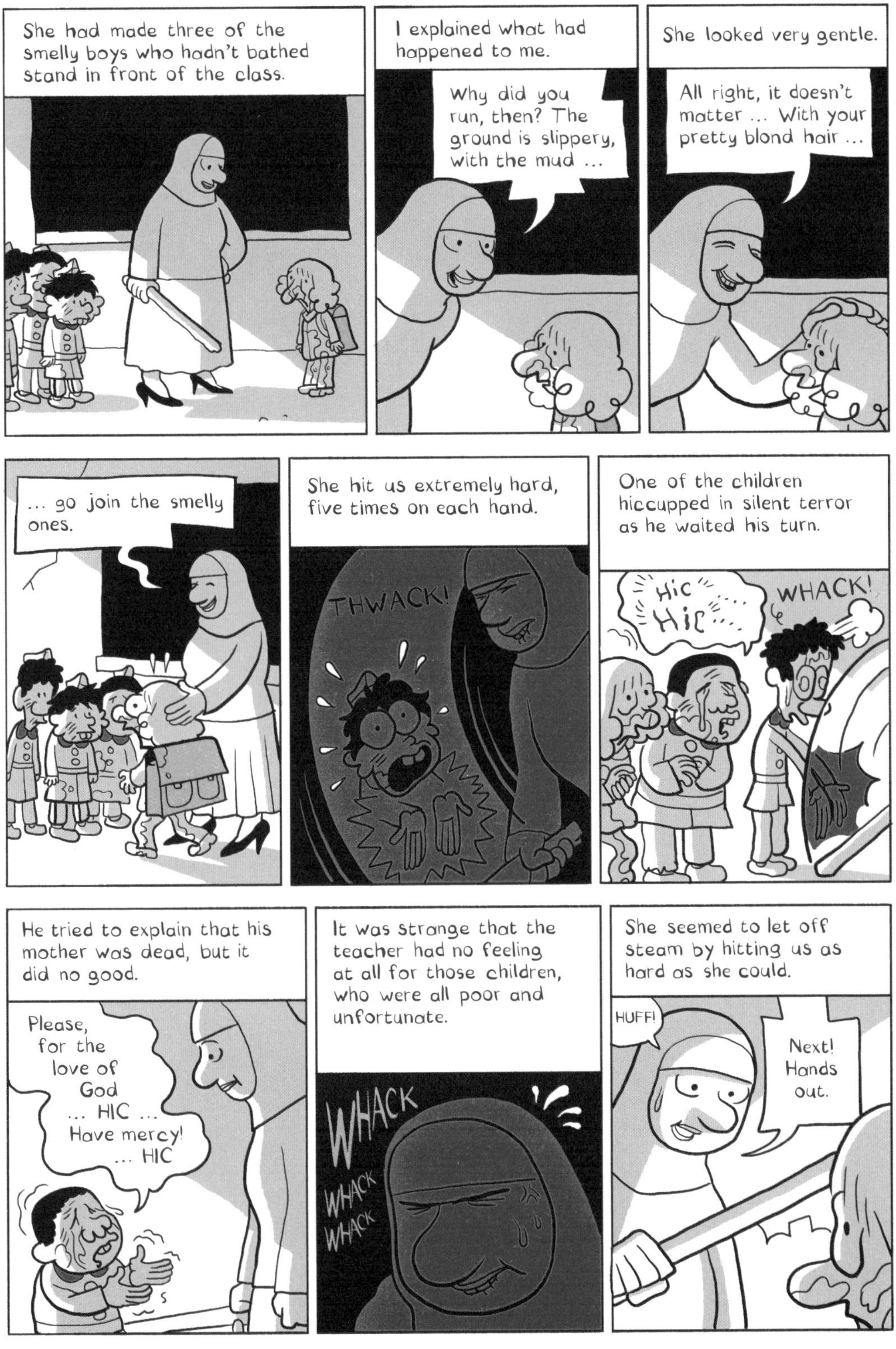
She had made three of the smelly boys who hadn't bathed stand in front of the class.
I explained what had happened to me.
Why did you run, then? The ground is slippery, with the mud ...
She looked very gentle.
All right, it doesn't matter ... With your pretty blond hair ...
... go join the smelly ones.
She hit us extremely hard, five times on each hand.
THWACK!
One of the children hiccupped in silent terror as he waited his turn.
HIC HIC
WHACK!
He tried to explain that his mother was dead, but it did no good.
Please, for the love of God ... HIC ... Have mercy! ... HIC
It was strange that the teacher had no feeling at all for those children, who were all poor and unfortunate.
WHACK
WHACK
WHACK
She seemed to let off steam by hitting us as hard as she could.
HUFF!
Next! Hands out.

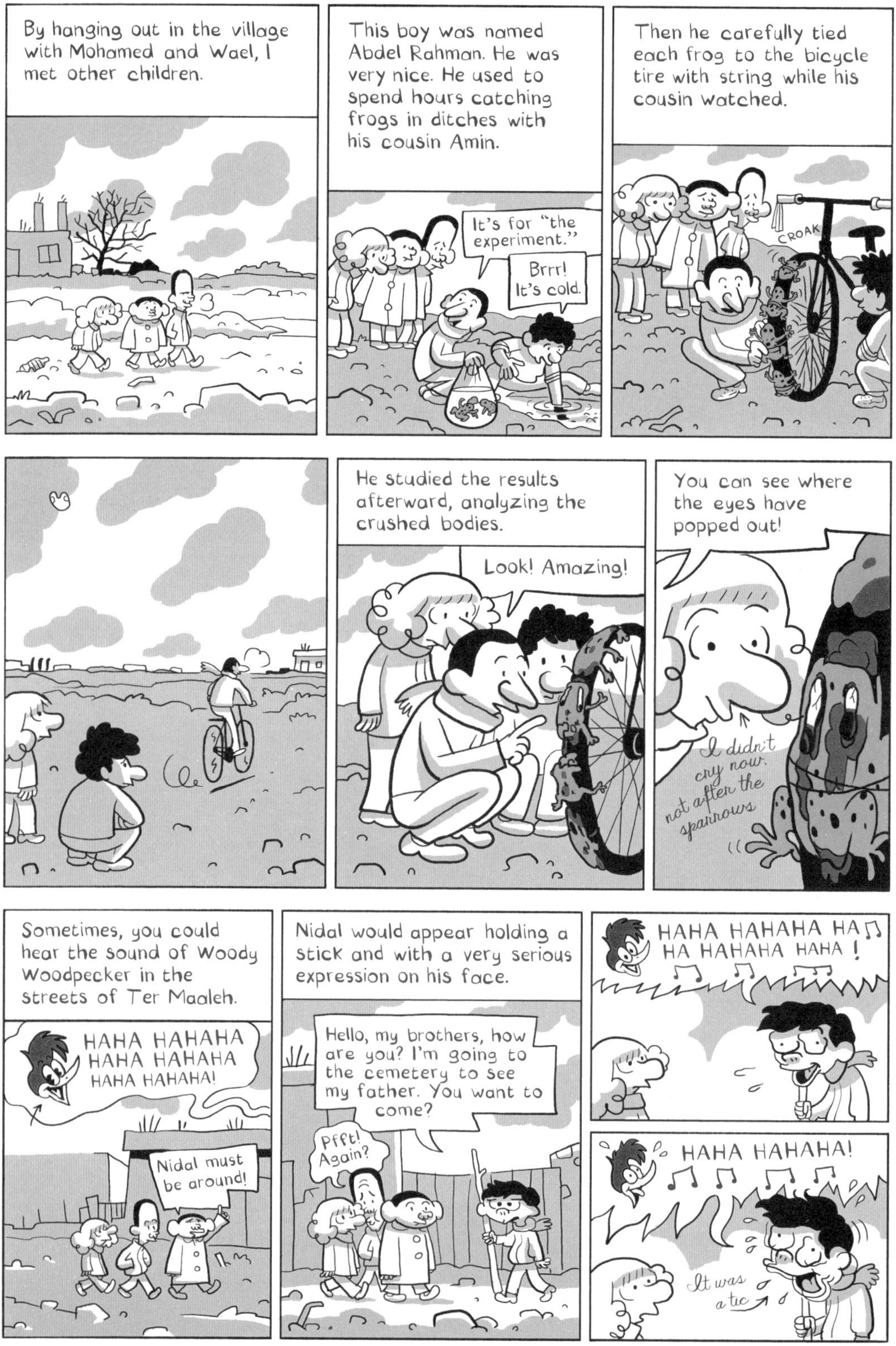
By hanging out in the village with Mohamed and Wael, I met other children.
This boy was named Abdel Rahman. He was very nice. He used to spend hours catching frogs in ditches with his cousin Amin.
It's for "the experiment."
Brrr! It's cold.
Then he carefully tied each frog to the bicycle tire with string while his cousin watched.
CROAK
He studied the results afterward, analyzing the crushed bodies.
Look! Amazing!
You can see where the eyes have popped out!
I didn't cry now, not after the sparrows
Sometimes, you could hear the sound of Woody Woodpecker in the streets of Ter Maaleh.
HAHA HAHAHA HAHA HAHAHA HAHA HAHAHA!
Nidal must be around!
Nidal would appear holding a stick and with a very serious expression on his face.
Hello, my brothers, how are you? I'm going to the cemetery to see my father. You want to come?
Pfft! Again?
HAHA HAHAHA HA HA HAHAHA HAHA !
HAHA HAHAHA!
It was a tic

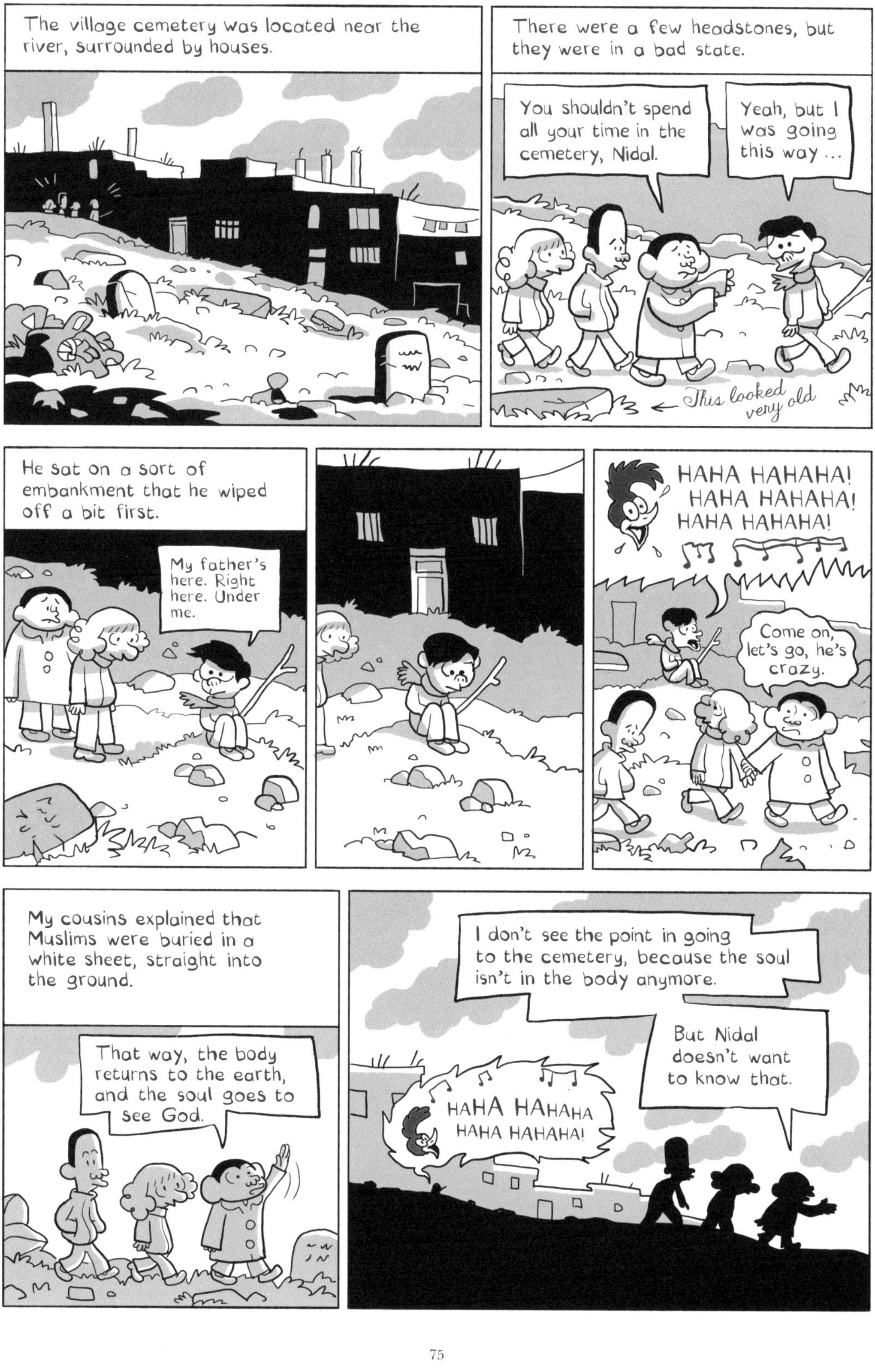
The village cemetery was located near the river, surrounded by houses.
There were a few headstones, but they were in a bad state.
You shouldn't spend all your time in the cemetery, Nidal.
Yeah, but I was going this way ...
This looked very old
He sat on a sort of embankment that he wiped off a bit first.
My father's here. Right here. Under me.
HAHA HAHAHA! HAHA HAHAHA! HAHA HAHAHA!
Come on, let's go, he's crazy.
My cousins explained that Muslims were buried in a white sheet, straight into the ground.
That way, the body returns to the earth, and the soul goes to see God.
I don't see the point in going to the cemetery, because the soul isn't in the body anymore.
But Nidal doesn't want to know that.
HAHA HAHAHA HAHA HAHAHA!

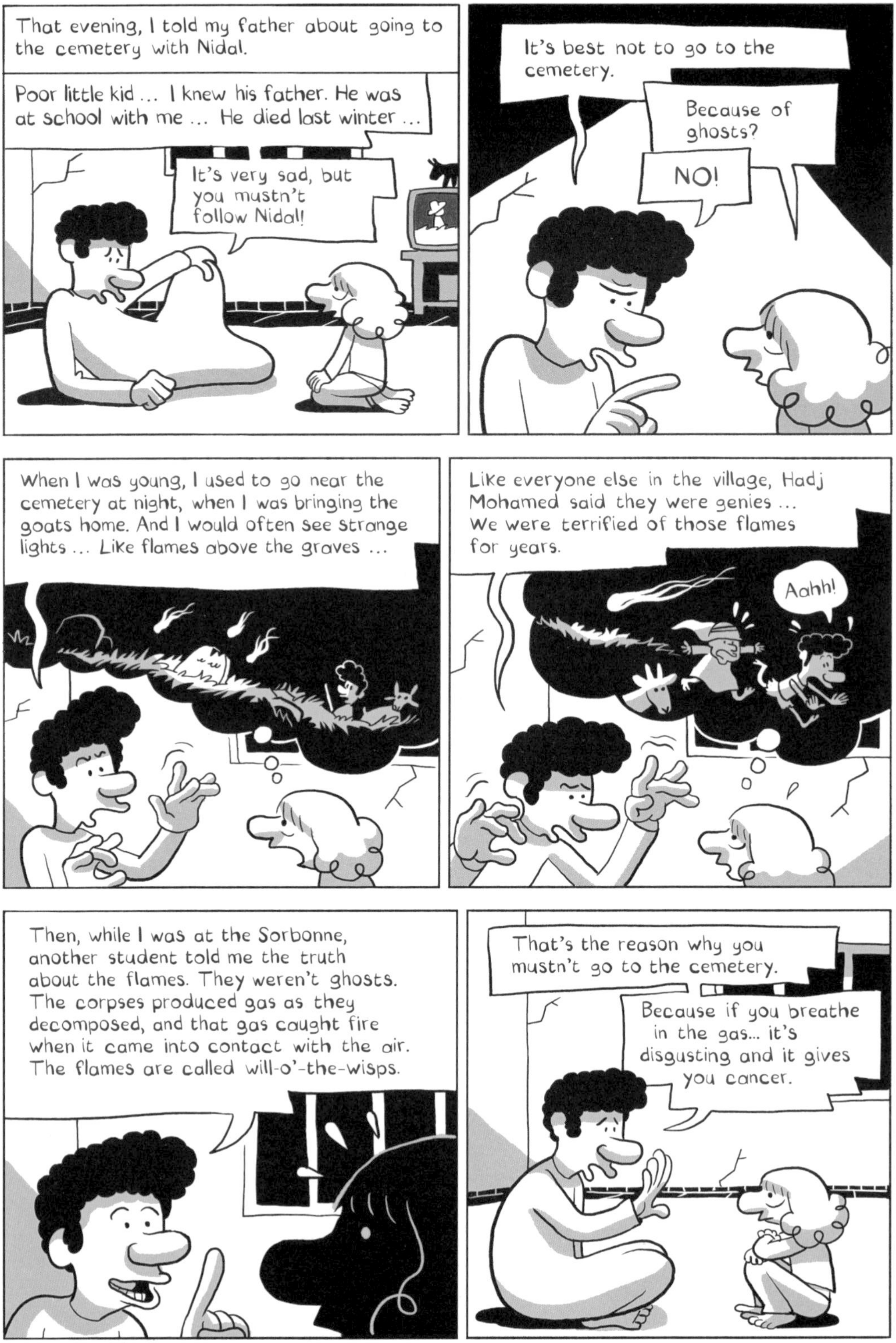

That evening, I told my father about going to the cemetery with Nidal.
Poor little kid ... I knew his father. He was at school with me ... He died last winter ...
It's very sad, but you mustn't follow Nidal!
It's best not to go to the cemetery.
Because of ghosts?
NO!
When I was young, I used to go near the cemetery at night, when I was bringing the goats home. And I would often see strange lights ... Like flames above the graves ...
Like everyone else in the village, Hadj Mohamed said they were genies ... We were terrified of those flames for years.
Aahh!
Then, while I was at the Sorbonne, another student told me the truth about the flames. They weren't ghosts. The corpses produced gas as they decomposed, and that gas caught fire when it came into contact with the air. The flames are called will-o'-the-wisps.
That's the reason why you mustn't go to the cemetery.
Because if you breathe in the gas... it's disgusting and it gives you cancer.

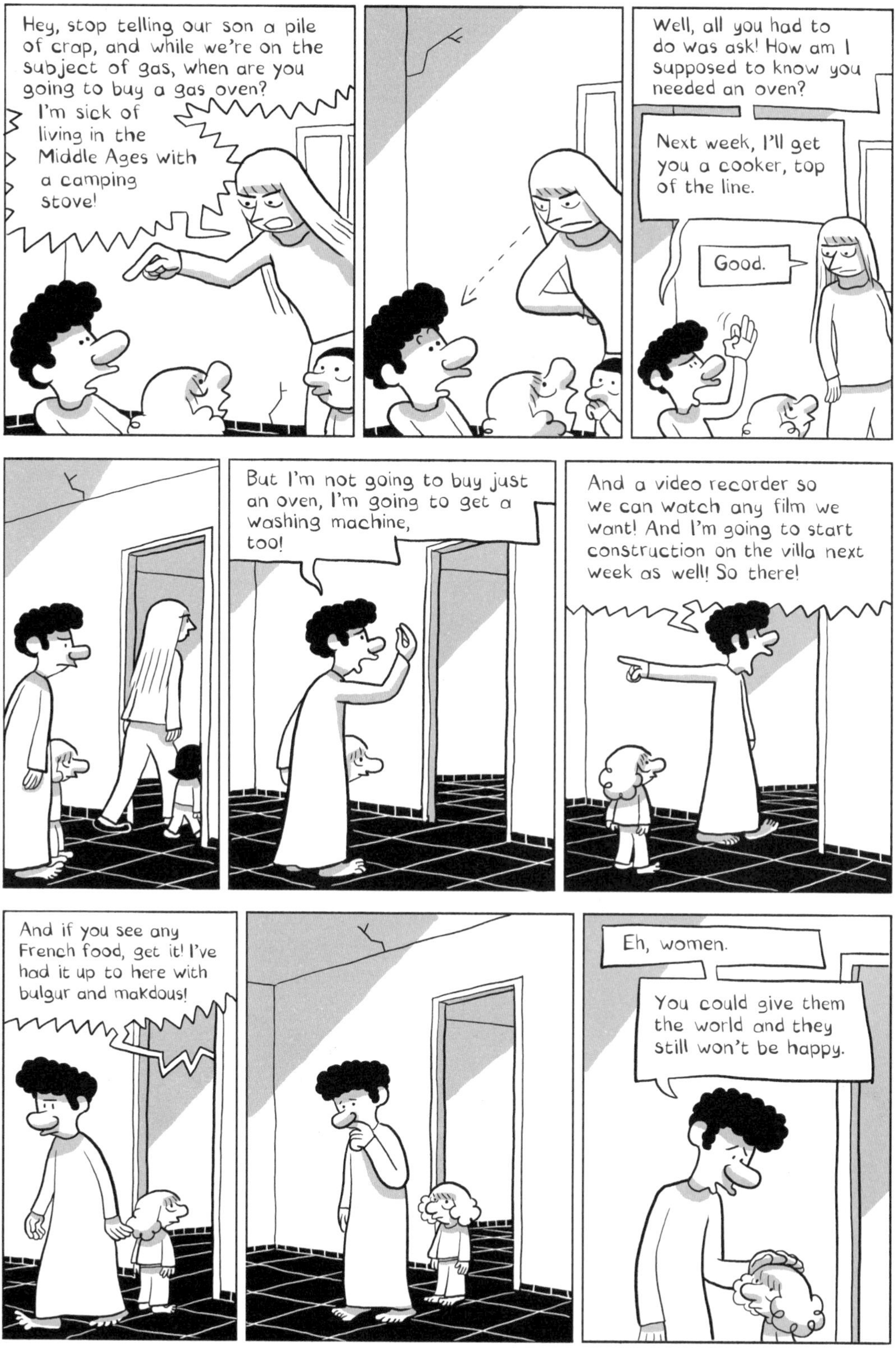
Hey, stop telling our son a pile of crap, and while we're on the subject of gas, when are you going to buy a gas oven?
I'm sick of living in the Middle Ages with a camping stove!
Well, all you had to do was ask! How am I supposed to know you needed an oven?
Next week, I'll get you a cooker, top of the line.
Good.
But I'm not going to buy just an oven, I'm going to get a washing machine, too!
And a video recorder so we can watch any film we want! And I'm going to start construction on the villa next week as well! So there!
And if you see any French food, get it! I've had it up to here with bulgur and makdous!
Eh, women.
You could give them the world and they still won't be happy.

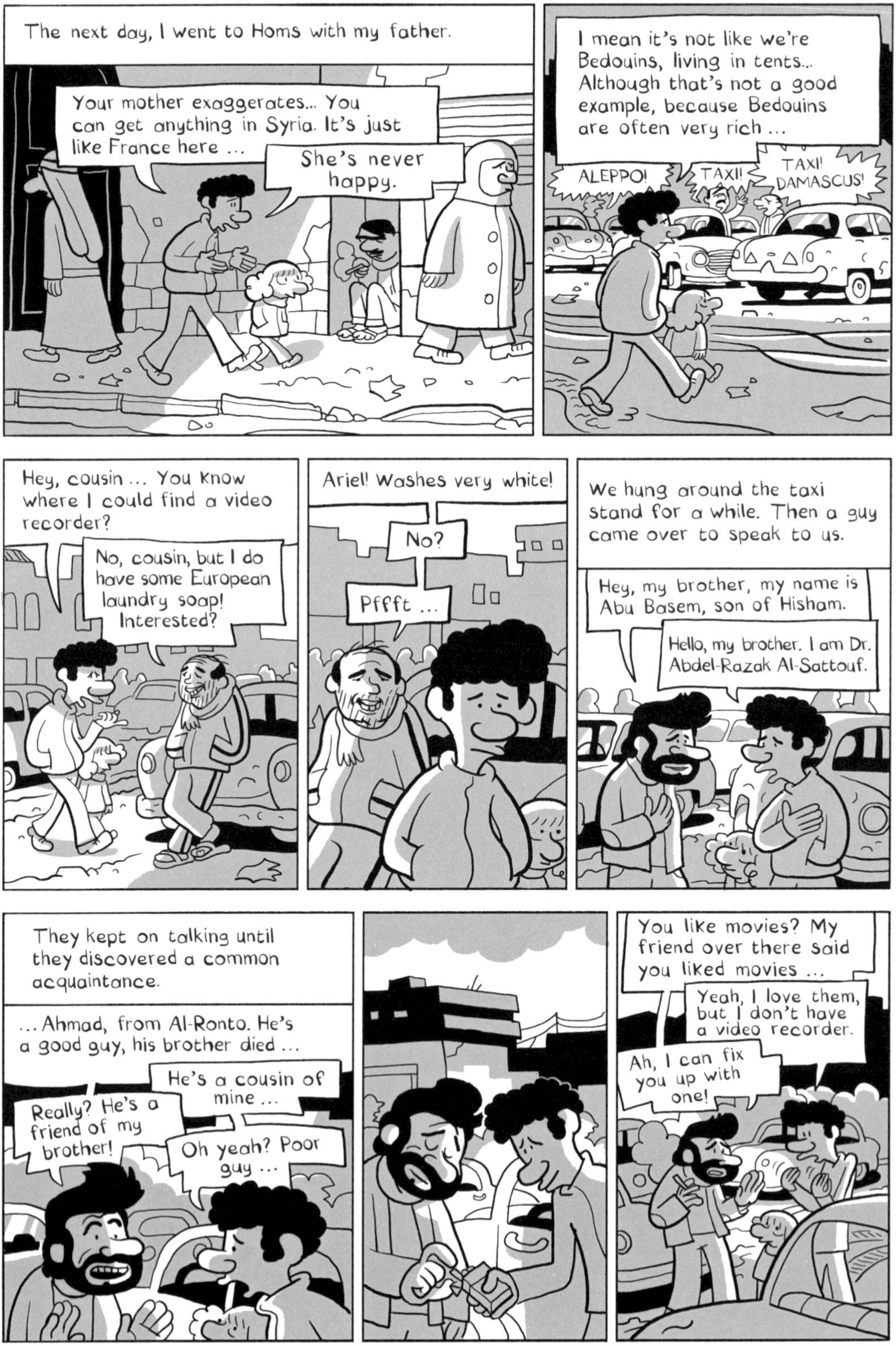

The next day, I went to Homs with my father.
Your mother exaggerates... You can get anything in Syria. It's just like France here ...
She's never happy.
I mean it's not like we're Bedouins, living in tents... Although that's not a good example, because Bedouins are often very rich ...
ALEPPO!
TAXI!
TAXI! DAMASCUS!
Hey, cousin ... You know where I could find a video recorder?
No, cousin, but I do have some European laundry soap! Interested?
Ariel! Washes very white!
No?
Pffft ...
We hung around the taxi stand for a while. Then a guy came over to speak to us.
Hey, my brother, my name is Abu Basem, son of Hisham.
Hello, my brother. I am Dr. Abdel-Razak Al-Sattouf.
They kept on talking until they discovered a common acquaintance.
... Ahmad, from Al-Ronto. He's a good guy, his brother died ...
Really? He's a friend of my brother!
He's a cousin of mine ...
Oh yeah? Poor guy ...
You like movies? My friend over there said you liked movies ...
Yeah, I love them, but I don't have a video recorder.
Ah, I can fix you up with one!

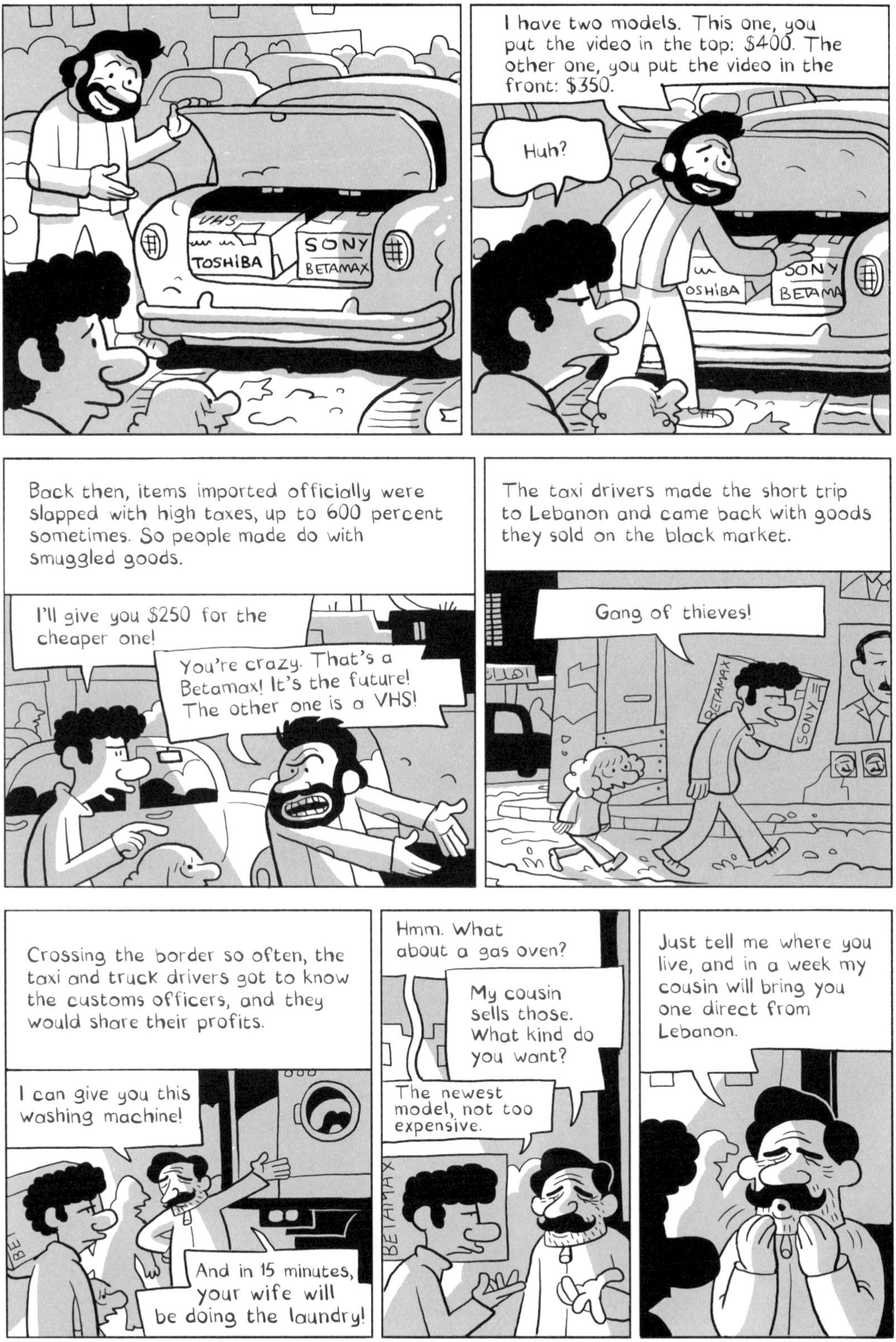
VHS
TOSHIBA
SONY
BETAMAX
I have two models. This one, you put the video in the top: $400. The other one, you put the video in the front: $350.
Huh?
OSHIBA
SONY
BETAMA
Back then, items imported officially were slapped with high taxes, up to 600 percent sometimes. So people made do with smuggled goods.
I'll give you $250 for the cheaper one!
You're crazy. That's a Betamax! It's the future! The other one is a VHS!
The taxi drivers made the short trip to Lebanon and came back with goods they sold on the black market.
Gang of thieves!
BETAMAX
SONY
Crossing the border so often, the taxi and truck drivers got to know the customs officers, and they would share their profits.
I can give you this washing machine!
And in 15 minutes, your wife will be doing the laundry!
Hmm. What about a gas oven?
My cousin sells those. What kind do you want?
The newest model, not too expensive.
BETAMAX
Just tell me where you live, and in a week my cousin will bring you one direct from Lebanon.

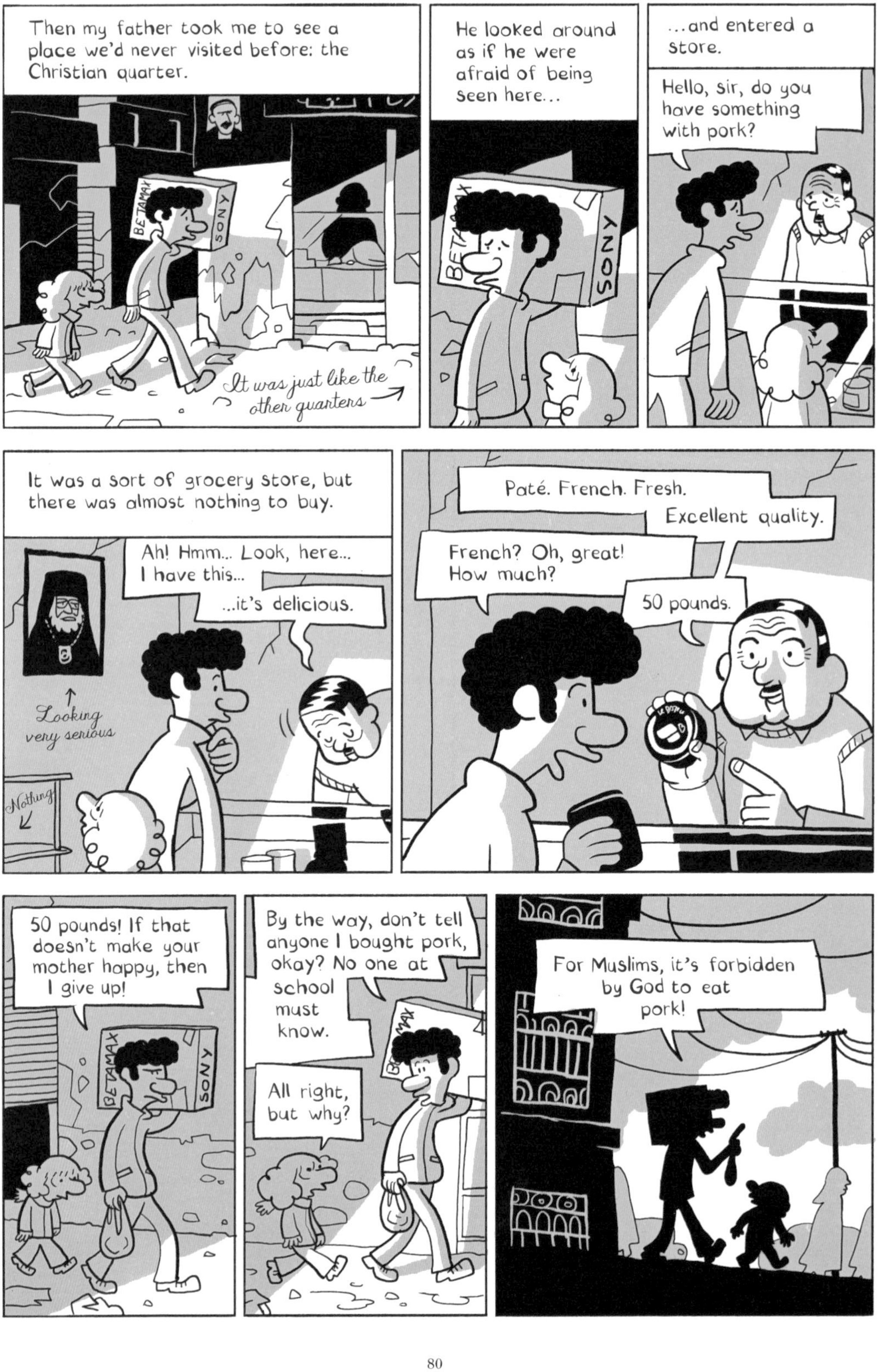

Then my father took me to see a place we'd never visited before: the Christian quarter.
BETAMAX
SONY
It was just like the other quarters
He looked around as if he were afraid of being seen here...
BETAMAX
SONY
...and entered a store.
Hello, sir, do you have something with pork?
It was a sort of grocery store, but there was almost nothing to buy.
Ah! Hmm... Look, here... I have this...
...it's delicious.
Looking very serious
Nothing
Paté. French. Fresh.
Excellent quality.
French? Oh, great! How much?
50 pounds.
50 pounds! If that doesn't make your mother happy, then I give up!
BETAMAX
SONY
By the way, don't tell anyone I bought pork, okay? No one at school must know.
All right, but why?
For Muslims, it's forbidden by God to eat pork!

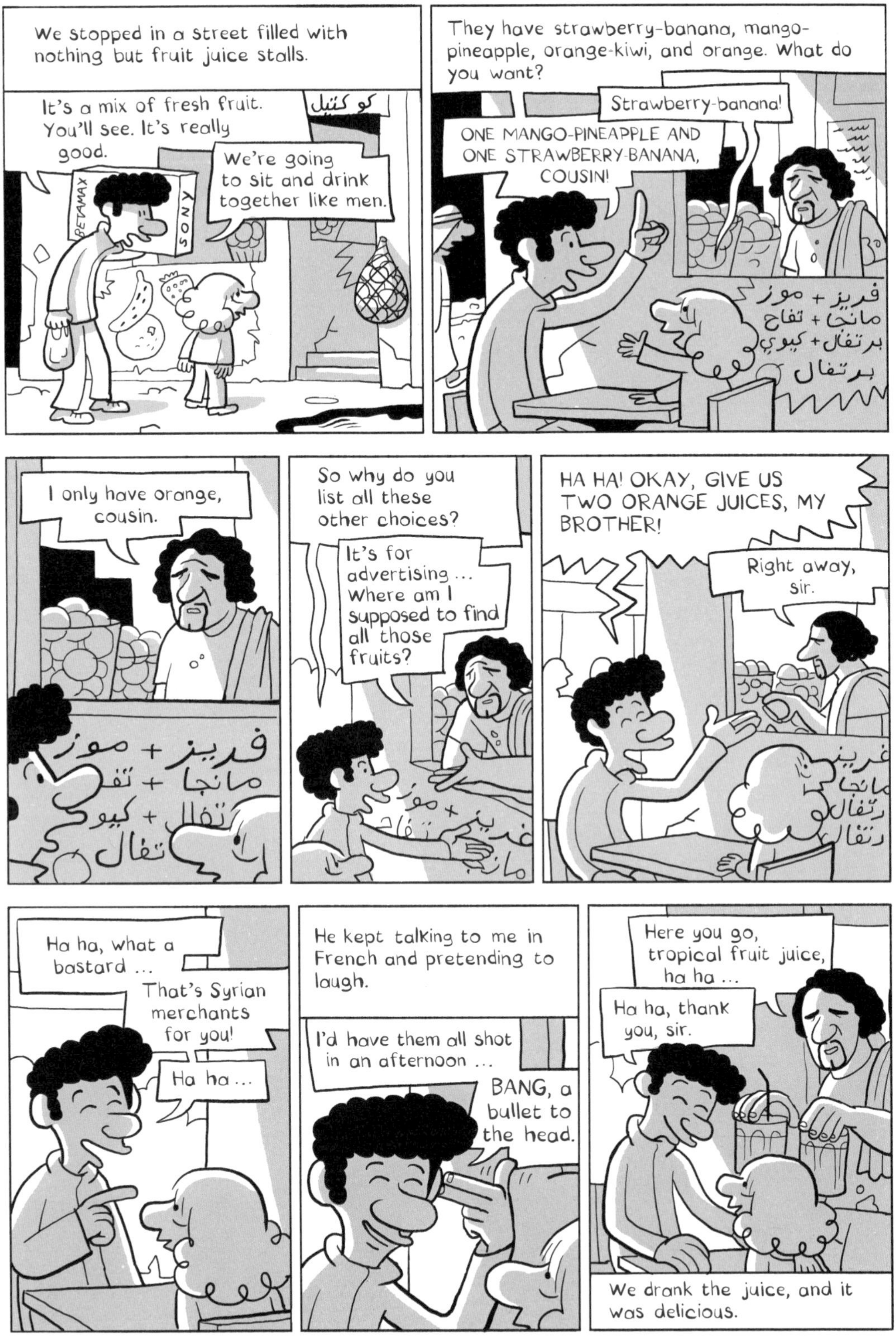

We stopped in a street filled with nothing but fruit juice stalls.
It's a mix of fresh fruit. You'll see. It's really good.
كوكتيل
BETAMAX
SONY
We're going to sit and drink together like men.
They have strawberry-banana, mango-pineapple, orange-kiwi, and orange. What do you want?
Strawberry-banana!
ONE MANGO-PINEAPPLE AND ONE STRAWBERRY-BANANA, COUSIN!
فريز + موز
مانجا + تفاح
برتفال + كيوي
برتفال
I only have orange, cousin.
So why do you list all these other choices?
It's for advertising ... Where am I supposed to find all those fruits?
HA HA! OKAY, GIVE US TWO ORANGE JUICES, MY BROTHER!
Right away, sir.
Ha ha, what a bastard ...
That's Syrian merchants for you!
Ha ha ...
He kept talking to me in French and pretending to laugh.
I'd have them all shot in an afternoon ...
BANG, a bullet to the head.
Here you go, tropical fruit juice, ha ha ...
Ha ha, thank you, sir.
We drank the juice, and it was delicious.

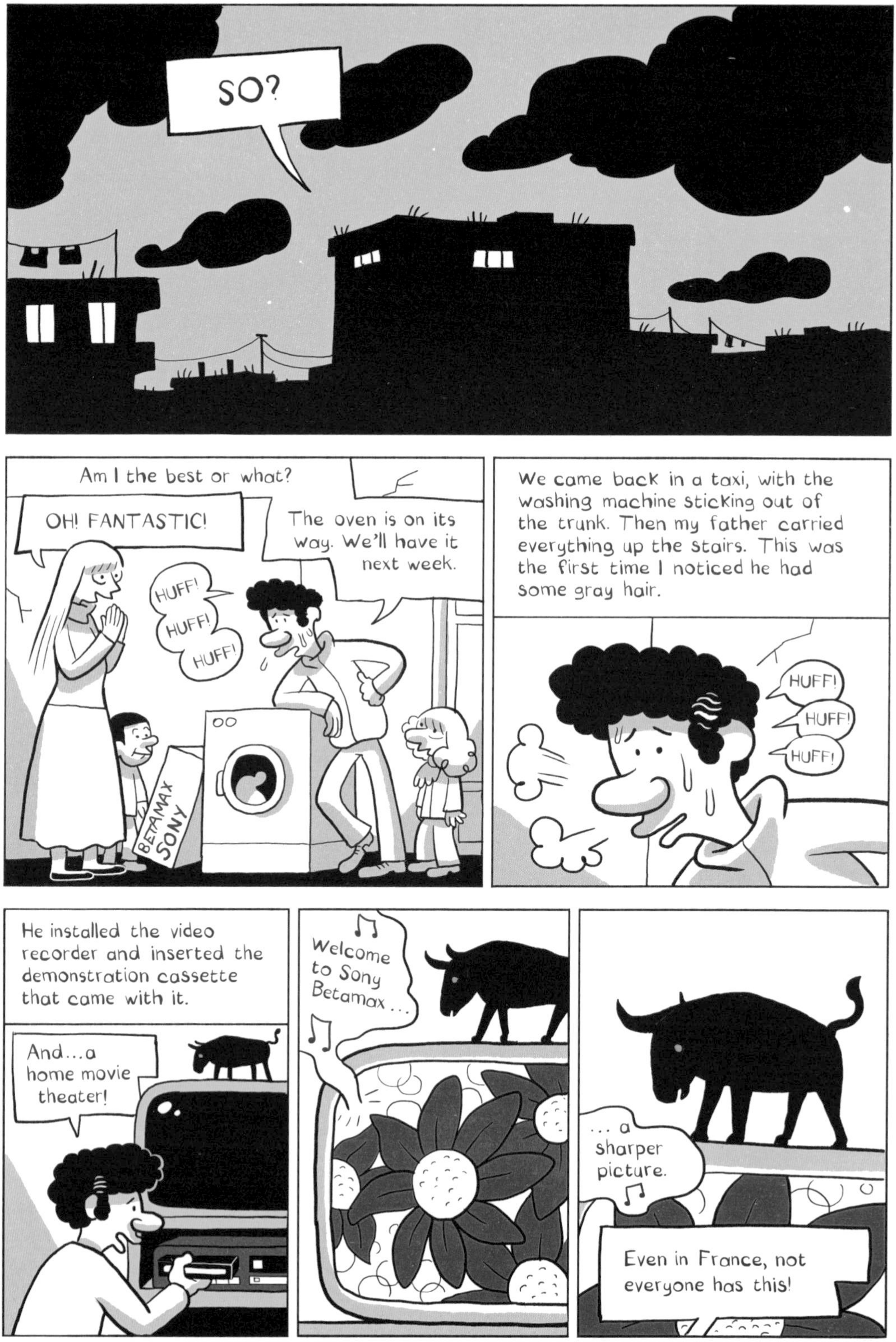
SO?
Am I the best or what?
OH! FANTASTIC!
HUFF!
HUFF!
HUFF!
The oven is on its way. We'll have it next week.
BETAMAX SONY
We came back in a taxi, with the washing machine sticking out of the trunk. Then my father carried everything up the stairs. This was the first time I noticed he had some gray hair.
HUFF!
HUFF!
HUFF!
He installed the video recorder and inserted the demonstration cassette that came with it.
And...a home movie theater!
Welcome to Sony Betamax...
...a sharper picture.
Even in France, not everyone has this!

CHAPTER 3

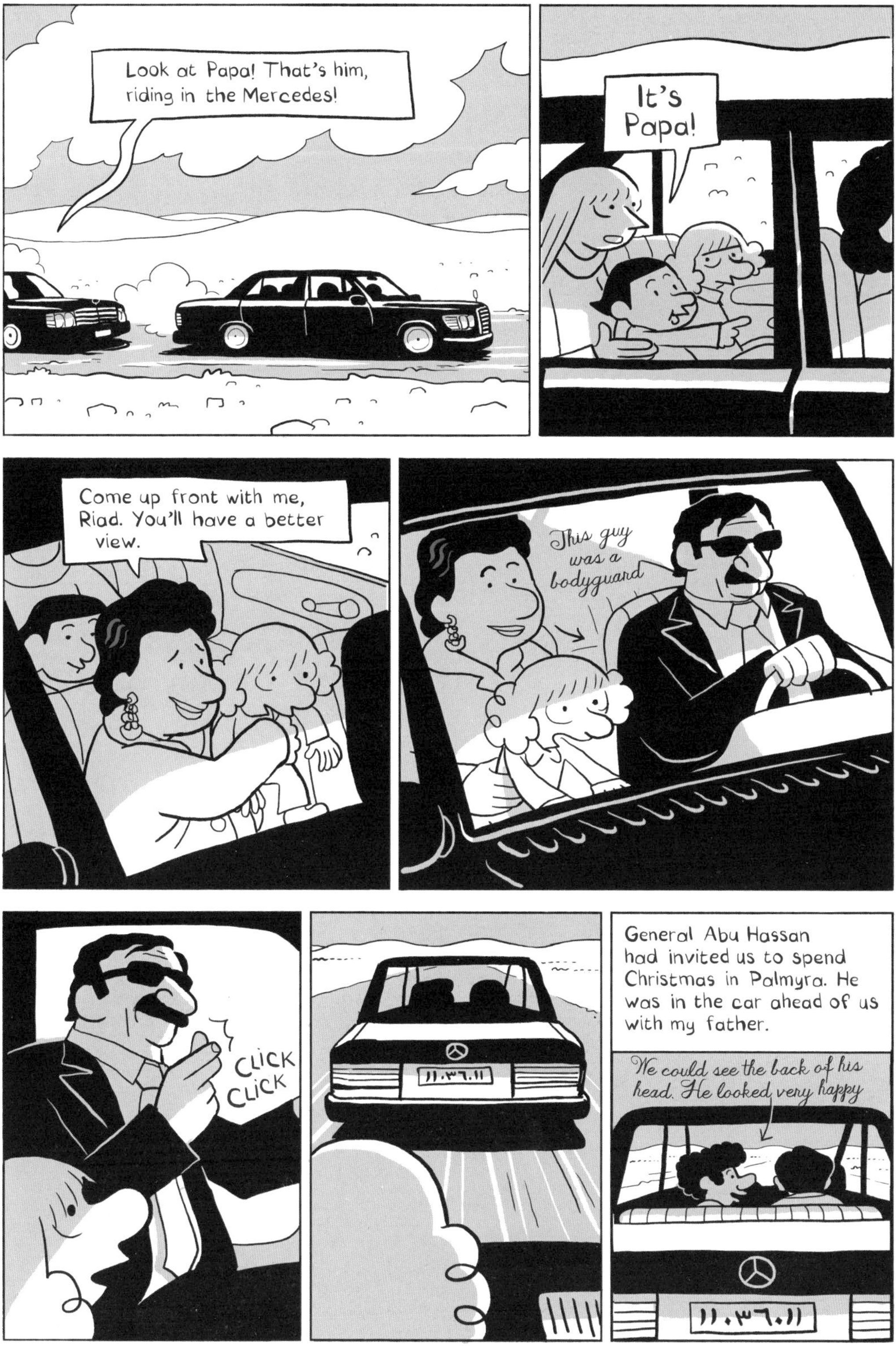
Look at Papa! That's him, riding in the Mercedes!
It's Papa!
Come up front with me, Riad. You'll have a better view.
This guy was a bodyguard
CLICK CLICK
General Abu Hassan had invited us to spend Christmas in Palmyra. He was in the car ahead of us with my father.
We could see the back of his head. He looked very happy

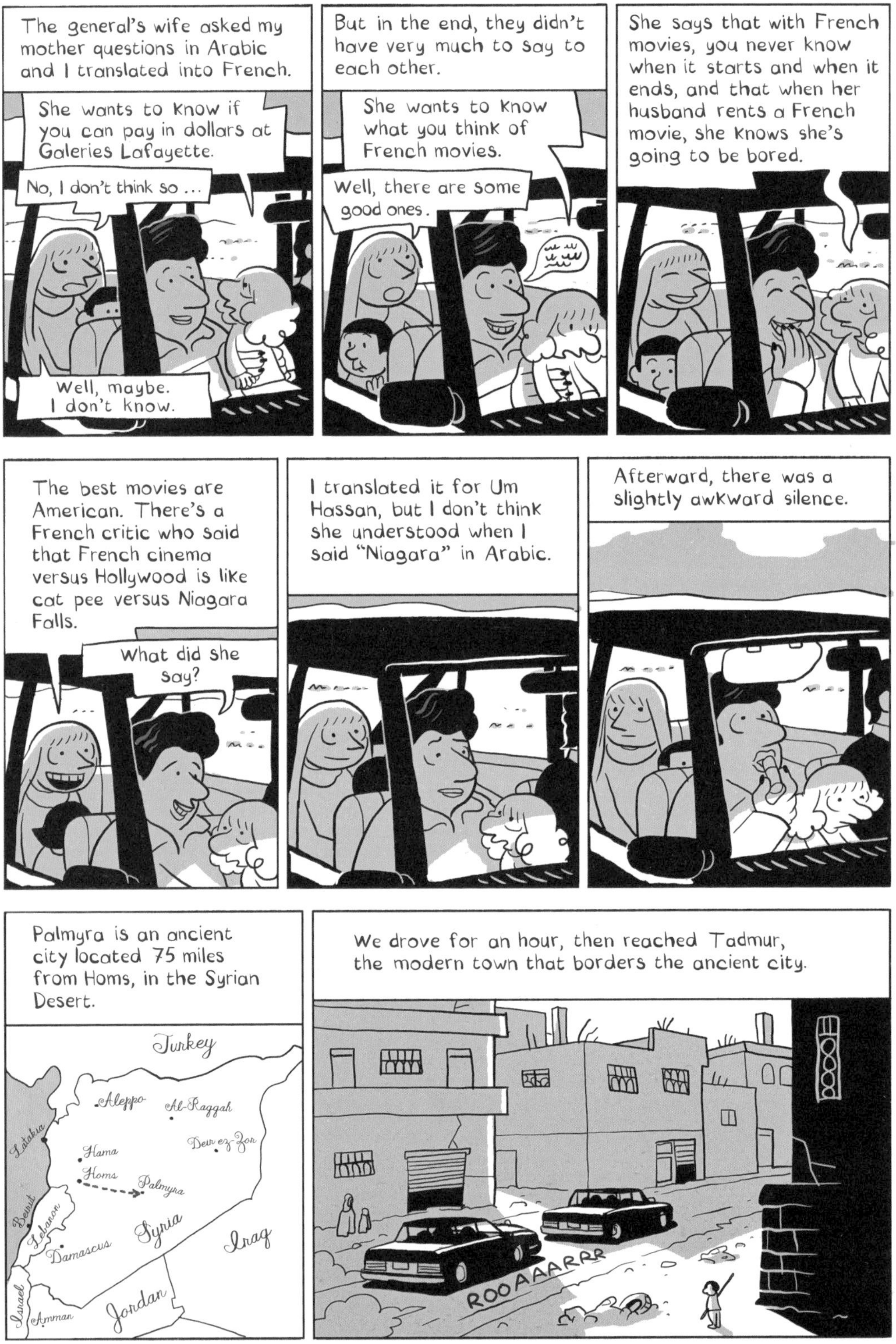
The general's wife asked my mother questions in Arabic and I translated into French.
She wants to know if you can pay in dollars at Galeries Lafayette.
No, I don't think so ...
Well, maybe. I don't know.
But in the end, they didn't have very much to say to each other.
She wants to know what you think of French movies.
Well, there are some good ones.
She says that with French movies, you never know when it starts and when it ends, and that when her husband rents a French movie, she knows she's going to be bored.
The best movies are American. There's a French critic who said that French cinema versus Hollywood is like cat pee versus Niagara Falls.
What did she say?
I translated it for Um Hassan, but I don't think she understood when I said "Niagara" in Arabic.
Afterward, there was a slightly awkward silence.
Palmyra is an ancient city located 75 miles from Homs, in the Syrian Desert.
Turkey
Aleppo
Al-Raqqah
Latakia
Hama
Deir ez-Zor
Homs
Palmyra
Beirut
Lebanon
Syria
Damascus
Iraq
Israel
Amman
Jordan
We drove for an hour, then reached Tadmur, the modern town that borders the ancient city.
ROOAAARRR

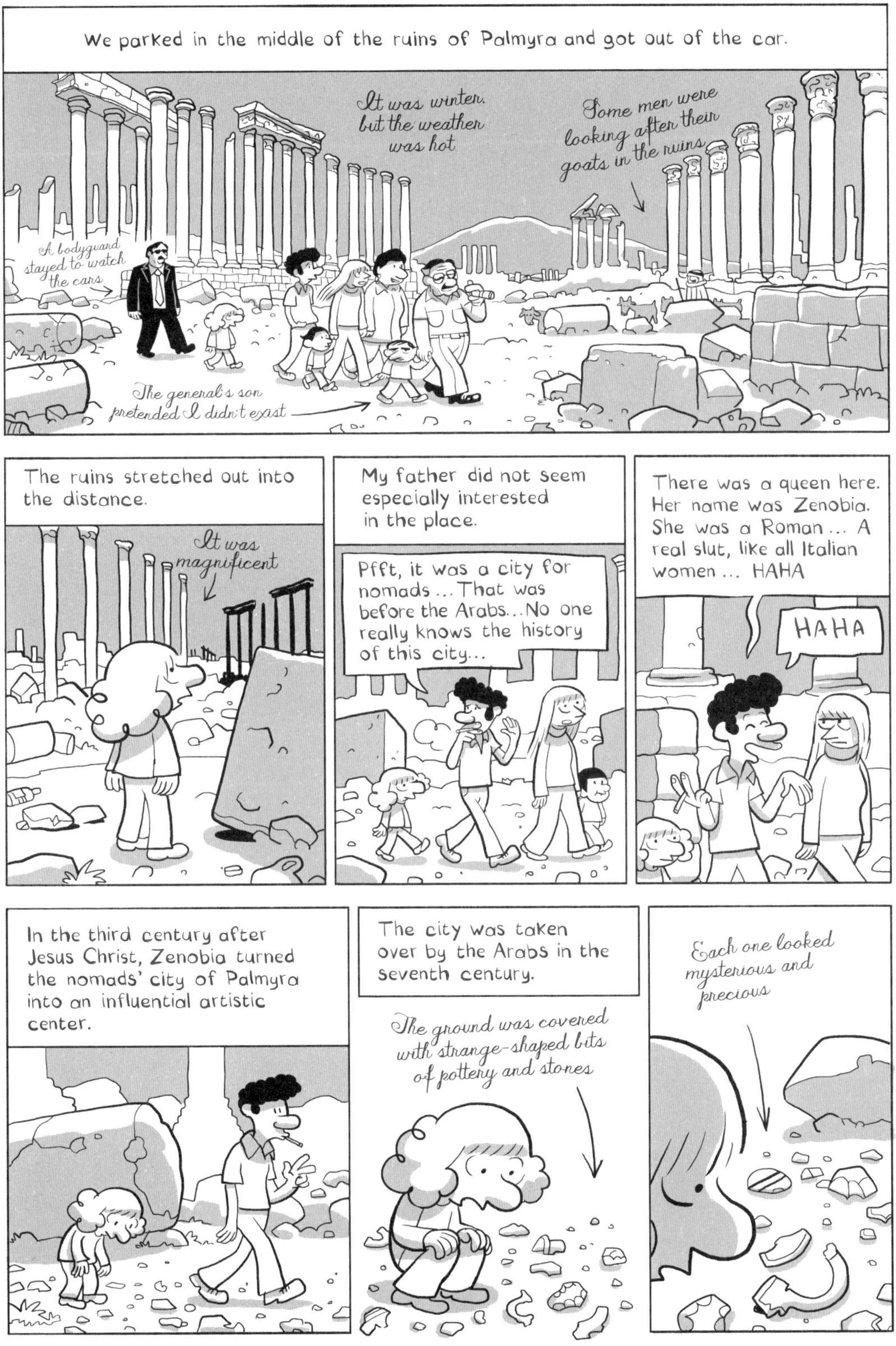
We parked in the middle of the ruins of Palmyra and got out of the car.
A bodyguard stayed to watch the cars
It was winter. but the weather was hot
Some men were looking after their goats in the ruins
The general's son pretended I didn't exist
The ruins stretched out into the distance.
It was magnificent
My father did not seem especially interested in the place.
Pfft, it was a city for nomads... That was before the Arabs... No one really knows the history of this city...
There was a queen here. Her name was Zenobia. She was a Roman... A real slut, like all Italian women... HAHA
HAHA
In the third century after Jesus Christ, Zenobia turned the nomads' city of Palmyra into an influential artistic center.
The city was taken over by the Arabs in the seventh century.
The ground was covered with strange-shaped bits of pottery and stones
Each one looked mysterious and precious

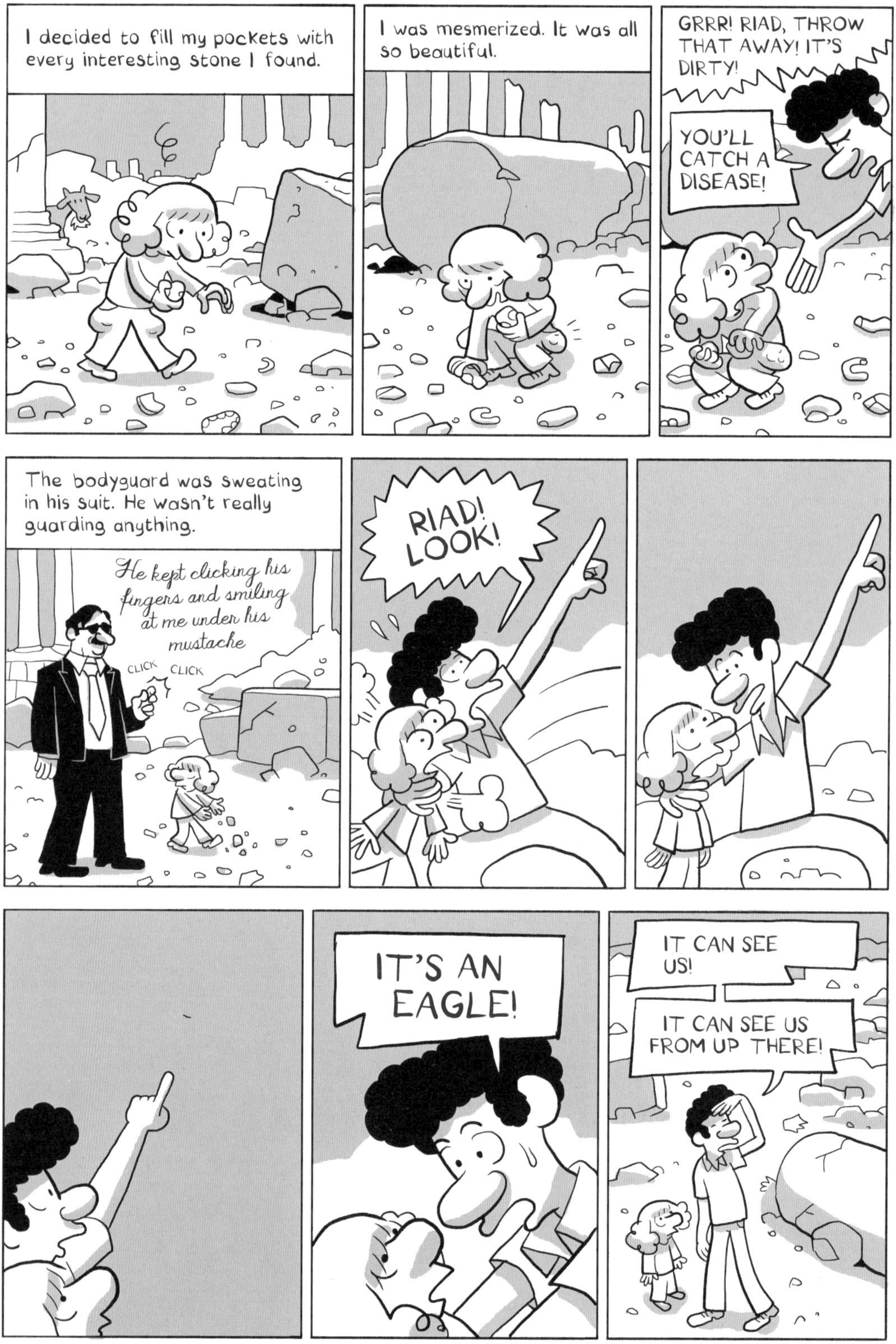
I decided to fill my pockets with every interesting stone I found.
I was mesmerized. It was all so beautiful.
GRRR! RIAD, THROW THAT AWAY! IT'S DIRTY!
YOU'LL CATCH A DISEASE!
The bodyguard was sweating in his suit. He wasn't really guarding anything.
He kept clicking his fingers and smiling at me under his mustache
CLICK
CLICK
RIAD! LOOK!
IT'S AN EAGLE!
IT CAN SEE US!
IT CAN SEE US FROM UP THERE!

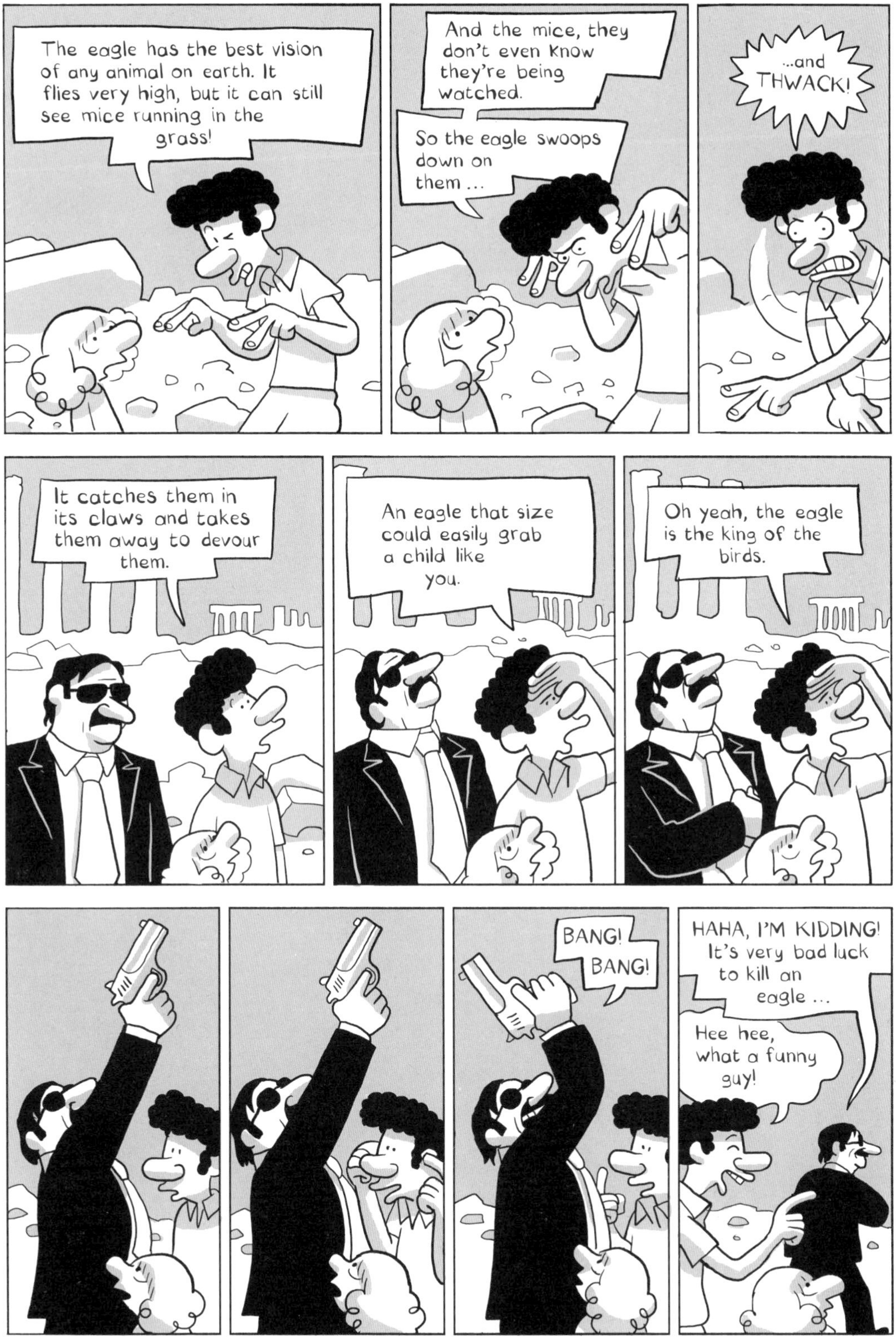
The eagle has the best vision of any animal on earth. It flies very high, but it can still see mice running in the grass!
And the mice, they don't even know they're being watched.
So the eagle swoops down on them ...
...and THWACK!
It catches them in its claws and takes them away to devour them.
An eagle that size could easily grab a child like you.
Oh yeah, the eagle is the king of the birds.
BANG! BANG!
HAHA, I'M KIDDING! It's very bad luck to kill an eagle ...
Hee hee, what a funny guy!

A child turned up with a bucket full of water bottles for sale.

Water, gentlemen? Nice cold water?

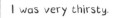

I was very thirsty.

It's poison, what this poor kid is selling! If you drink his stagnant water, you'll catch dysentery and die.

In French

Water?

This is the devil tempting you!

My father gave the kid a coin.

Here. And keep your water.

Oh, thank you, sir! May God bless you. You are a good man!

Let's go.

Thank you! May God protect your children!

You see? We should always look after those less fortunate than us. We must be sensitive and generous!

We must love doing good to others...

For me, it comes naturally.

I'm thirsty!

YOU'LL DRINK TONIGHT! SPOILED LITTLE BRAT WHINING ALL THE TIME!

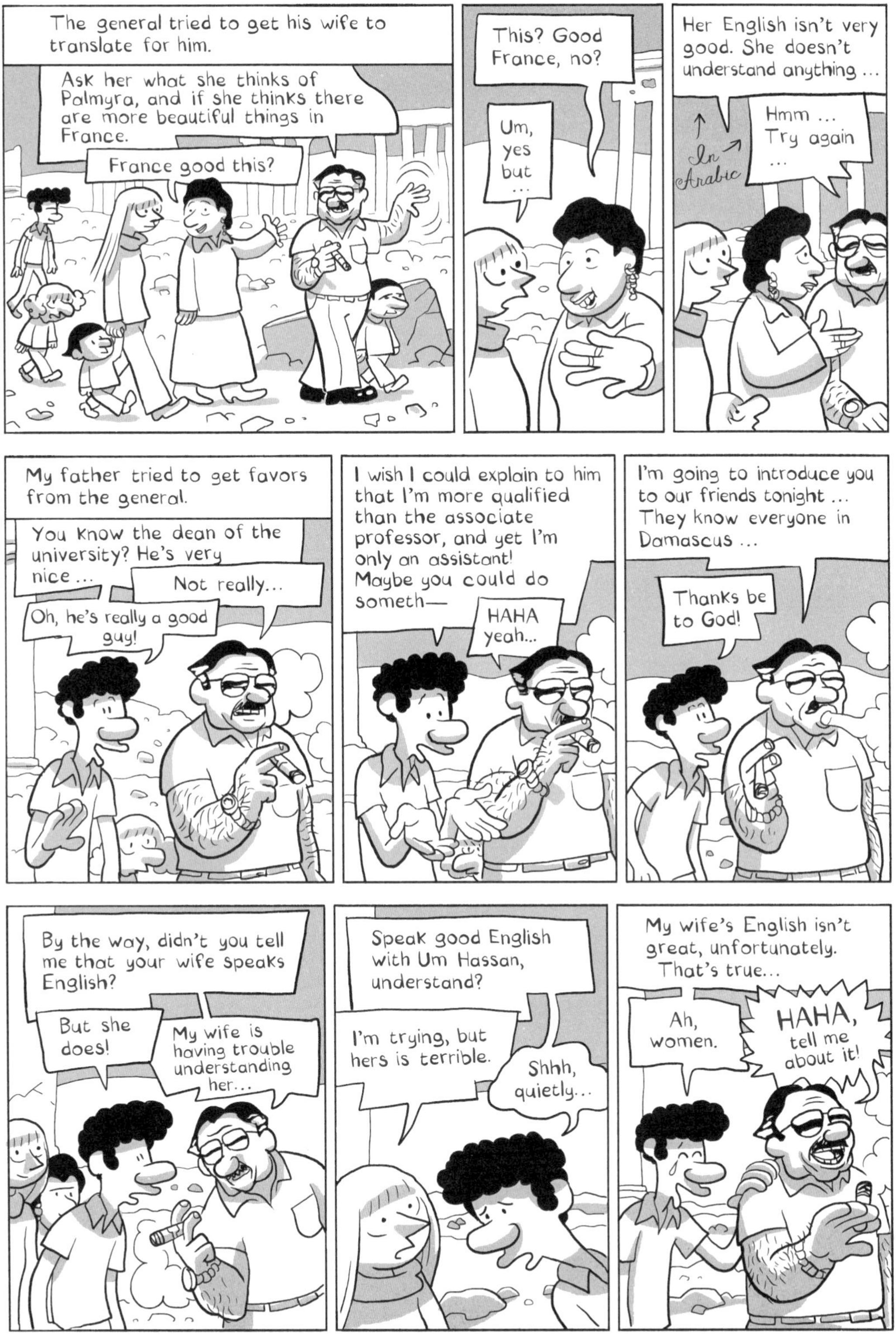
The general tried to get his wife to translate for him.
Ask her what she thinks of Palmyra, and if she thinks there are more beautiful things in France.
France good this?
This? Good France, no?
Um, yes but ...
Her English isn't very good. She doesn't understand anything ...
In Arabic
Hmm ... Try again ...
My father tried to get favors from the general.
You know the dean of the university? He's very nice ...
Not really...
Oh, he's really a good guy!
I wish I could explain to him that I'm more qualified than the associate professor, and yet I'm only an assistant! Maybe you could do someth—
HAHA yeah...
I'm going to introduce you to our friends tonight ... They know everyone in Damascus ...
Thanks be to God!
By the way, didn't you tell me that your wife speaks English?
But she does!
My wife is having trouble understanding her...
Speak good English with Um Hassan, understand?
I'm trying, but hers is terrible.
Shhh, quietly...
My wife's English isn't great, unfortunately. That's true...
Ah, women.
HAHA, tell me about it!

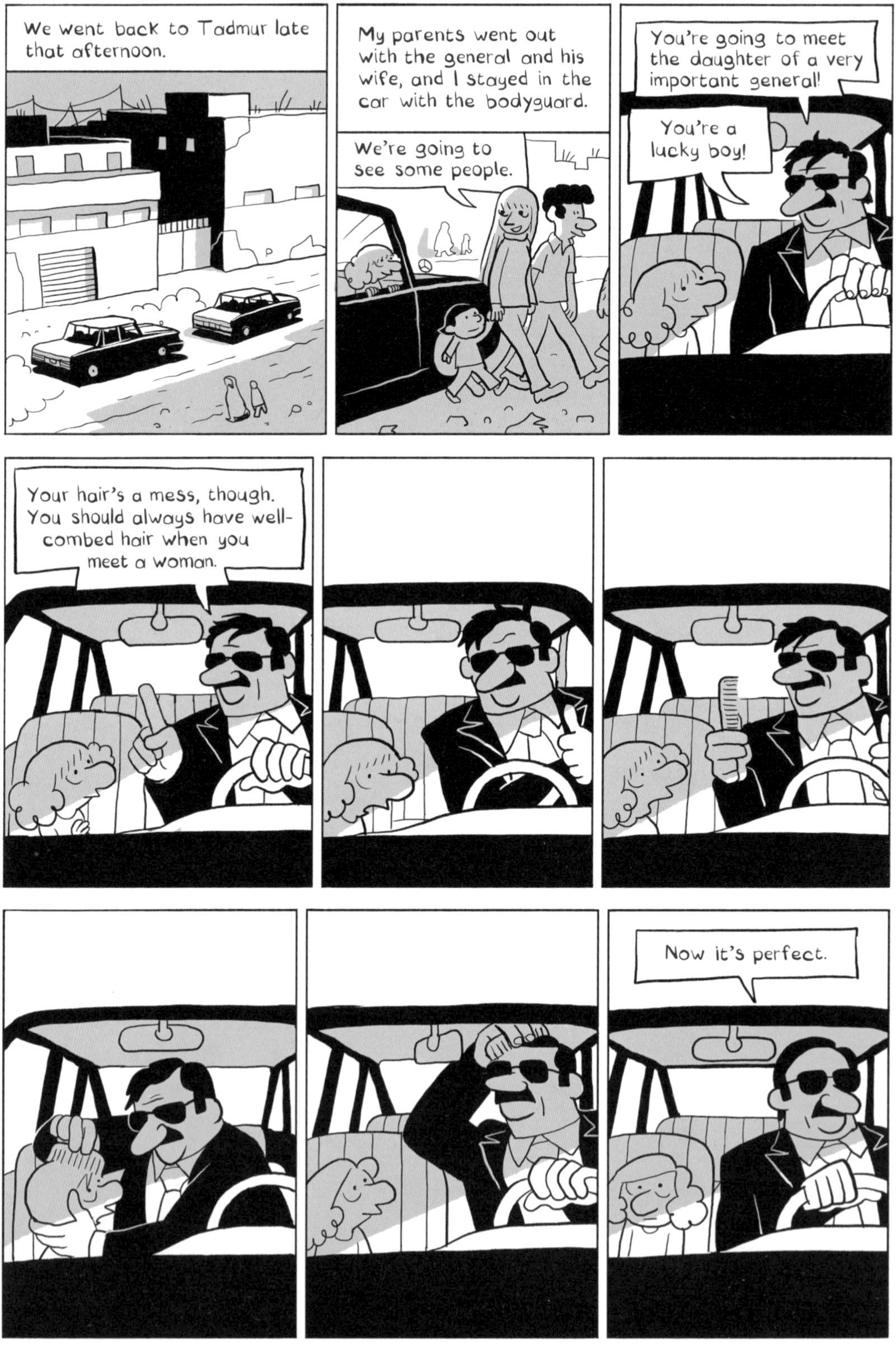
We went back to Tadmur late that afternoon.
My parents went out with the general and his wife, and I stayed in the car with the bodyguard.
We're going to see some people.
You're going to meet the daughter of a very important general!
You're a lucky boy!
Your hair's a mess, though. You should always have well-combed hair when you meet a woman.
Now it's perfect.

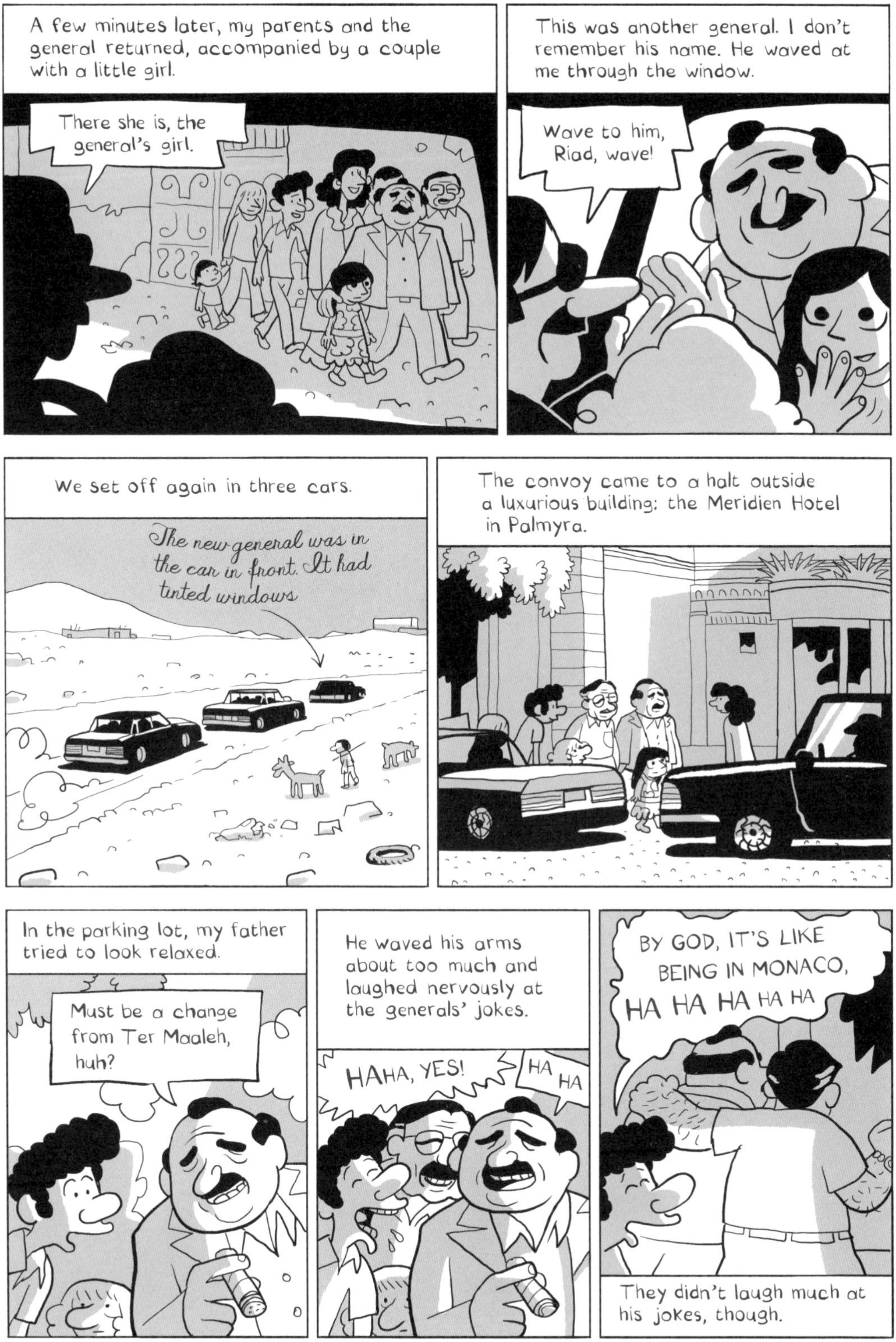
A few minutes later, my parents and the general returned, accompanied by a couple with a little girl.
There she is, the general's girl.
This was another general. I don't remember his name. He waved at me through the window.
Wave to him, Riad, wave!
We set off again in three cars.
The new general was in the car in front. It had tinted windows
The convoy came to a halt outside a luxurious building: the Meridien Hotel in Palmyra.
In the parking lot, my father tried to look relaxed.
Must be a change from Ter Maaleh, huh?
He waved his arms about too much and laughed nervously at the generals' jokes.
HAHA, YES!
HA HA
BY GOD, IT'S LIKE BEING IN MONACO, HA HA HA HA HA
They didn't laugh much at his jokes, though.

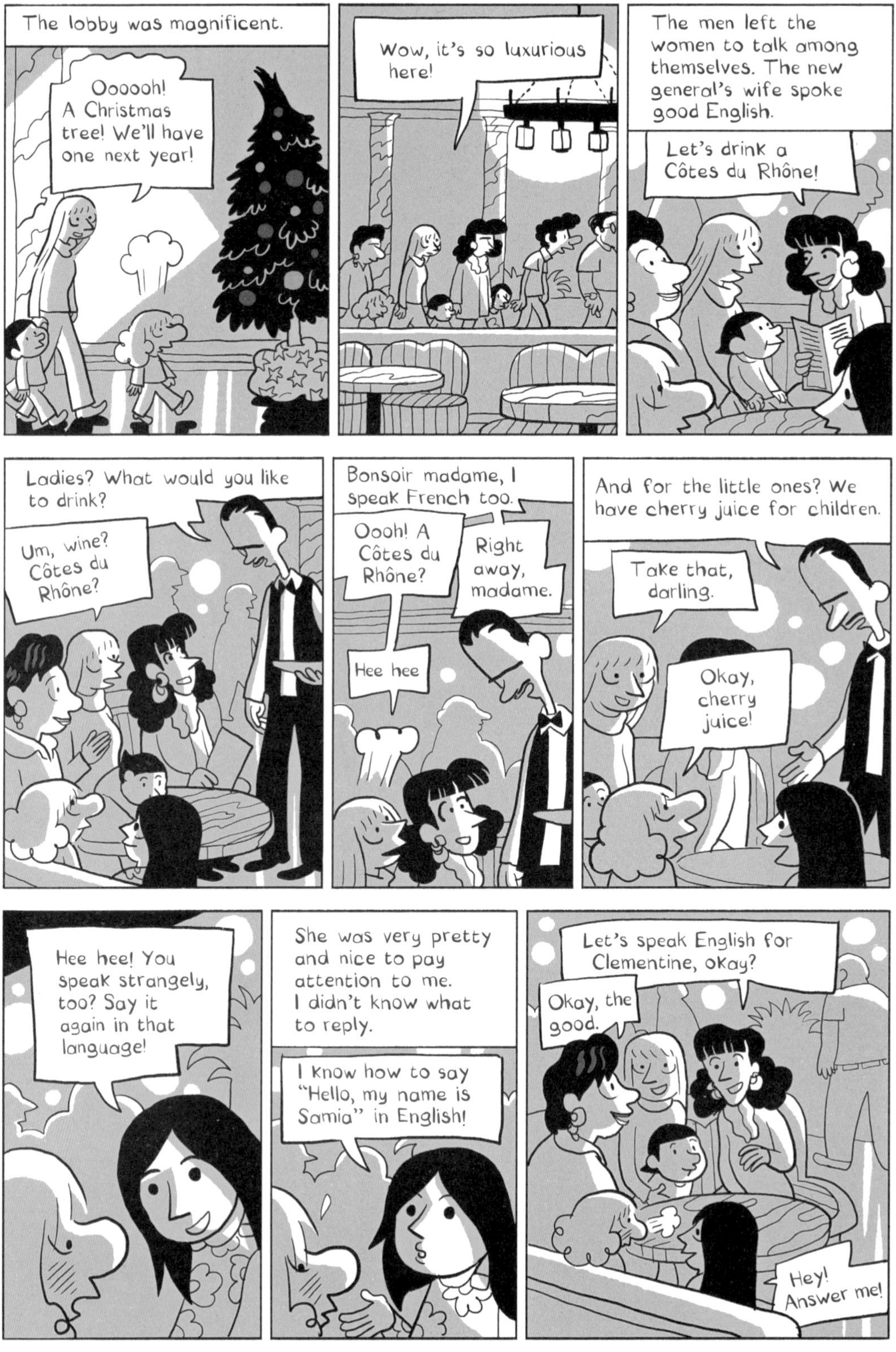
The lobby was magnificent.
Oooooh! A Christmas tree! We'll have one next year!
Wow, it's so luxurious here!
The men left the women to talk among themselves. The new general's wife spoke good English.
Let's drink a Côtes du Rhône!
Ladies? What would you like to drink?
Um, wine? Côtes du Rhône?
Bonsoir madame, I speak French too.
Oooh! A Côtes du Rhône?
Right away, madame.
Hee hee
And for the little ones? We have cherry juice for children.
Take that, darling.
Okay, cherry juice!
Hee hee! You speak strangely, too? Say it again in that language!
She was very pretty and nice to pay attention to me. I didn't know what to reply.
I know how to say "Hello, my name is Samia" in English!
Let's speak English for Clementine, okay?
Okay, the good.
Hey! Answer me!

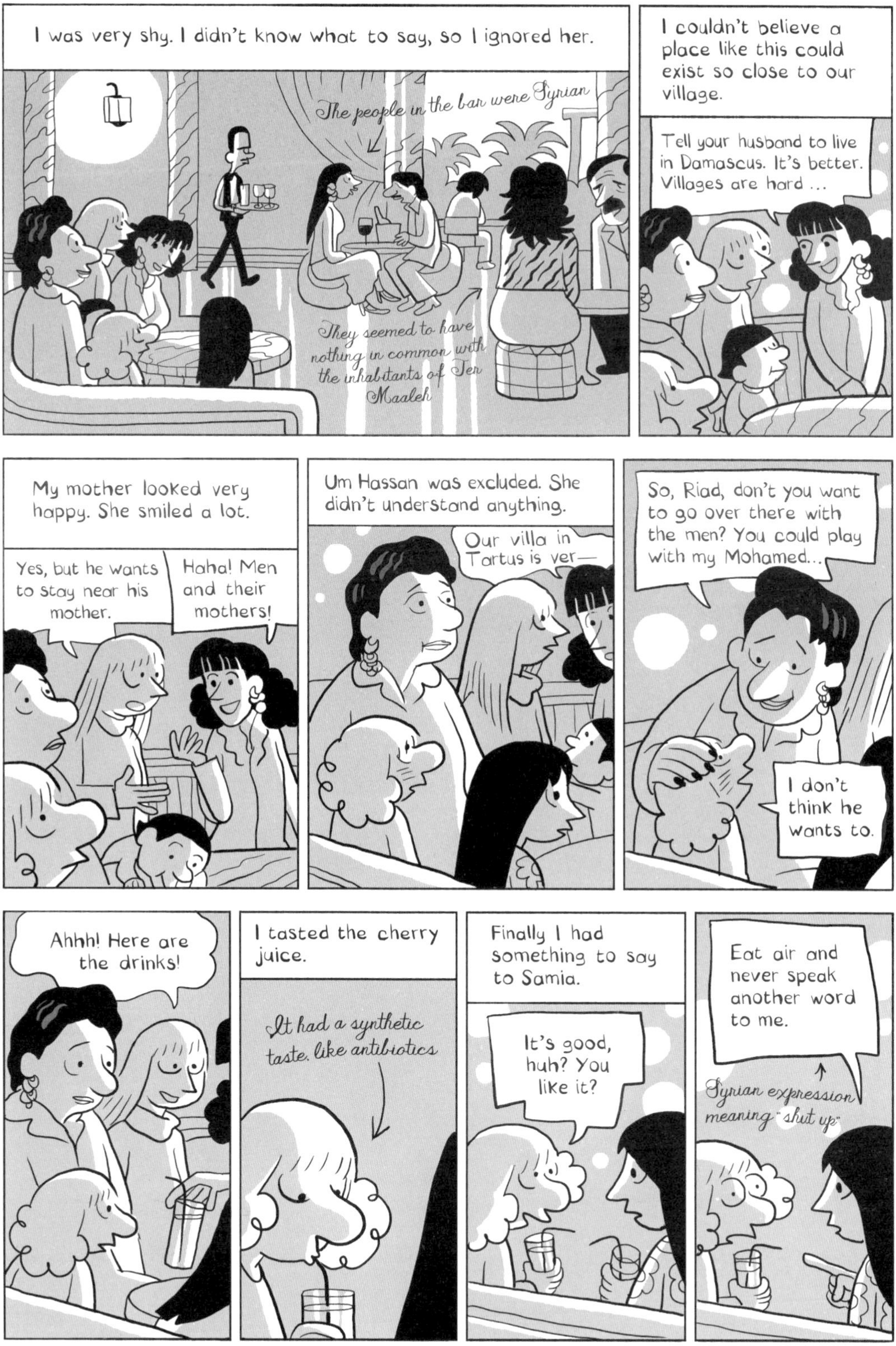
I was very shy. I didn't know what to say, so I ignored her.
The people in the bar were Syrian
They seemed to have nothing in common with the inhabitants of Ter Maaleh
I couldn't believe a place like this could exist so close to our village.
Tell your husband to live in Damascus. It's better. Villages are hard ...
My mother looked very happy. She smiled a lot.
Yes, but he wants to stay near his mother.
Haha! Men and their mothers!
Um Hassan was excluded. She didn't understand anything.
Our villa in Tartus is ver—
So, Riad, don't you want to go over there with the men? You could play with my Mohamed...
I don't think he wants to.
Ahhh! Here are the drinks!
I tasted the cherry juice.
It had a synthetic taste. like antibiotics
Finally I had something to say to Samia.
It's good, huh? You like it?
Eat air and never speak another word to me.
Syrian expression meaning "shut up"

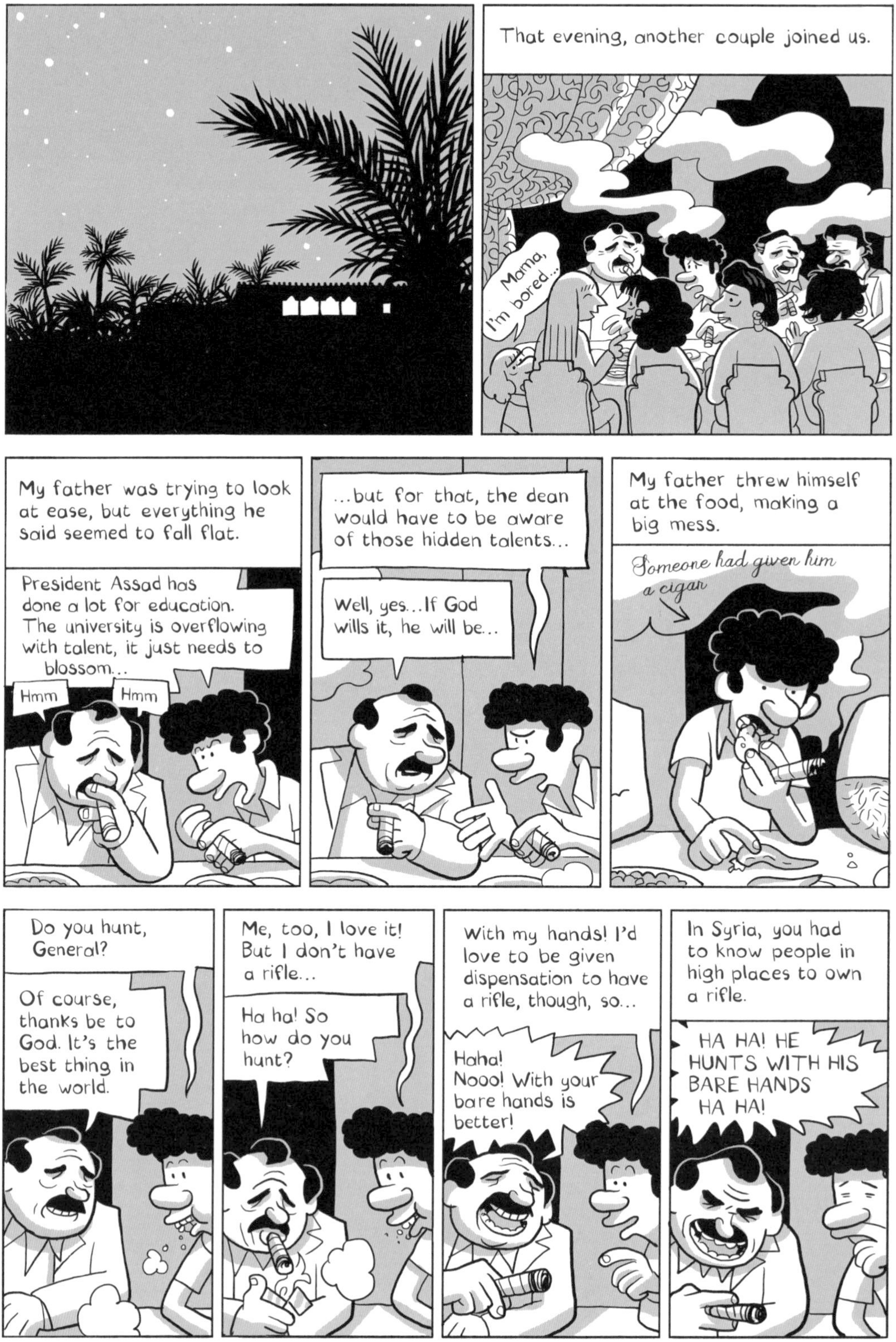
That evening, another couple joined us.
Mama, I'm bored...
My father was trying to look at ease, but everything he said seemed to fall flat.
President Assad has done a lot for education. The university is overflowing with talent, it just needs to blossom...
Hmm
Hmm
...but for that, the dean would have to be aware of those hidden talents...
Well, yes... If God wills it, he will be...
My father threw himself at the food, making a big mess.
Someone had given him a cigar
Do you hunt, General?
Of course, thanks be to God. It's the best thing in the world.
Me, too, I love it! But I don't have a rifle...
Ha ha! So how do you hunt?
With my hands! I'd love to be given dispensation to have a rifle, though, so...
Haha! Nooo! With your bare hands is better!
In Syria, you had to know people in high places to own a rifle.
HA HA! HE HUNTS WITH HIS BARE HANDS HA HA!

The general called to me.

CLICK! CLICK! CLICK!

CLICK! CLICK! CLICK!

He seemed gentle but powerful.

You like?

Wow!

Good! This kid's wonderful.

Here!

There's a playground for children outside! Go out and play if you like!

I'll look after your coin.

In the yard, Samia was playing with Mohamed and a little boy I had never seen before.

His hair was slicked back and he was wearing a gold-embroidered waistcoat.

Ice-cold velvet eyes

Six years old at most

Little polished slippers

Golden belt buckle

I looked at Samia and Mohamed, but they turned away.

But he stared at me

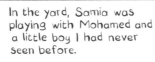

I headed straight for the playground.

What are you doing, dog?

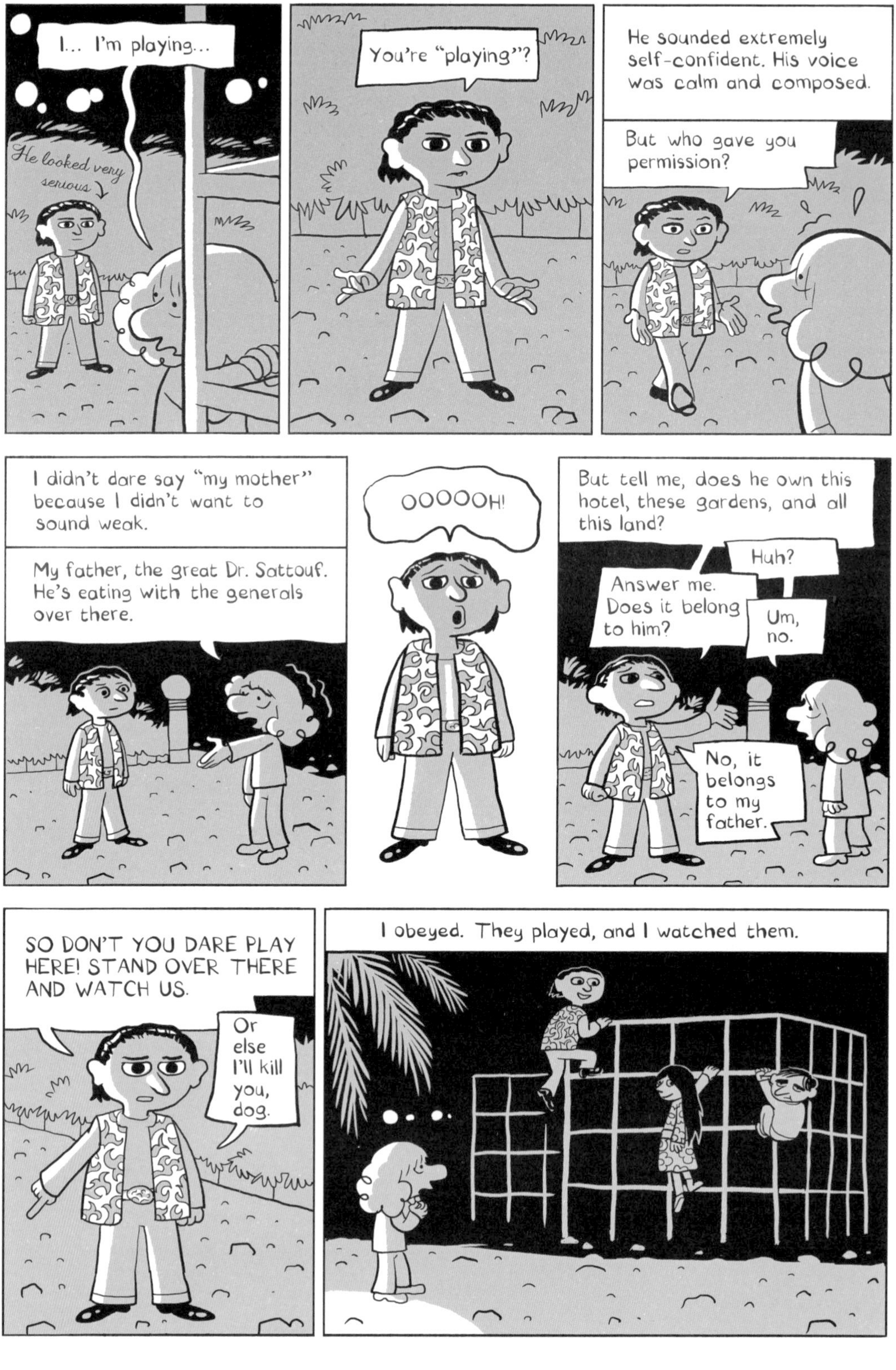

I... I'm playing...
He looked very serious
You're "playing"?
He sounded extremely self-confident. His voice was calm and composed.
But who gave you permission?
I didn't dare say "my mother" because I didn't want to sound weak.
My father, the great Dr. Sattouf. He's eating with the generals over there.
OOOOOH!
But tell me, does he own this hotel, these gardens, and all this land?
Huh?
Answer me. Does it belong to him?
Um, no.
No, it belongs to my father.
SO DON'T YOU DARE PLAY HERE! STAND OVER THERE AND WATCH US.
Or else I'll kill you, dog.
I obeyed. They played, and I watched them.

CHAPTER 4

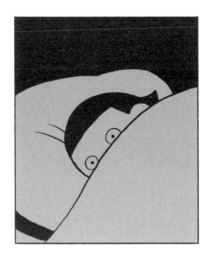

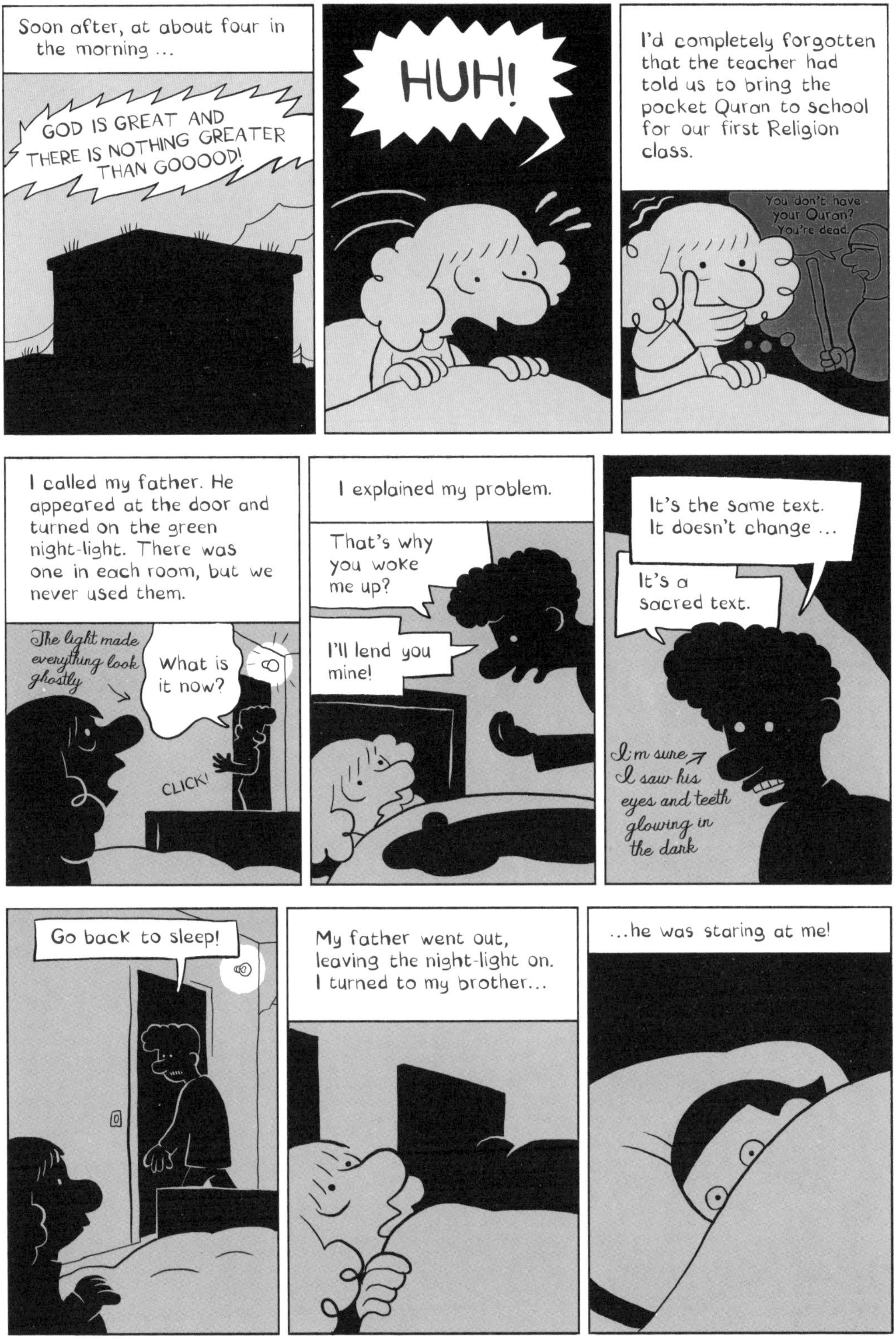
Soon after, at about four in the morning ...
GOD IS GREAT AND THERE IS NOTHING GREATER THAN GOOOOD!
HUH!
I'd completely forgotten that the teacher had told us to bring the pocket Quran to school for our first Religion class.
You don't have your Quran? You're dead.
I called my father. He appeared at the door and turned on the green night-light. There was one in each room, but we never used them.
The light made everything look ghostly
What is it now?
CLICK!
I explained my problem.
That's why you woke me up?
I'll lend you mine!
It's the same text. It doesn't change ...
It's a sacred text.
I'm sure I saw his eyes and teeth glowing in the dark
Go back to sleep!
My father went out, leaving the night-light on. I turned to my brother...
...he was staring at me!

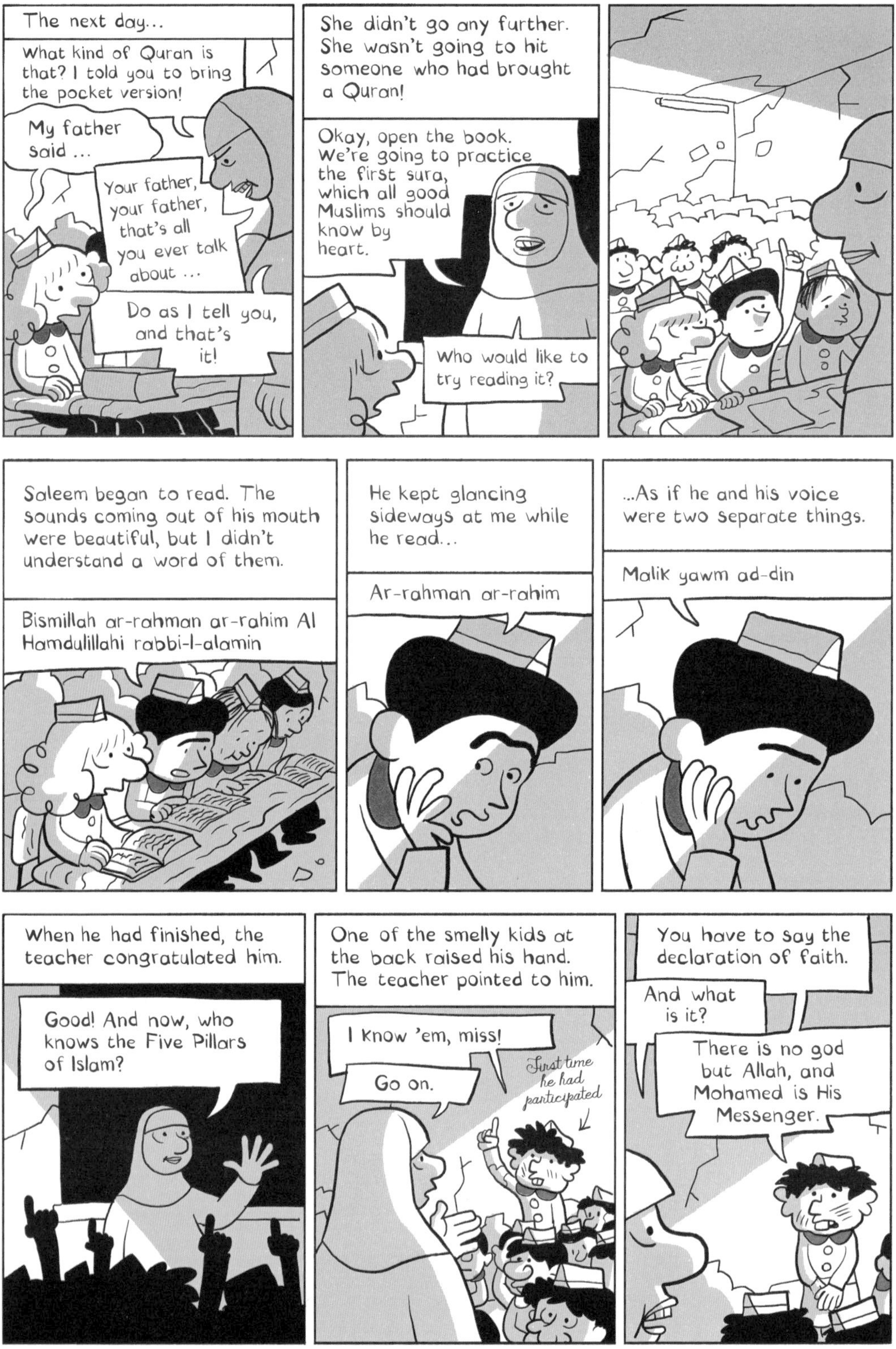
The next day...
What kind of Quran is that? I told you to bring the pocket version!
My father said ...
Your father, your father, that's all you ever talk about ...
Do as I tell you, and that's it!
She didn't go any further. She wasn't going to hit someone who had brought a Quran!
Okay, open the book. We're going to practice the first sura, which all good Muslims should know by heart.
Who would like to try reading it?
Saleem began to read. The sounds coming out of his mouth were beautiful, but I didn't understand a word of them.
Bismillah ar-rahman ar-rahim Al Hamdulillahi rabbi-l-alamin
He kept glancing sideways at me while he read...
Ar-rahman ar-rahim
...As if he and his voice were two separate things.
Malik yawm ad-din
When he had finished, the teacher congratulated him.
Good! And now, who knows the Five Pillars of Islam?
One of the smelly kids at the back raised his hand. The teacher pointed to him.
I know 'em, miss!
Go on.
First time he had participated
You have to say the declaration of faith.
And what is it?
There is no god but Allah, and Mohamed is His Messenger.

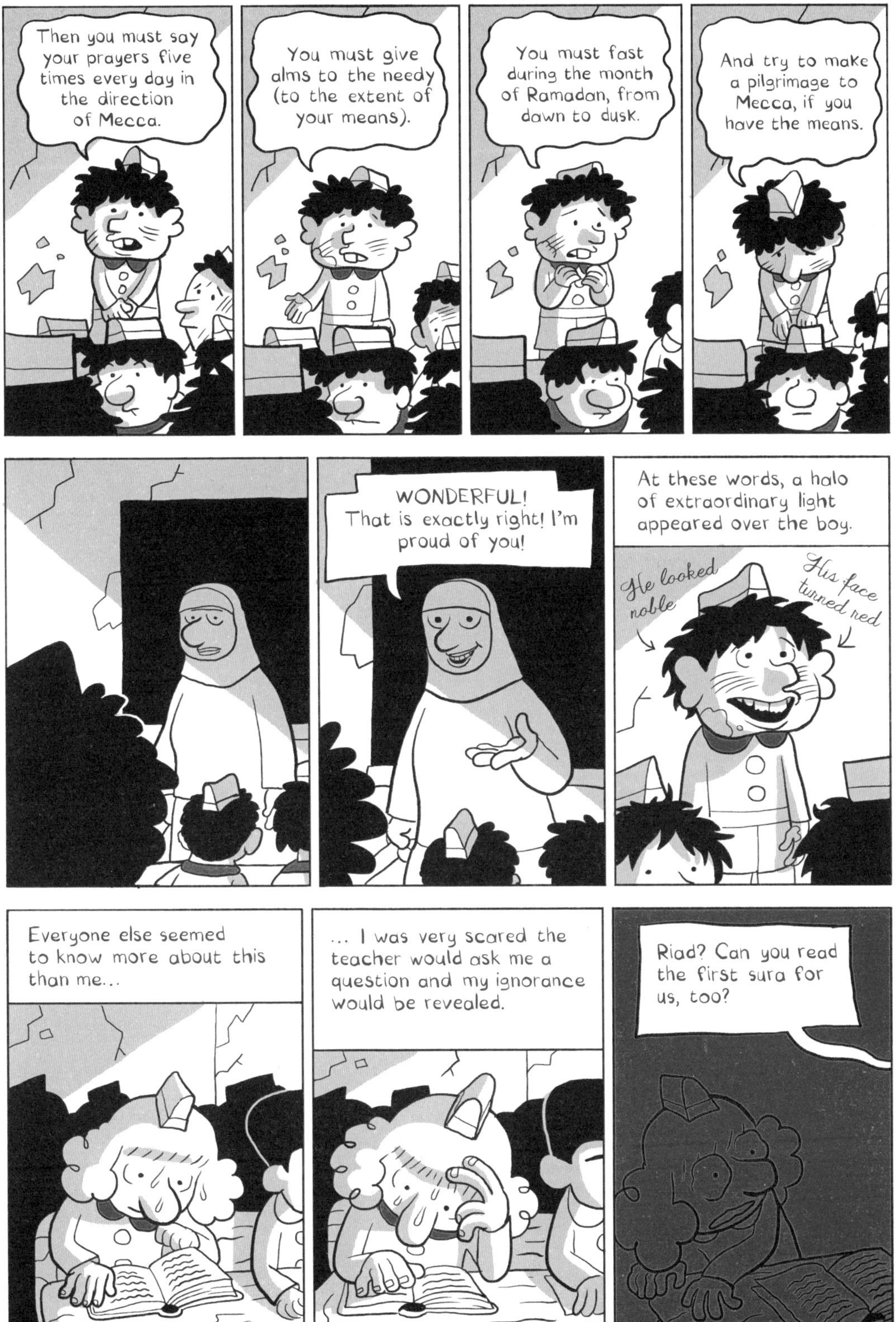
Then you must say your prayers five times every day in the direction of Mecca.
You must give alms to the needy (to the extent of your means).
You must fast during the month of Ramadan, from dawn to dusk.
And try to make a pilgrimage to Mecca, if you have the means.
WONDERFUL! That is exactly right! I'm proud of you!
At these words, a halo of extraordinary light appeared over the boy.
He looked noble
His face turned red
Everyone else seemed to know more about this than me...
... I was very scared the teacher would ask me a question and my ignorance would be revealed.
Riad? Can you read the first sura for us, too?

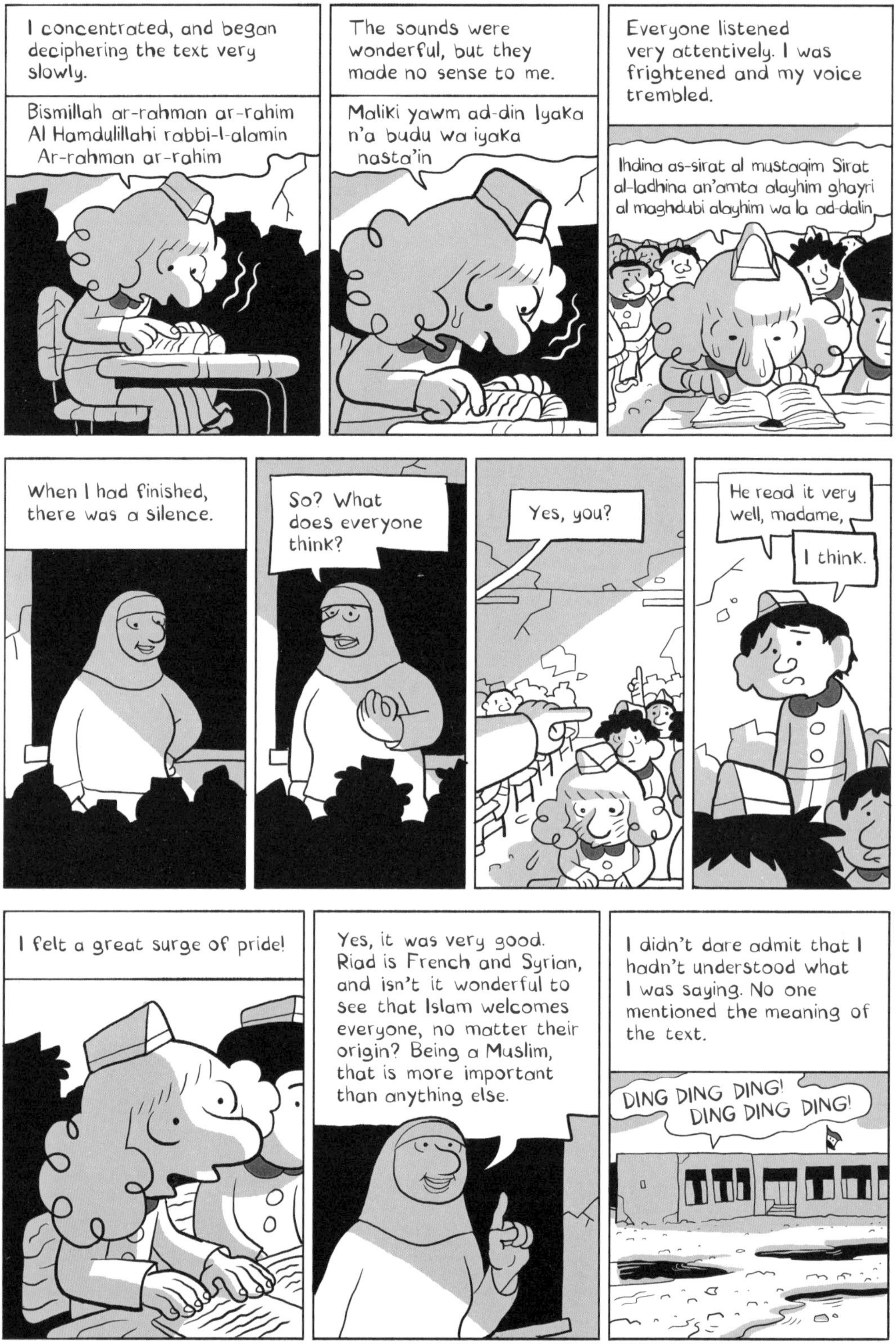
I concentrated, and began deciphering the text very slowly.
Bismillah ar-rahman ar-rahim Al Hamdulillahi rabbi-l-alamin Ar-rahman ar-rahim
The sounds were wonderful, but they made no sense to me.
Maliki yawm ad-din Iyaka n'a budu wa iyaka nasta'in
Everyone listened very attentively. I was frightened and my voice trembled.
Ihdina as-sirat al mustaqim Sirat al-ladhina an'amta alayhim ghayri al maghdubi alayhim wa la ad-dalin
When I had finished, there was a silence.
So? What does everyone think?
Yes, you?
He read it very well, madame,
I think.
I felt a great surge of pride!
Yes, it was very good. Riad is French and Syrian, and isn't it wonderful to see that Islam welcomes everyone, no matter their origin? Being a Muslim, that is more important than anything else.
I didn't dare admit that I hadn't understood what I was saying. No one mentioned the meaning of the text.
DING DING DING! DING DING DING!

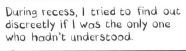

During recess, I tried to find out discreetly if I was the only one who hadn't understood.

It's beautiful, isn't it, the first sura?

Oh yeah, very beautiful!

Cough cough

... and it's interesting what it says, don't you think?

Yes, yes, by God.

Could you just explain the end to me? I didn't understand it.

Open your heart and you will understand.

Anyway, I'm going to play.

Cough! Cough!

All the boys I asked about the text's meaning avoided the question.

Of course I understood it all! But I don't want to talk about it.

Saleem ended up admitting that he didn't understand it, either.

It's because we're young!

My father told me that the older we get, the more we understand. And that at a certain moment, everything becomes clear and we stop wondering.

Does that mean the teacher understands it?

Of course! She's the teacher!

105

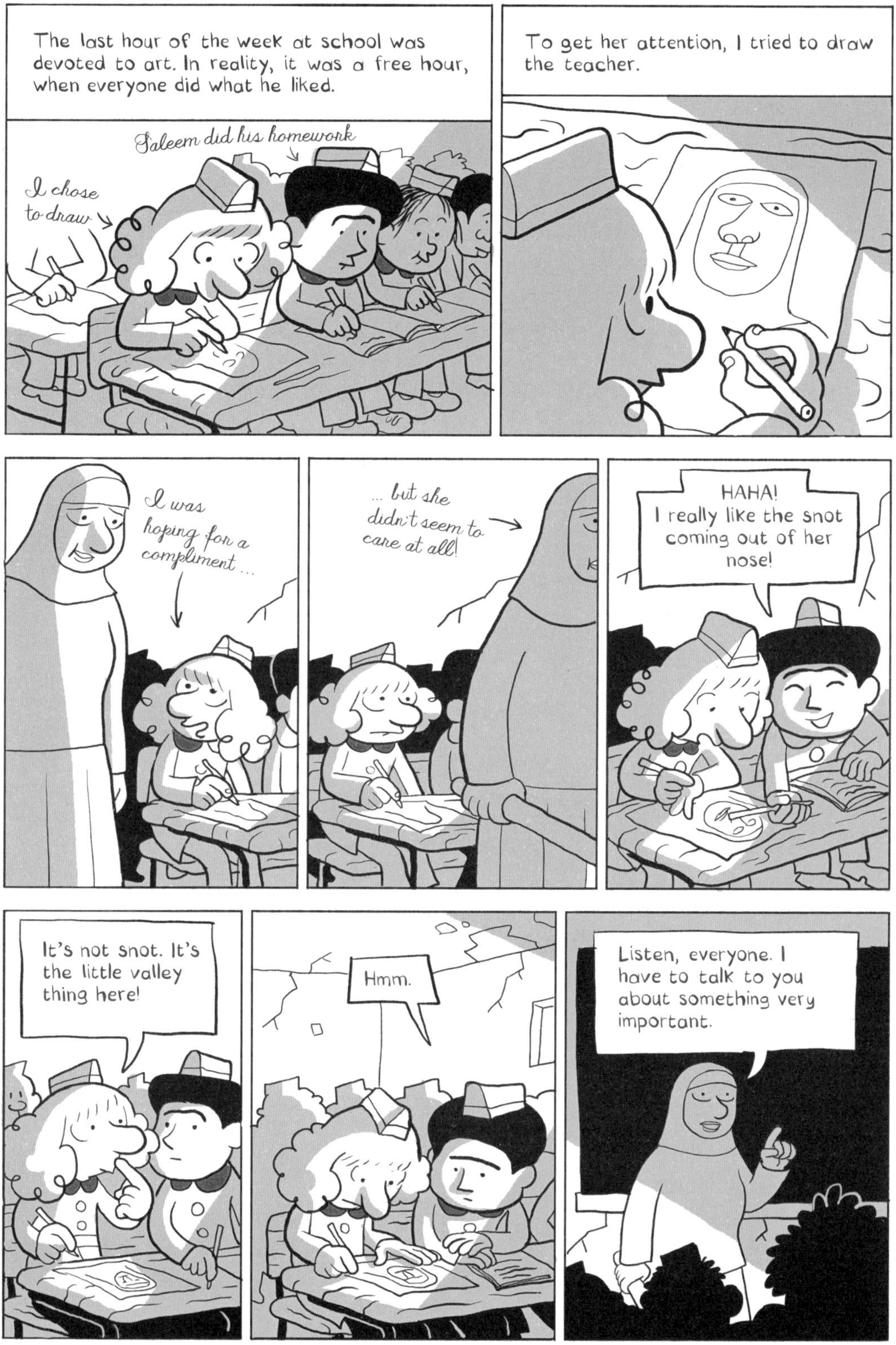
The last hour of the week at school was devoted to art. In reality, it was a free hour, when everyone did what he liked.
Saleem did his homework
I chose to draw
To get her attention, I tried to draw the teacher.
I was hoping for a compliment...
... but she didn't seem to care at all!
HAHA! I really like the snot coming out of her nose!
It's not snot. It's the little valley thing here!
Hmm.
Listen, everyone. I have to talk to you about something very important.

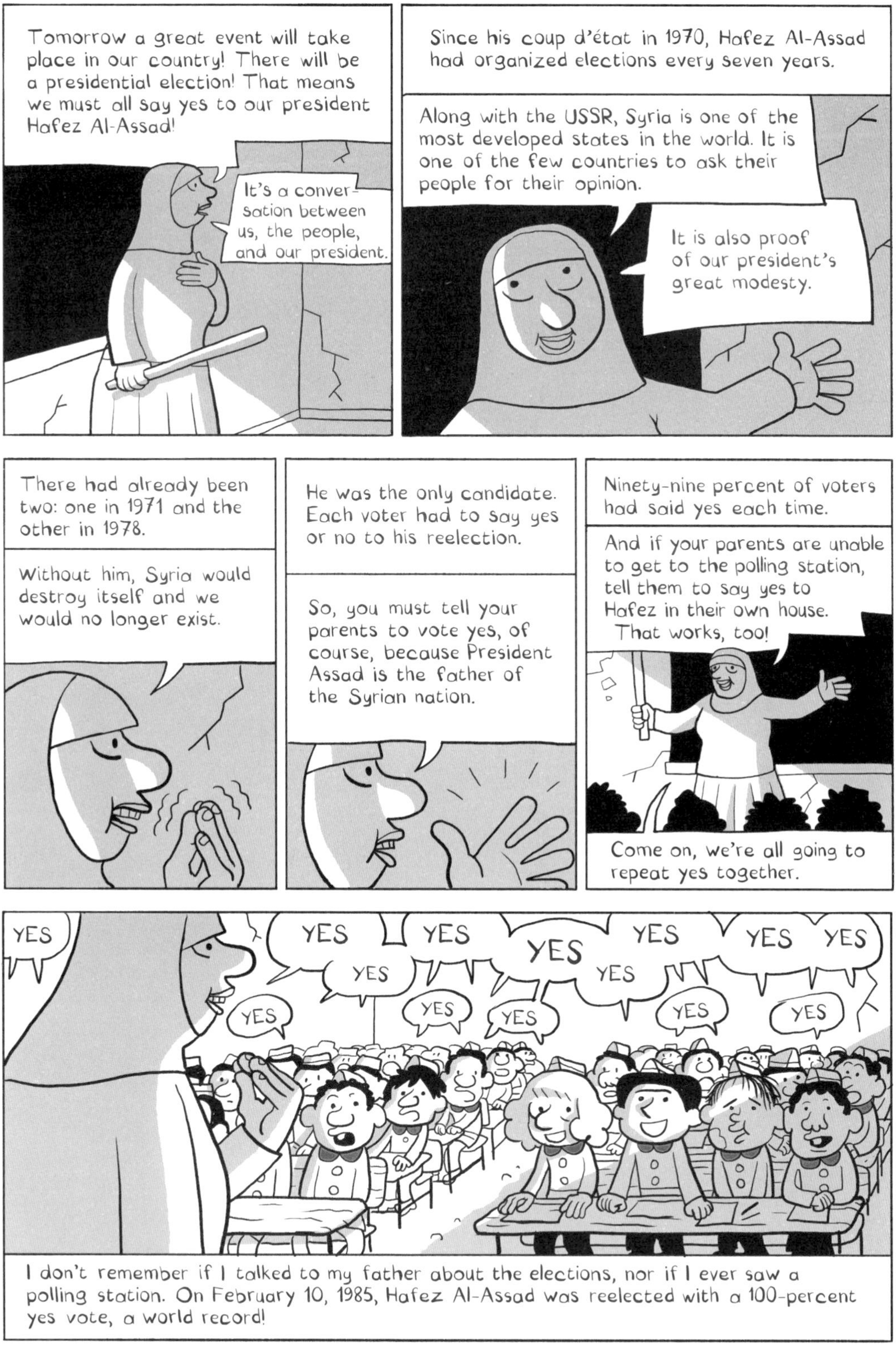
Tomorrow a great event will take place in our country! There will be a presidential election! That means we must all say yes to our president Hafez Al-Assad!
It's a conversation between us, the people, and our president.
Since his coup d'état in 1970, Hafez Al-Assad had organized elections every seven years.
Along with the USSR, Syria is one of the most developed states in the world. It is one of the few countries to ask their people for their opinion.
It is also proof of our president's great modesty.
There had already been two: one in 1971 and the other in 1978.
Without him, Syria would destroy itself and we would no longer exist.
He was the only candidate. Each voter had to say yes or no to his reelection.
So, you must tell your parents to vote yes, of course, because President Assad is the father of the Syrian nation.
Ninety-nine percent of voters had said yes each time.
And if your parents are unable to get to the polling station, tell them to say yes to Hafez in their own house. That works, too!
Come on, we're all going to repeat yes together.
YES
YES
YES
YES
YES
YES
YES
YES
YES
YES
YES
YES
YES
YES
YES
I don't remember if I talked to my father about the elections, nor if I ever saw a polling station. On February 10, 1985, Hafez Al-Assad was reelected with a 100-percent yes vote, a world record!

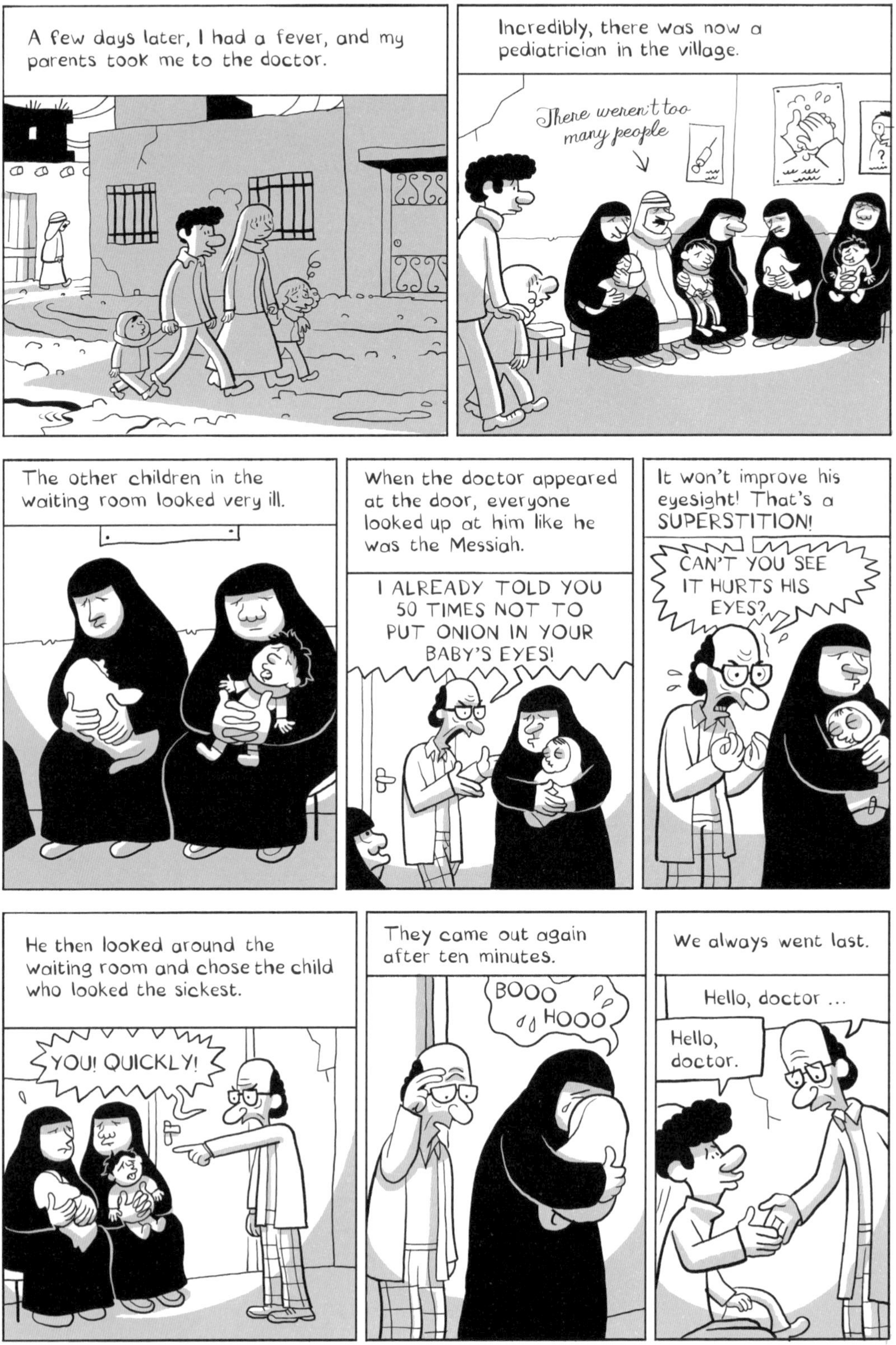
A few days later, I had a fever, and my parents took me to the doctor.
Incredibly, there was now a pediatrician in the village.
There weren't too many people
The other children in the waiting room looked very ill.
When the doctor appeared at the door, everyone looked up at him like he was the Messiah.
I ALREADY TOLD YOU 50 TIMES NOT TO PUT ONION IN YOUR BABY'S EYES!
It won't improve his eyesight! That's a SUPERSTITION!
CAN'T YOU SEE IT HURTS HIS EYES?
He then looked around the waiting room and chose the child who looked the sickest.
YOU! QUICKLY!
They came out again after ten minutes.
BOOO HOOO
We always went last.
Hello, doctor …
Hello, doctor.

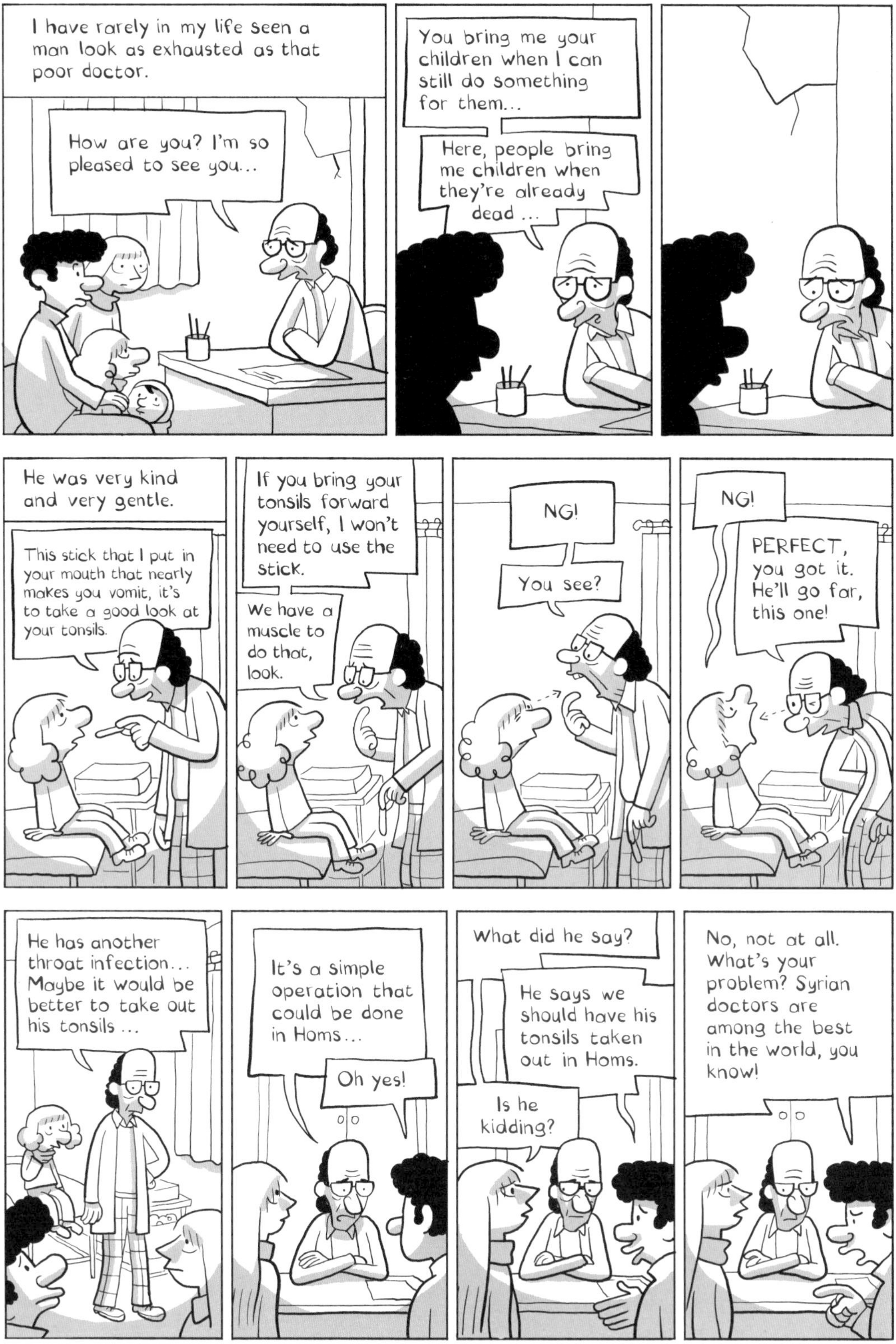
I have rarely in my life seen a man look as exhausted as that poor doctor.
How are you? I'm so pleased to see you...
You bring me your children when I can still do something for them...
Here, people bring me children when they're already dead ...
He was very kind and very gentle.
This stick that I put in your mouth that nearly makes you vomit, it's to take a good look at your tonsils.
If you bring your tonsils forward yourself, I won't need to use the stick.
We have a muscle to do that, look.
NG!
You see?
NG!
PERFECT, you got it. He'll go far, this one!
He has another throat infection... Maybe it would be better to take out his tonsils ...
It's a simple operation that could be done in Homs...
Oh yes!
What did he say?
He says we should have his tonsils taken out in Homs.
Is he kidding?
No, not at all. What's your problem? Syrian doctors are among the best in the world, you know!

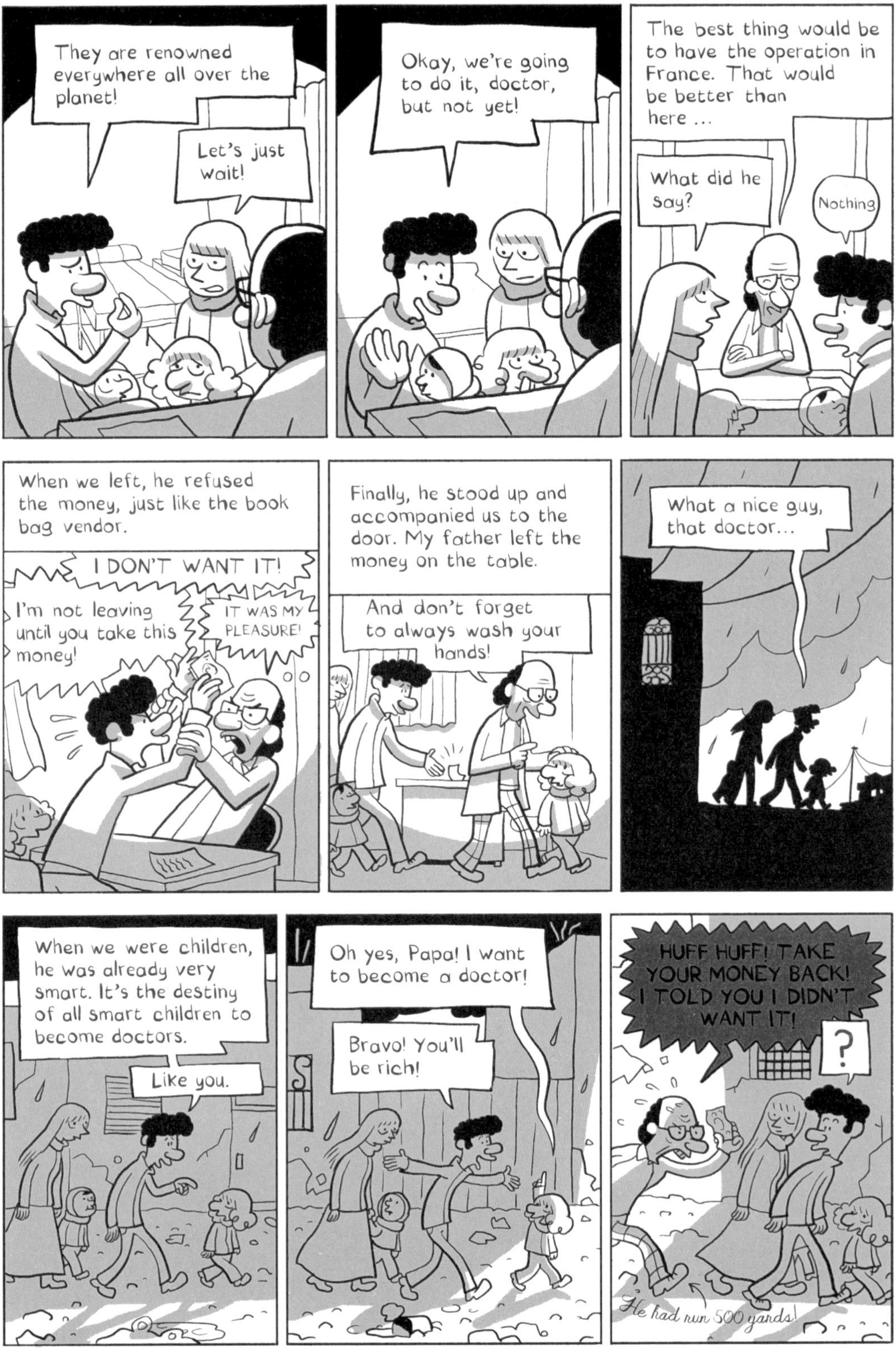
They are renowned everywhere all over the planet!
Let's just wait!
Okay, we're going to do it, doctor, but not yet!
The best thing would be to have the operation in France. That would be better than here ...
What did he say?
Nothing
When we left, he refused the money, just like the book bag vendor.
I DON'T WANT IT!
I'm not leaving until you take this money!
IT WAS MY PLEASURE!
Finally, he stood up and accompanied us to the door. My father left the money on the table.
And don't forget to always wash your hands!
What a nice guy, that doctor...
When we were children, he was already very smart. It's the destiny of all smart children to become doctors.
Like you.
Oh yes, Papa! I want to become a doctor!
Bravo! You'll be rich!
HUFF HUFF! TAKE YOUR MONEY BACK! I TOLD YOU I DIDN'T WANT IT!
?
He had run 500 yards!

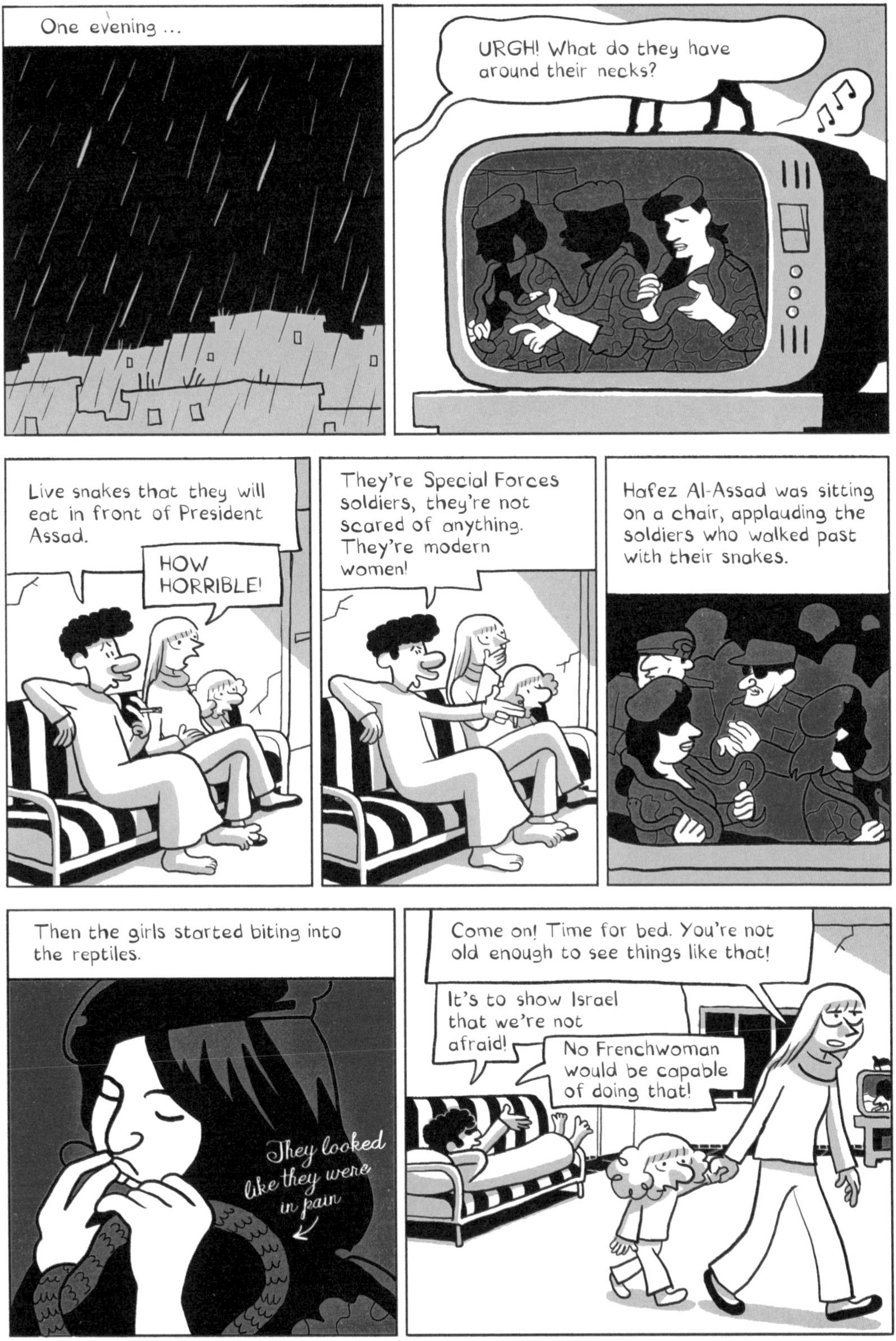
One evening ...
URGH! What do they have around their necks?
Live snakes that they will eat in front of President Assad.
HOW HORRIBLE!
They're Special Forces soldiers, they're not scared of anything. They're modern women!
Hafez Al-Assad was sitting on a chair, applauding the soldiers who walked past with their snakes.
Then the girls started biting into the reptiles.
They looked like they were in pain
Come on! Time for bed. You're not old enough to see things like that!
It's to show Israel that we're not afraid!
No Frenchwoman would be capable of doing that!

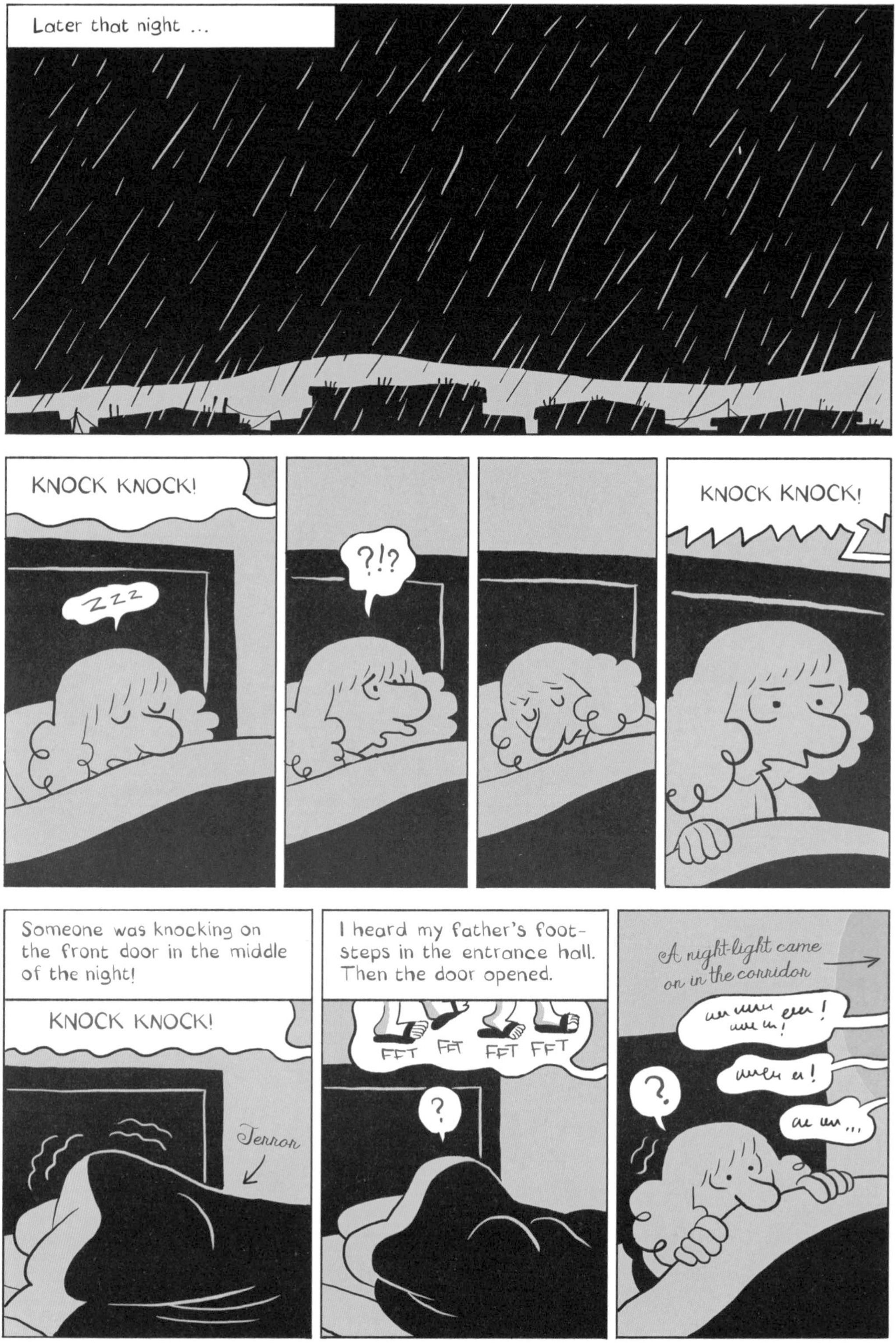
Later that night ...
KNOCK KNOCK!
ZZZ
?!?
KNOCK KNOCK!
Someone was knocking on the front door in the middle of the night!
KNOCK KNOCK!
Terror
I heard my father's foot-steps in the entrance hall. Then the door opened.
FFT FFT FFT FFT
?
A night-light came on in the corridor
?

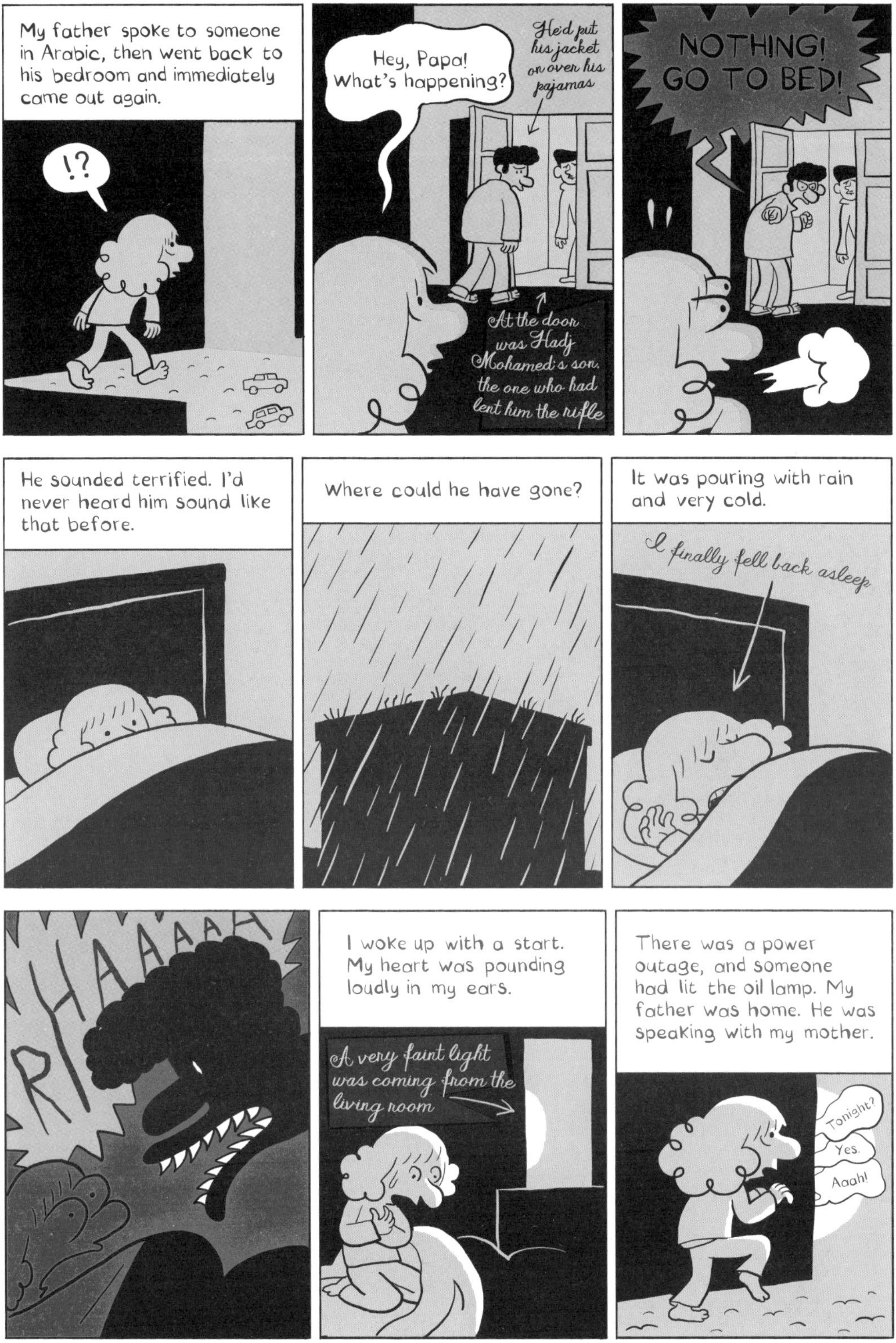

My father spoke to someone in Arabic, then went back to his bedroom and immediately came out again.
!?
Hey, Papa! What's happening?
He'd put his jacket on over his pajamas
At the door was Hadj Mohamed's son, the one who had lent him the rifle
NOTHING! GO TO BED!
He sounded terrified. I'd never heard him sound like that before.
Where could he have gone?
It was pouring with rain and very cold.
I finally fell back asleep
RHAAAAA
I woke up with a start. My heart was pounding loudly in my ears.
A very faint light was coming from the living room
There was a power outage, and someone had lit the oil lamp. My father was home. He was speaking with my mother.
Tonight?
Yes.
Aaah!

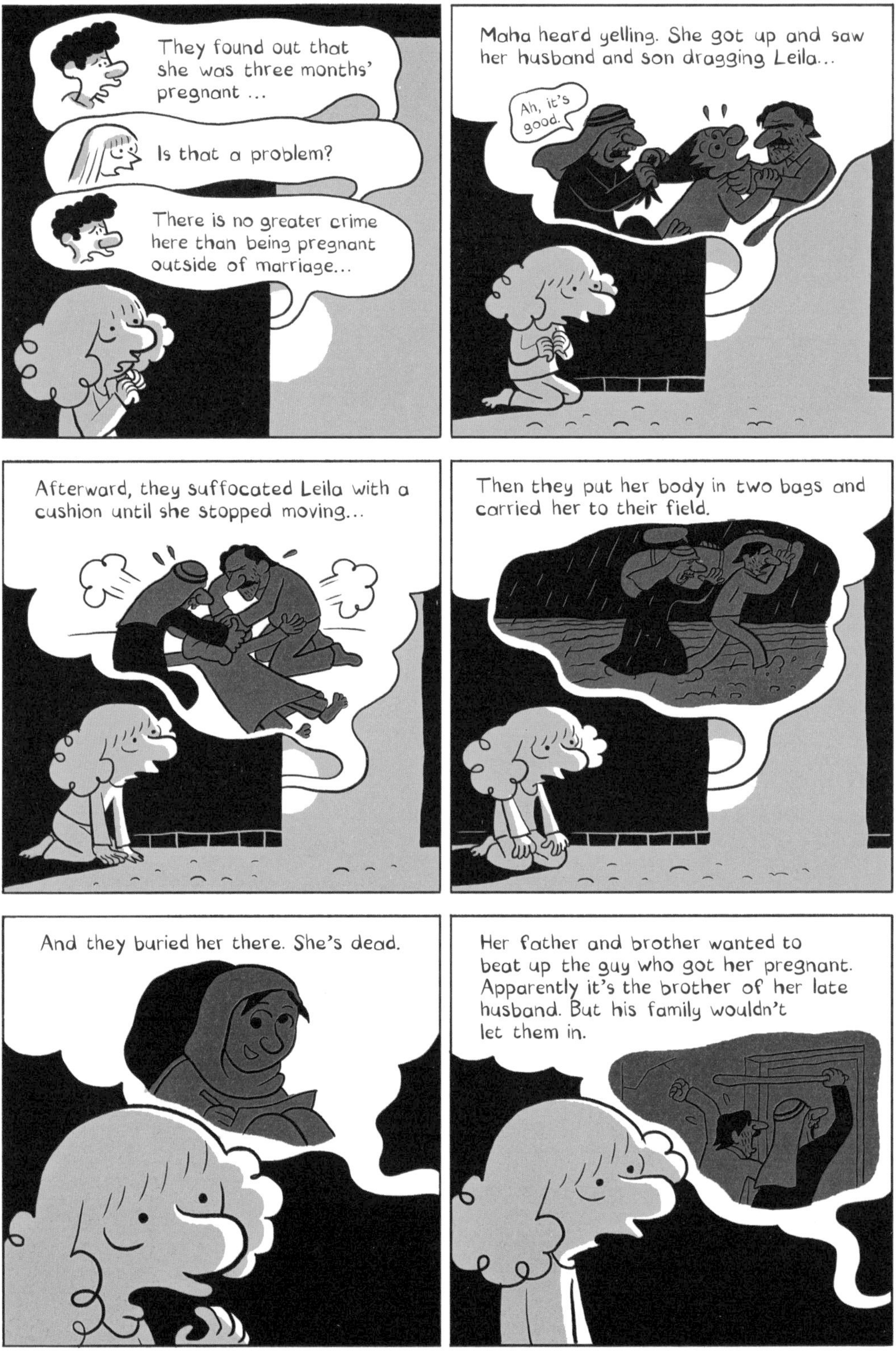
They found out that she was three months' pregnant ...
Is that a problem?
There is no greater crime here than being pregnant outside of marriage...
Maha heard yelling. She got up and saw her husband and son dragging Leila...
Ah, it's good.
Afterward, they suffocated Leila with a cushion until she stopped moving...
Then they put her body in two bags and carried her to their field.
And they buried her there. She's dead.
Her father and brother wanted to beat up the guy who got her pregnant. Apparently it's the brother of her late husband. But his family wouldn't let them in.

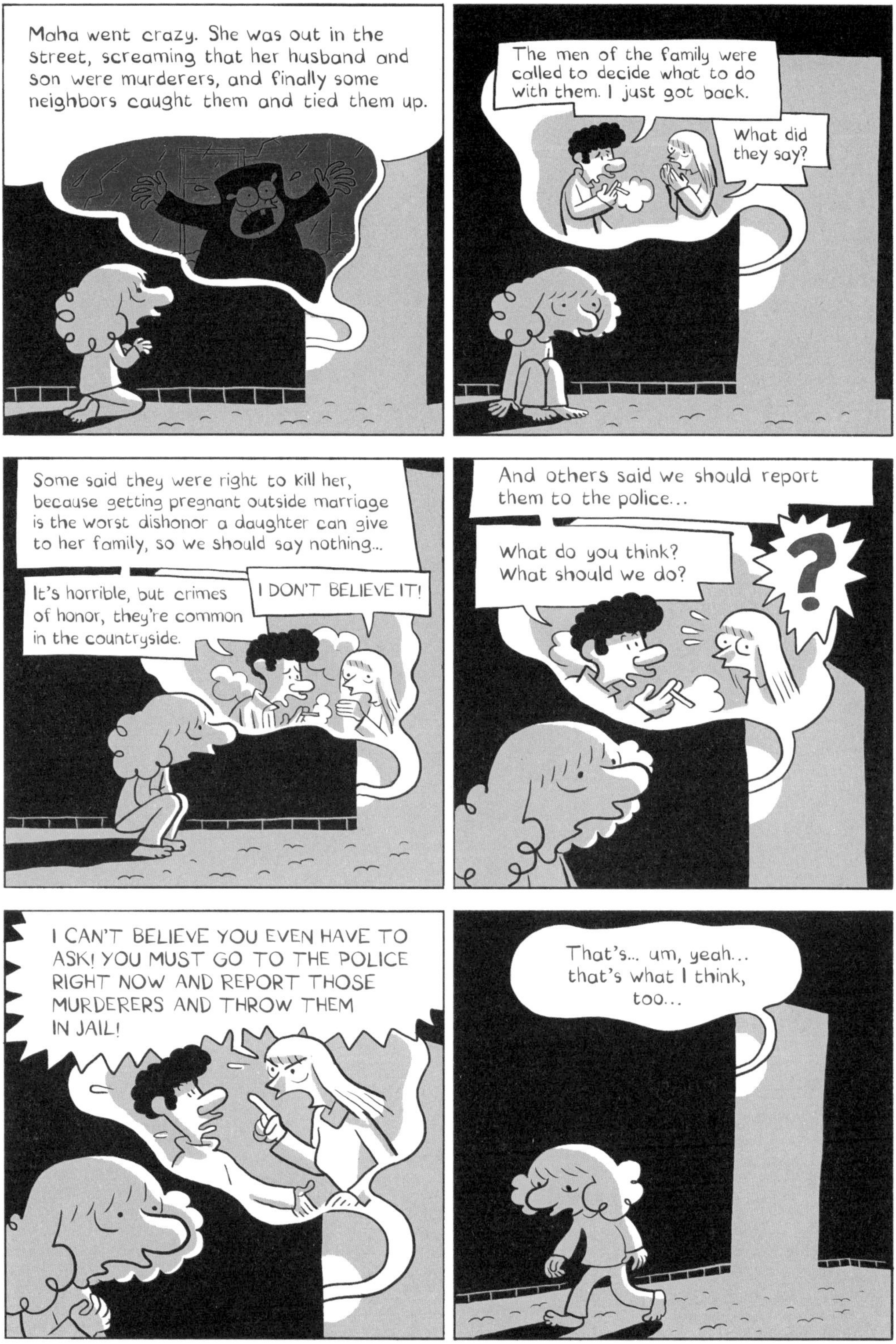
Maha went crazy. She was out in the street, screaming that her husband and son were murderers, and finally some neighbors caught them and tied them up.
The men of the family were called to decide what to do with them. I just got back.
What did they say?
Some said they were right to kill her, because getting pregnant outside marriage is the worst dishonor a daughter can give to her family, so we should say nothing...
It's horrible, but crimes of honor, they're common in the countryside.
I DON'T BELIEVE IT!
And others said we should report them to the police...
What do you think? What should we do?
?
I CAN'T BELIEVE YOU EVEN HAVE TO ASK! YOU MUST GO TO THE POLICE RIGHT NOW AND REPORT THOSE MURDERERS AND THROW THEM IN JAIL!
That's... um, yeah... that's what I think, too...

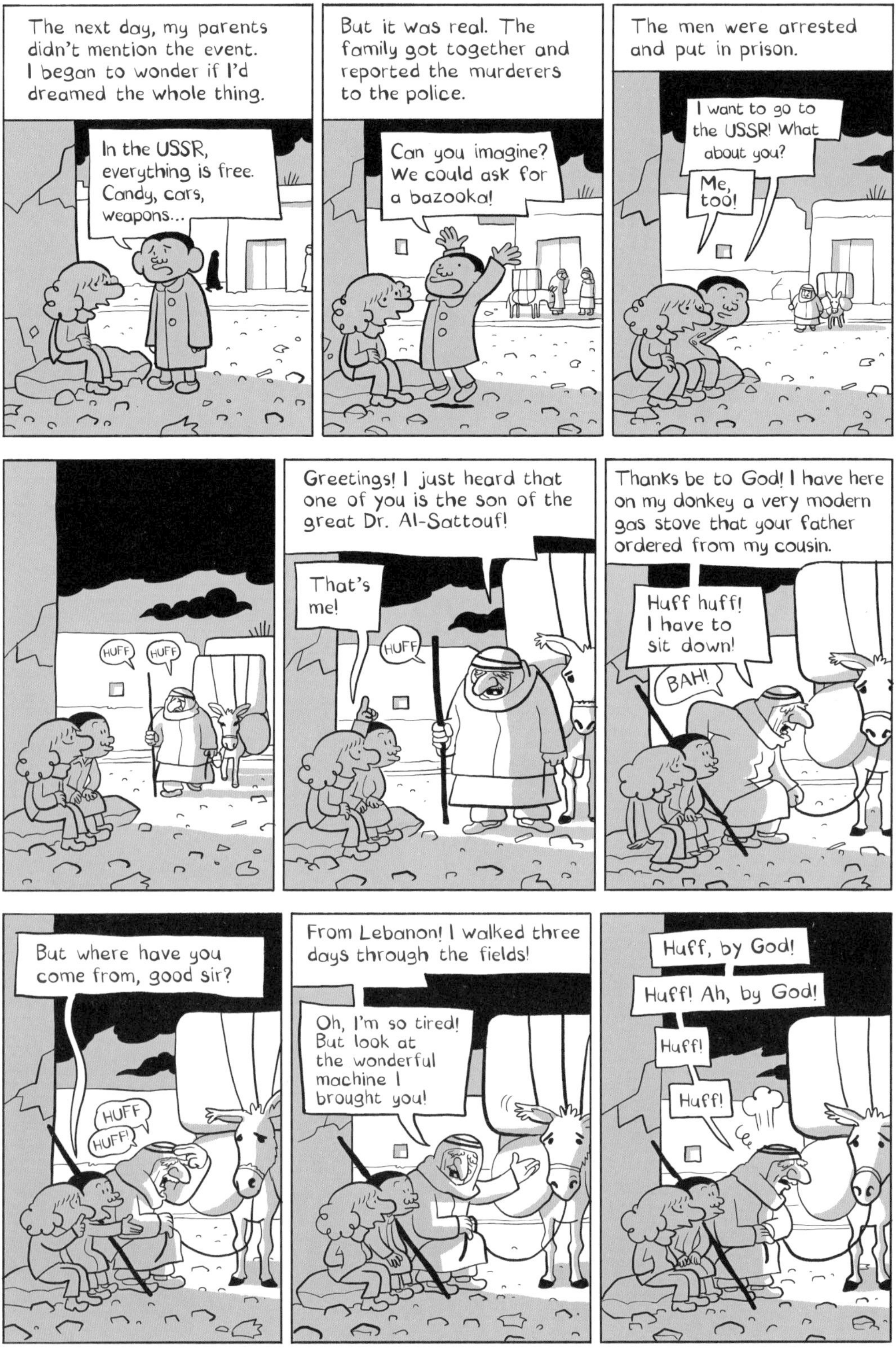
The next day, my parents didn't mention the event. I began to wonder if I'd dreamed the whole thing.
In the USSR, everything is free. Candy, cars, weapons...
But it was real. The family got together and reported the murderers to the police.
Can you imagine? We could ask for a bazooka!
The men were arrested and put in prison.
I want to go to the USSR! What about you?
Me, too!
HUFF
HUFF
Greetings! I just heard that one of you is the son of the great Dr. Al-Sattouf!
That's me!
HUFF
Thanks be to God! I have here on my donkey a very modern gas stove that your father ordered from my cousin.
Huff huff! I have to sit down!
BAH!
But where have you come from, good sir?
HUFF
HUFF!
From Lebanon! I walked three days through the fields!
Oh, I'm so tired! But look at the wonderful machine I brought you!
Huff, by God!
Huff! Ah, by God!
Huff!
Huff!

CHAPTER 5

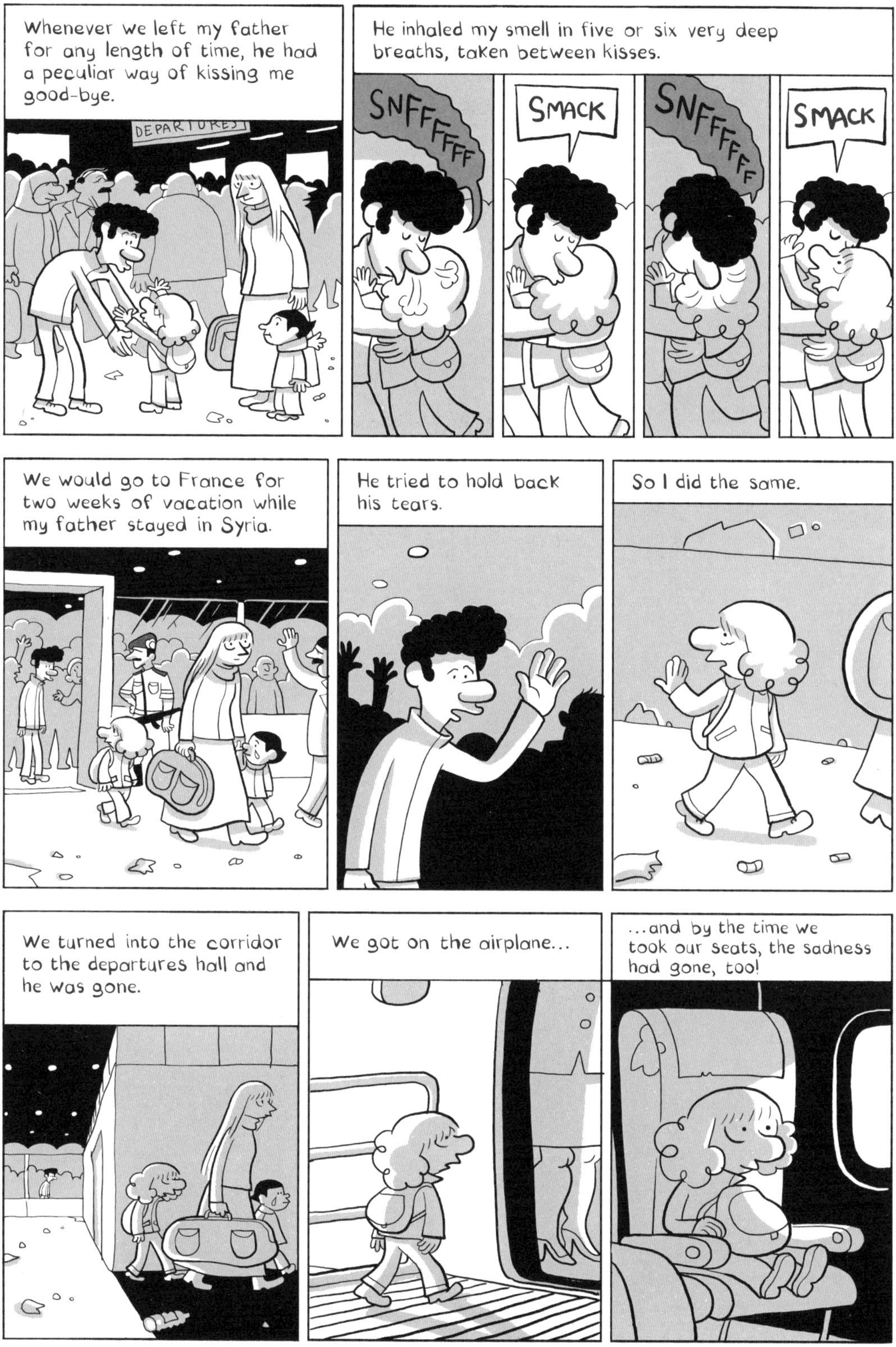

Whenever we left my father for any length of time, he had a peculiar way of kissing me good-bye.
DEPARTURES
He inhaled my smell in five or six very deep breaths, taken between kisses.
SNFFFFFF
SMACK
SNFFFFFF
SMACK
We would go to France for two weeks of vacation while my father stayed in Syria.
He tried to hold back his tears.
So I did the same.
We turned into the corridor to the departures hall and he was gone.
We got on the airplane...
...and by the time we took our seats, the sadness had gone, too!

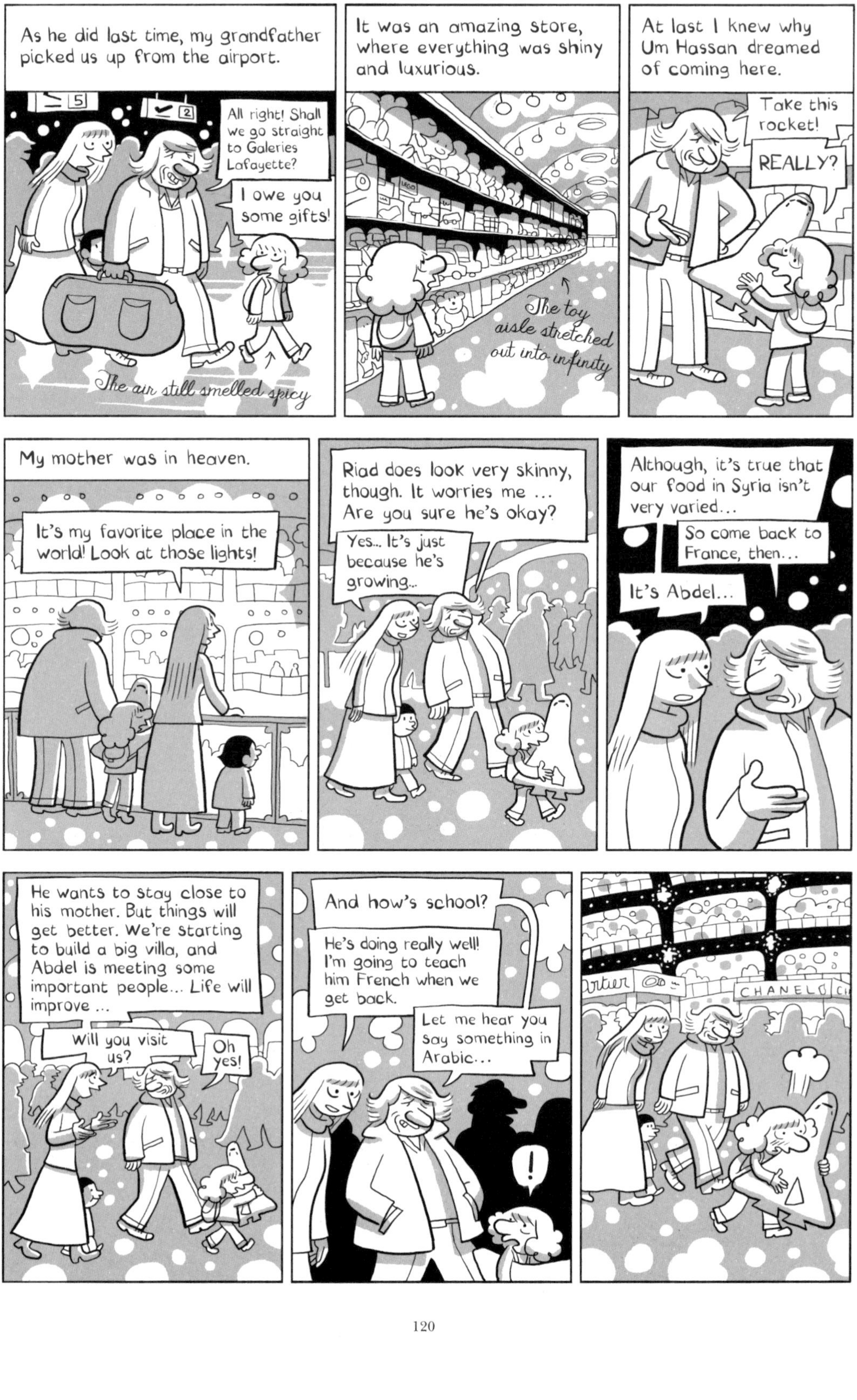
As he did last time, my grandfather picked us up from the airport.
All right! Shall we go straight to Galeries Lafayette?
I owe you some gifts!
The air still smelled spicy
It was an amazing store, where everything was shiny and luxurious.
The toy aisle stretched out into infinity
At last I knew why Um Hassan dreamed of coming here.
Take this rocket!
REALLY?
My mother was in heaven.
It's my favorite place in the world! Look at those lights!
Riad does look very skinny, though. It worries me ... Are you sure he's okay?
Yes... It's just because he's growing...
Although, it's true that our food in Syria isn't very varied...
So come back to France, then...
It's Abdel...
He wants to stay close to his mother. But things will get better. We're starting to build a big villa, and Abdel is meeting some important people... Life will improve ...
Will you visit us?
Oh yes!
And how's school?
He's doing really well! I'm going to teach him French when we get back.
Let me hear you say something in Arabic...
!
CHANEL

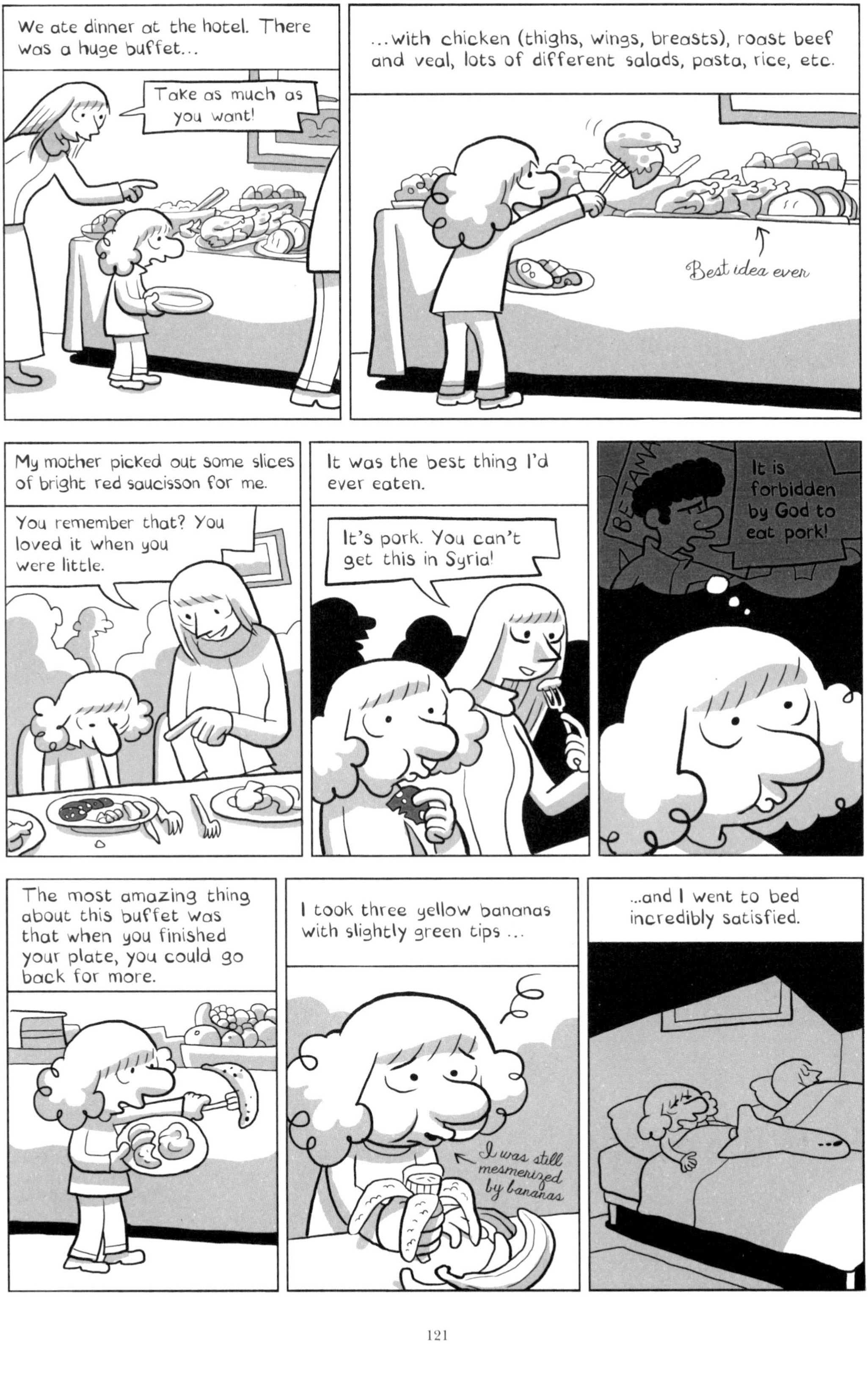
We ate dinner at the hotel. There was a huge buffet...
Take as much as you want!
...with chicken (thighs, wings, breasts), roast beef and veal, lots of different salads, pasta, rice, etc.
Best idea ever
My mother picked out some slices of bright red saucisson for me.
You remember that? You loved it when you were little.
It was the best thing I'd ever eaten.
It's pork. You can't get this in Syria!
It is forbidden by God to eat pork!
The most amazing thing about this buffet was that when you finished your plate, you could go back for more.
I took three yellow bananas with slightly green tips ...
I was still mesmerized by bananas
...and I went to bed incredibly satisfied.

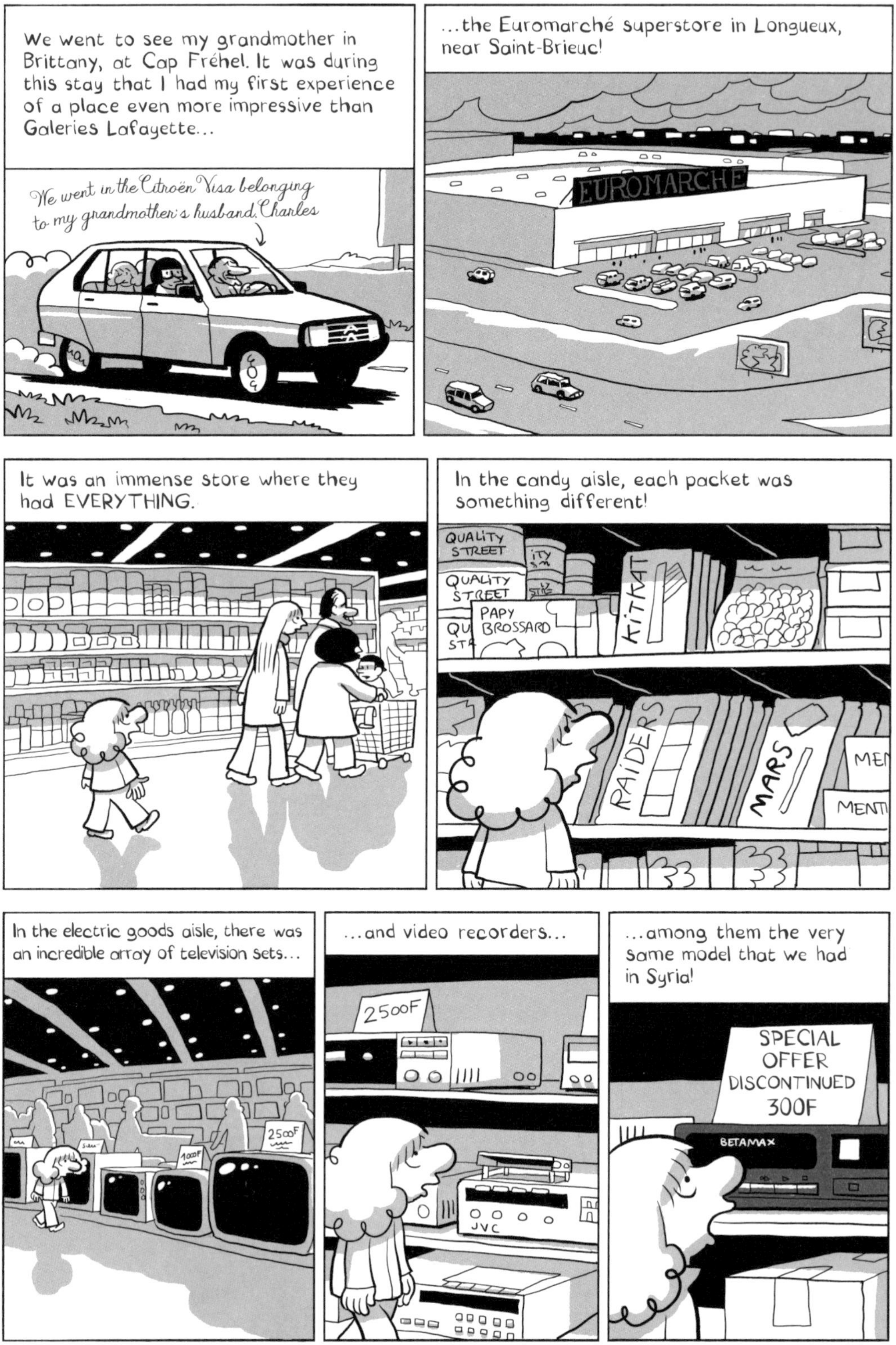
We went to see my grandmother in Brittany, at Cap Fréhel. It was during this stay that I had my first experience of a place even more impressive than Galeries Lafayette...
We went in the Citroën Visa belonging to my grandmother's husband, Charles
...the Euromarché superstore in Longueux, near Saint-Brieuc!
EUROMARCHE
It was an immense store where they had EVERYTHING.
In the candy aisle, each packet was something different!
QUALITY STREET
QUALITY STREET
PAPY BROSSARD
KitKat
RAIDERS
MARS
In the electric goods aisle, there was an incredible array of television sets...
2500F
1000F
...and video recorders...
2500F
JVC
...among them the very same model that we had in Syria!
SPECIAL OFFER DISCONTINUED 300F
BETAMAX

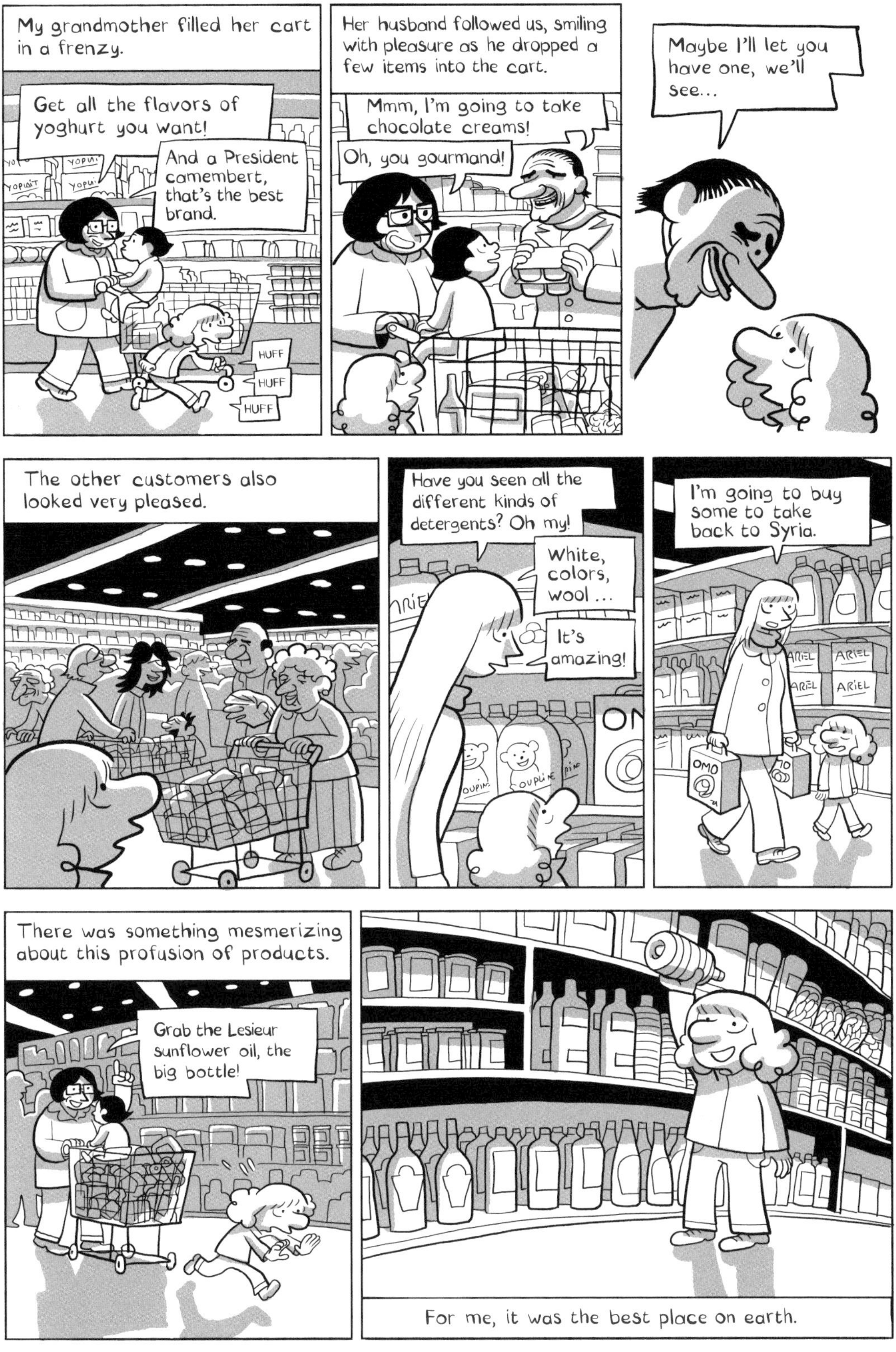
My grandmother filled her cart in a frenzy.
Get all the flavors of yoghurt you want!
And a President camembert, that's the best brand.
YOPLAIT
HUFF
HUFF
HUFF
Her husband followed us, smiling with pleasure as he dropped a few items into the cart.
Mmm, I'm going to take chocolate creams!
Oh, you gourmand!
Maybe I'll let you have one, we'll see...
The other customers also looked very pleased.
Have you seen all the different kinds of detergents? Oh my!
White, colors, wool ...
It's amazing!
I'm going to buy some to take back to Syria.
ARIEL
ARIEL
ARIEL
ARIEL
OMO
There was something mesmerizing about this profusion of products.
Grab the Lesieur sunflower oil, the big bottle!
For me, it was the best place on earth.

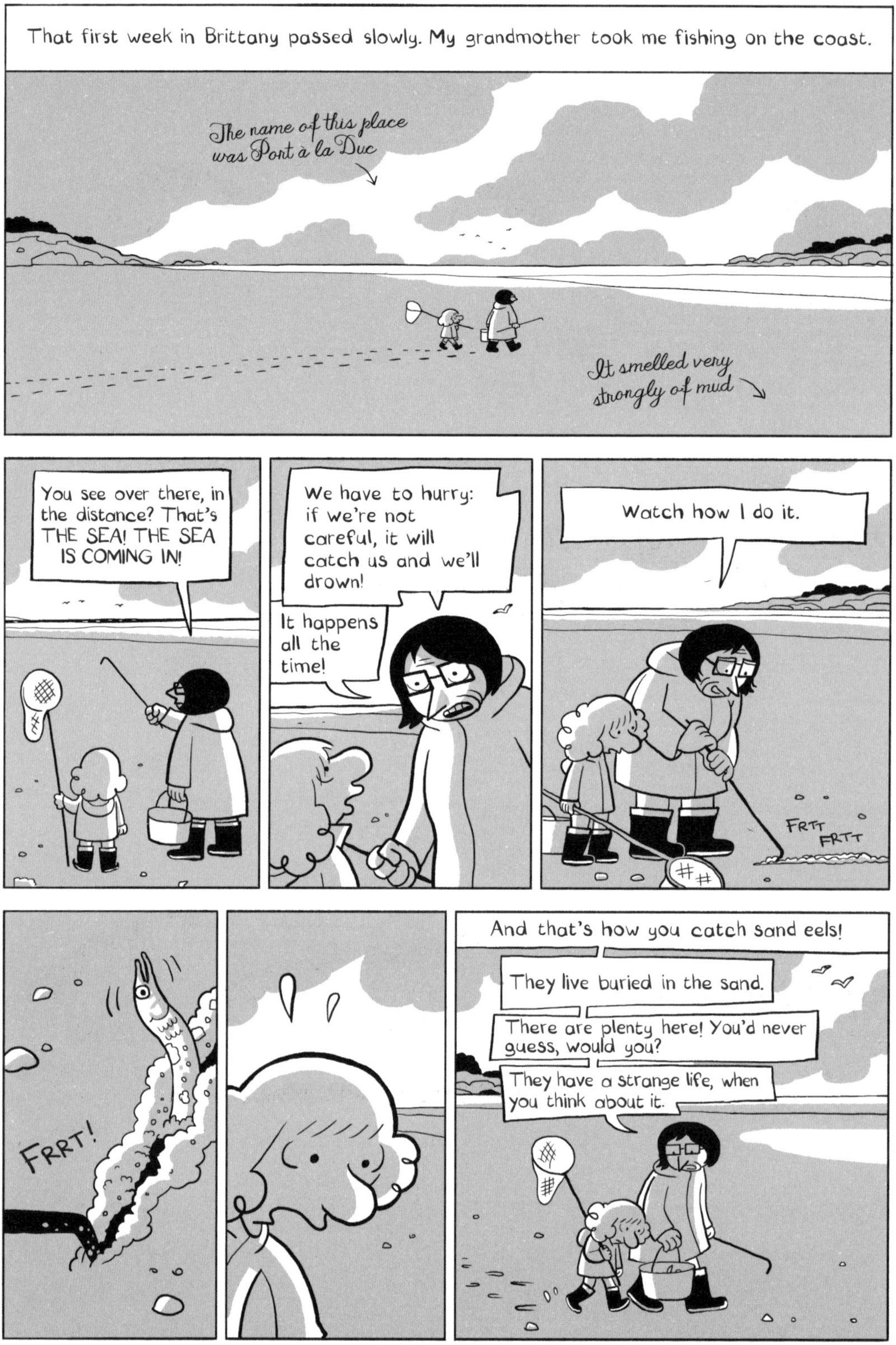

That first week in Brittany passed slowly. My grandmother took me fishing on the coast.
The name of this place was Port à la Duc
It smelled very strongly of mud
You see over there, in the distance? That's THE SEA! THE SEA IS COMING IN!
We have to hurry: if we're not careful, it will catch us and we'll drown!
It happens all the time!
Watch how I do it.
FRTT FRTT
FRRT!
And that's how you catch sand eels!
They live buried in the sand.
There are plenty here! You'd never guess, would you?
They have a strange life, when you think about it.

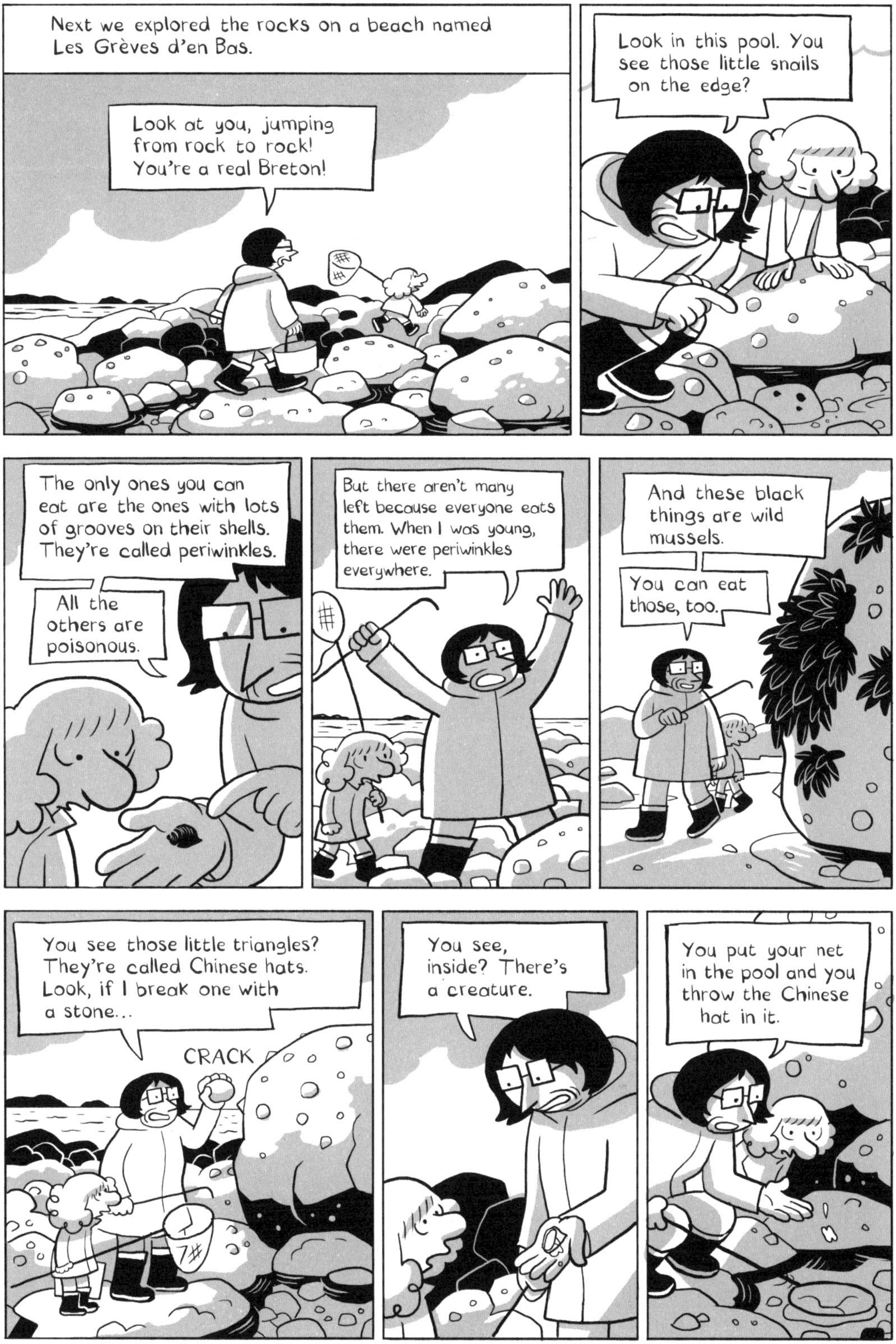

Next we explored the rocks on a beach named Les Grèves d'en Bas.
Look at you, jumping from rock to rock! You're a real Breton!
Look in this pool. You see those little snails on the edge?
The only ones you can eat are the ones with lots of grooves on their shells. They're called periwinkles.
All the others are poisonous.
But there aren't many left because everyone eats them. When I was young, there were periwinkles everywhere.
And these black things are wild mussels.
You can eat those, too.
You see those little triangles? They're called Chinese hats. Look, if I break one with a stone...
CRACK
You see, inside? There's a creature.
You put your net in the pool and you throw the Chinese hat in it.

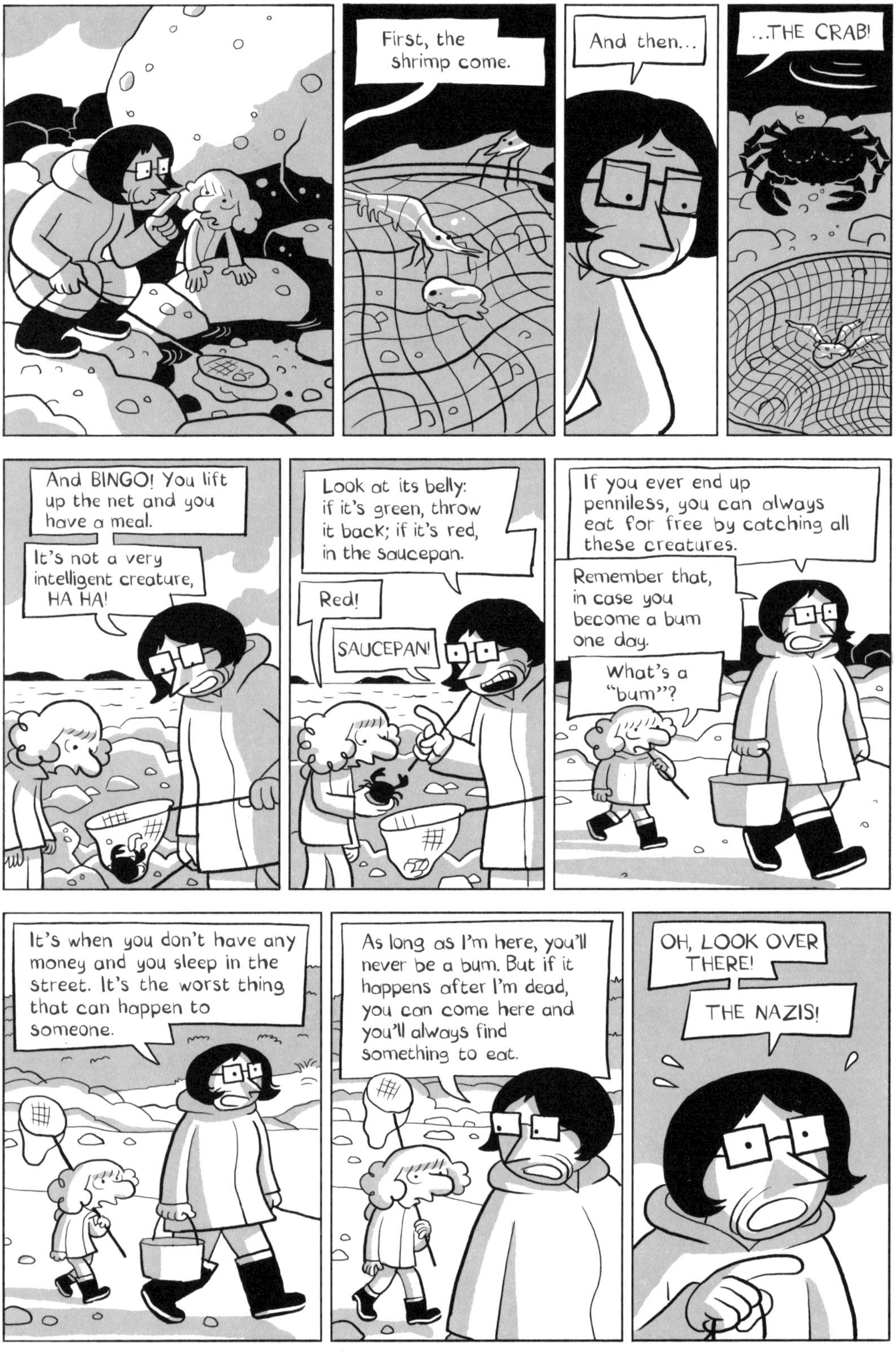
First, the shrimp come.
And then...
...THE CRAB!
And BINGO! You lift up the net and you have a meal.
It's not a very intelligent creature, HA HA!
Look at its belly: if it's green, throw it back; if it's red, in the saucepan.
Red!
SAUCEPAN!
If you ever end up penniless, you can always eat for free by catching all these creatures.
Remember that, in case you become a bum one day.
What's a "bum"?
It's when you don't have any money and you sleep in the street. It's the worst thing that can happen to someone.
As long as I'm here, you'll never be a bum. But if it happens after I'm dead, you can come here and you'll always find something to eat.
OH, LOOK OVER THERE!
THE NAZIS!

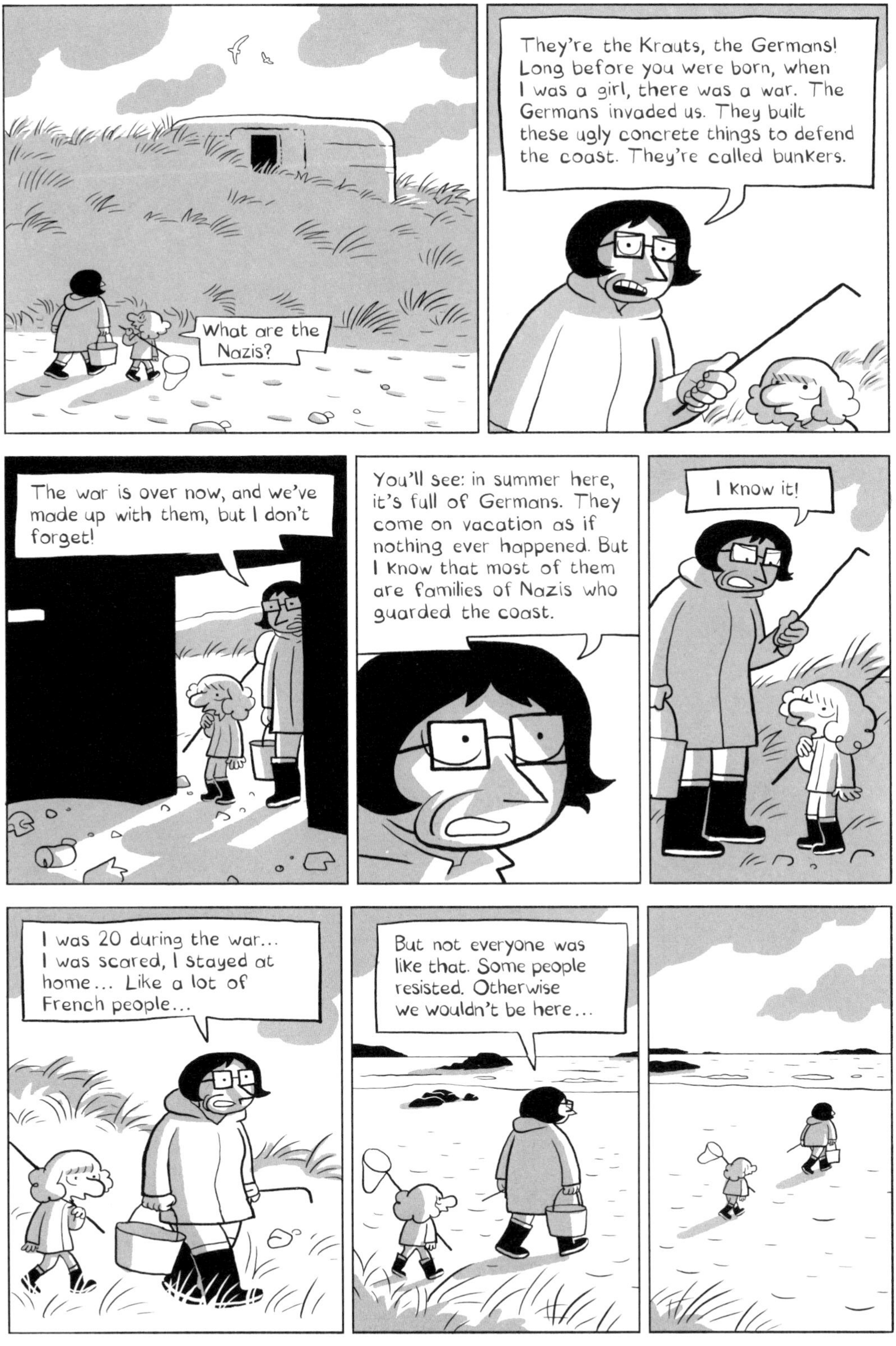
What are the Nazis?
They're the Krauts, the Germans! Long before you were born, when I was a girl, there was a war. The Germans invaded us. They built these ugly concrete things to defend the coast. They're called bunkers.
The war is over now, and we've made up with them, but I don't forget!
You'll see: in summer here, it's full of Germans. They come on vacation as if nothing ever happened. But I know that most of them are families of Nazis who guarded the coast.
I know it!
I was 20 during the war... I was scared, I stayed at home... Like a lot of French people...
But not everyone was like that. Some people resisted. Otherwise we wouldn't be here...

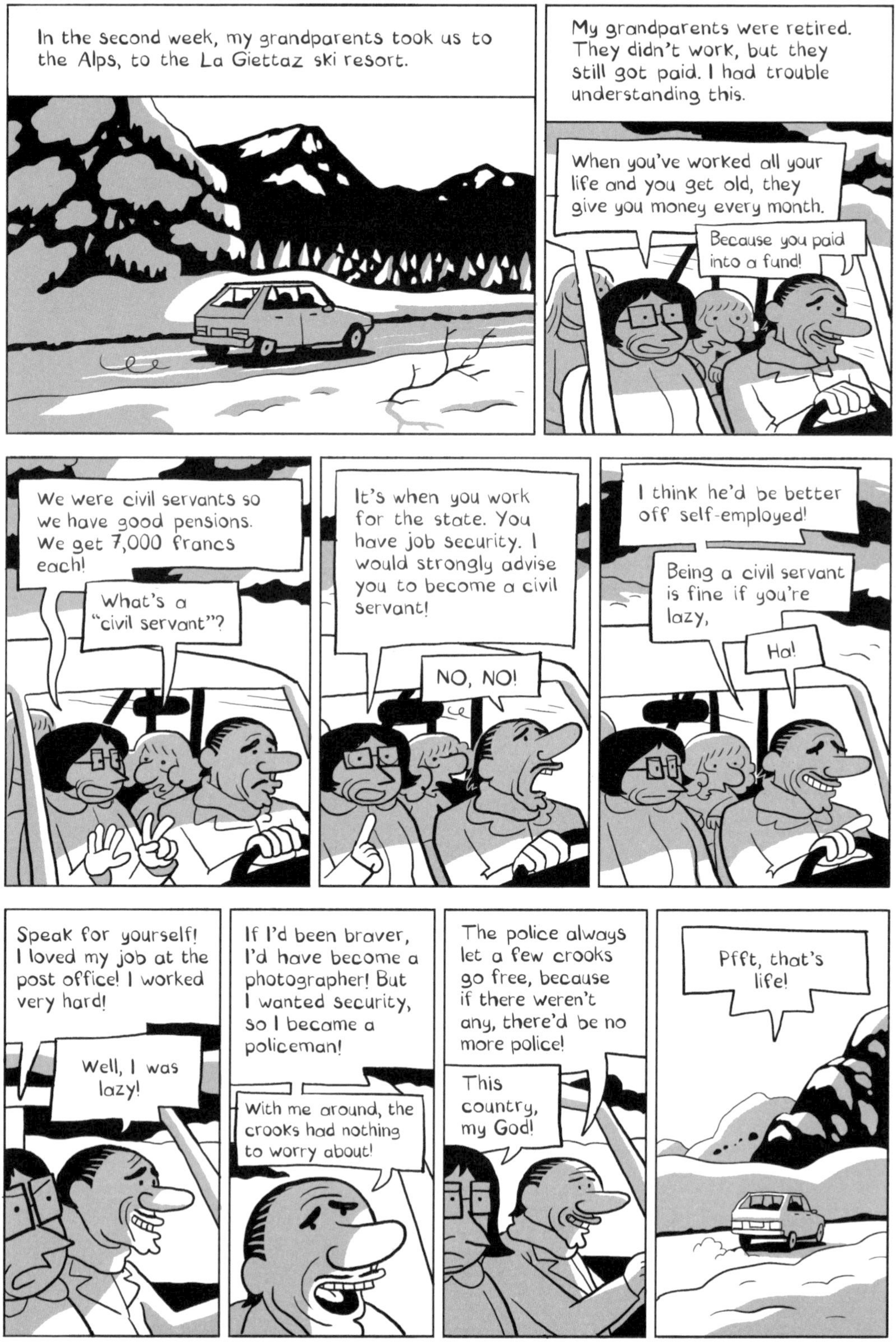
In the second week, my grandparents took us to the Alps, to the La Giettaz ski resort.
My grandparents were retired. They didn't work, but they still got paid. I had trouble understanding this.
When you've worked all your life and you get old, they give you money every month.
Because you paid into a fund!
We were civil servants so we have good pensions. We get 7,000 francs each!
What's a "civil servant"?
It's when you work for the state. You have job security. I would strongly advise you to become a civil servant!
NO, NO!
I think he'd be better off self-employed!
Being a civil servant is fine if you're lazy,
Ha!
Speak for yourself! I loved my job at the post office! I worked very hard!
Well, I was lazy!
If I'd been braver, I'd have become a photographer! But I wanted security, so I became a policeman!
With me around, the crooks had nothing to worry about!
The police always let a few crooks go free, because if there weren't any, there'd be no more police!
This country, my God!
Pfft, that's life!

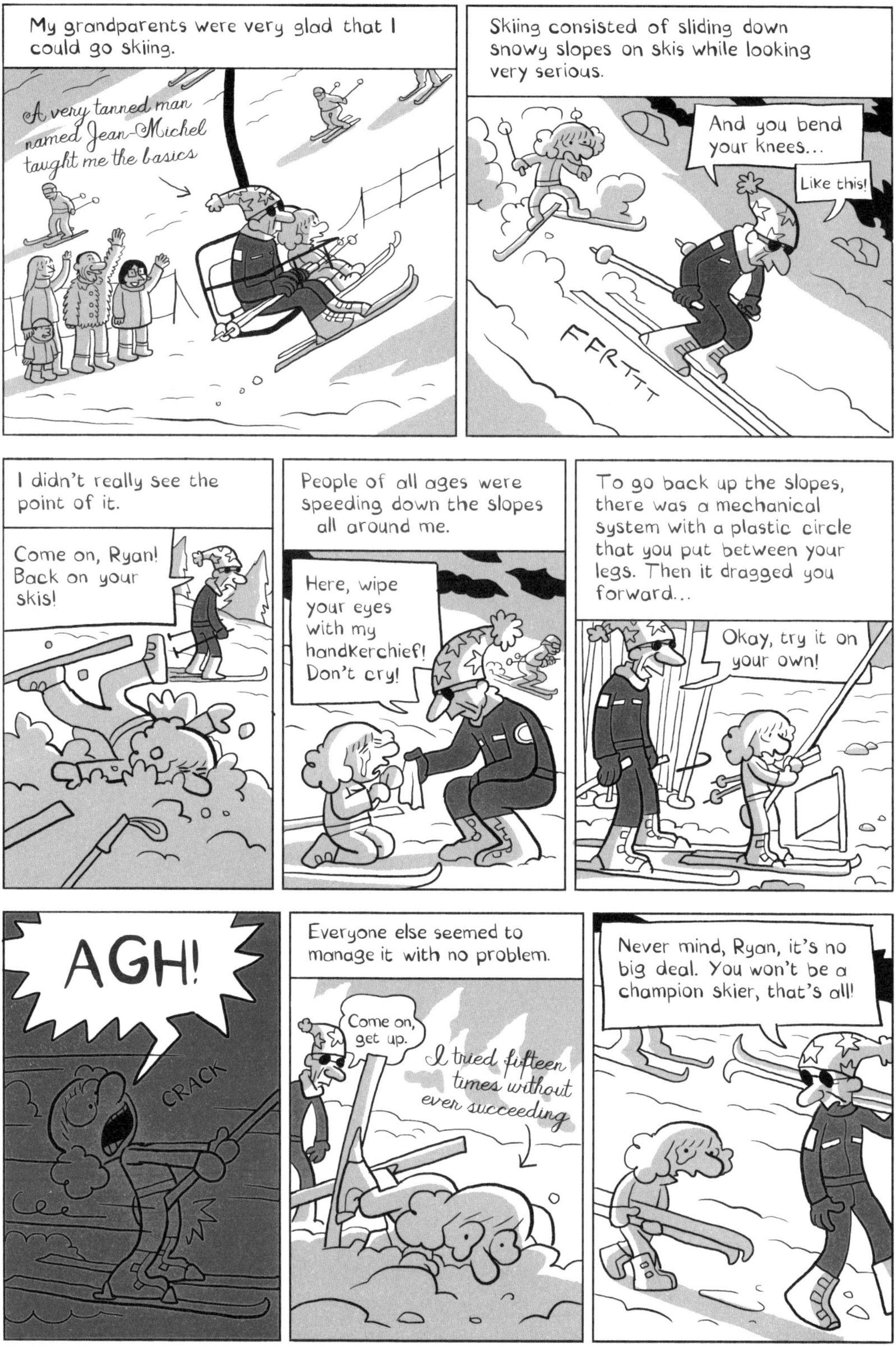
My grandparents were very glad that I could go skiing.
A very tanned man named Jean-Michel taught me the basics
Skiing consisted of sliding down snowy slopes on skis while looking very serious.
And you bend your knees...
Like this!
FFRTTT
I didn't really see the point of it.
Come on, Ryan! Back on your skis!
People of all ages were speeding down the slopes all around me.
Here, wipe your eyes with my handkerchief! Don't cry!
To go back up the slopes, there was a mechanical system with a plastic circle that you put between your legs. Then it dragged you forward...
Okay, try it on your own!
AGH!
CRACK
Everyone else seemed to manage it with no problem.
Come on, get up.
I tried fifteen times without ever succeeding
Never mind, Ryan, it's no big deal. You won't be a champion skier, that's all!

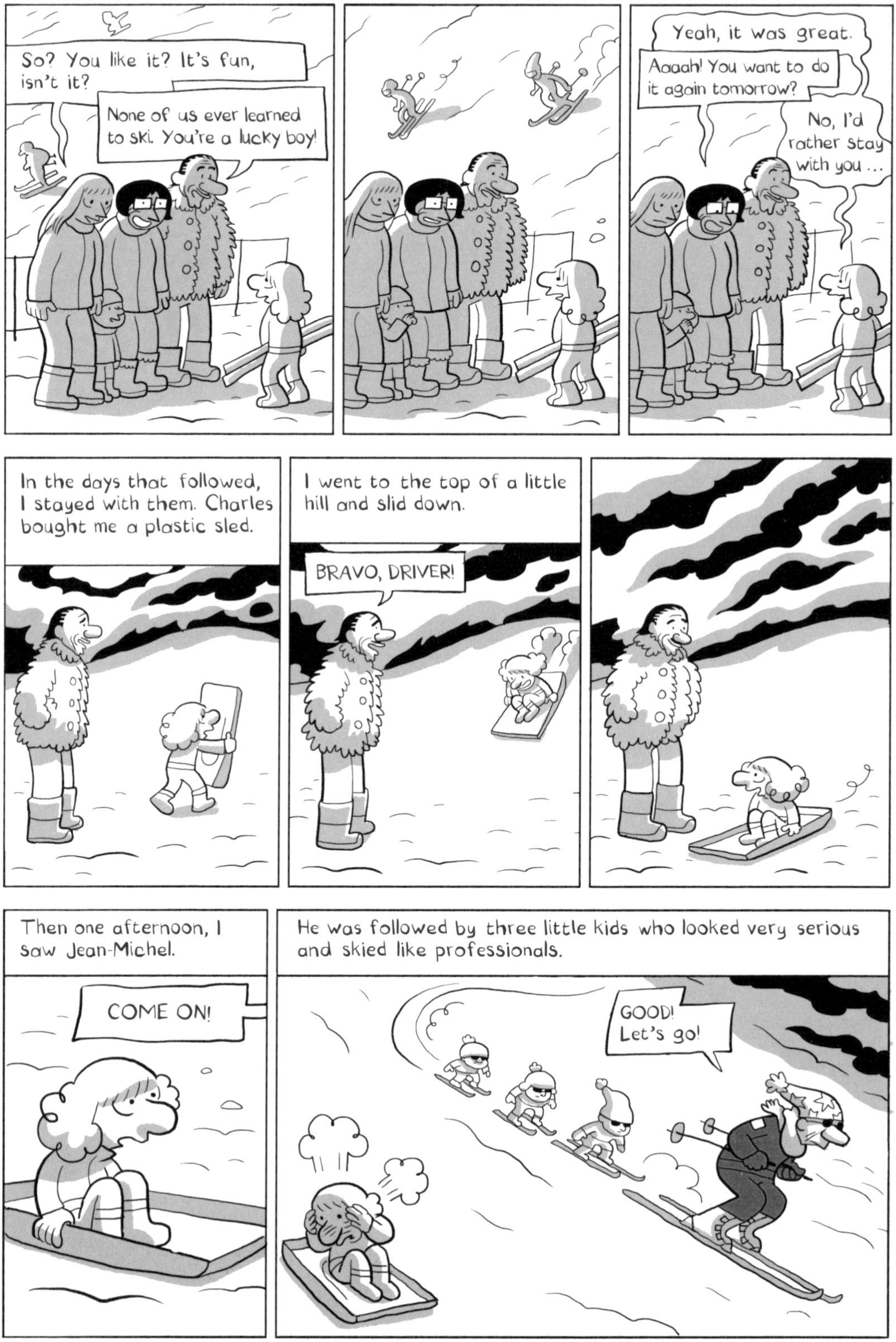
So? You like it? It's fun, isn't it?
None of us ever learned to ski. You're a lucky boy!
Yeah, it was great.
Aaaah! You want to do it again tomorrow?
No, I'd rather stay with you …
In the days that followed, I stayed with them. Charles bought me a plastic sled.
I went to the top of a little hill and slid down.
BRAVO, DRIVER!
Then one afternoon, I saw Jean-Michel.
COME ON!
He was followed by three little kids who looked very serious and skied like professionals.
GOOD! Let's go!

CHAPTER 6

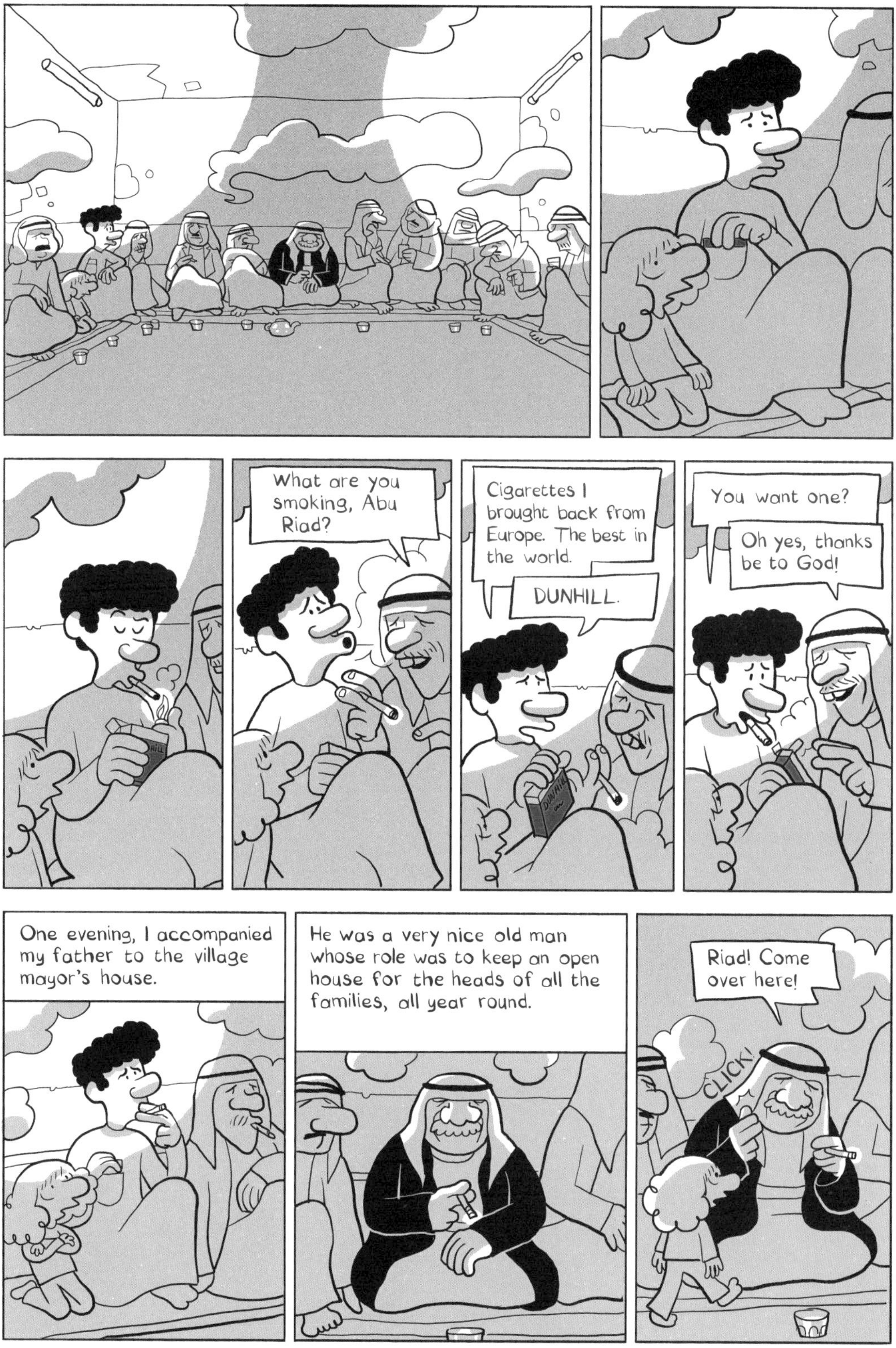
What are you smoking, Abu Riad?
Cigarettes I brought back from Europe. The best in the world.
DUNHILL.
You want one?
Oh yes, thanks be to God!
One evening, I accompanied my father to the village mayor's house.
He was a very nice old man whose role was to keep an open house for the heads of all the families, all year round.
Riad! Come over here!
CLICK!

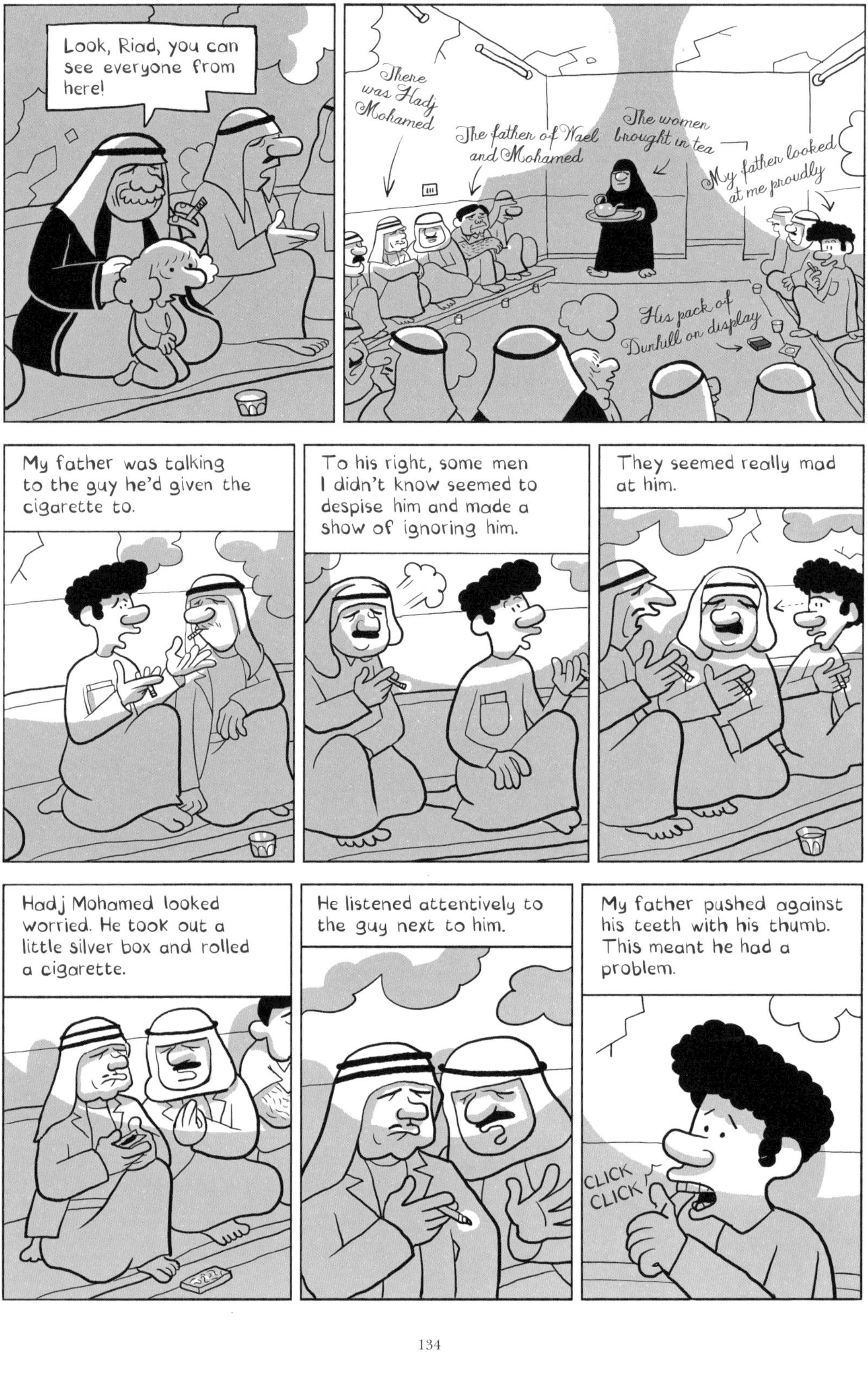

Look, Riad, you can see everyone from here!
There was Hadj Mohamed
The women brought in tea
The father of Wael and Mohamed
My father looked at me proudly
His pack of Dunhill on display
My father was talking to the guy he'd given the cigarette to.
To his right, some men I didn't know seemed to despise him and made a show of ignoring him.
They seemed really mad at him.
Hadj Mohamed looked worried. He took out a little silver box and rolled a cigarette.
He listened attentively to the guy next to him.
My father pushed against his teeth with his thumb. This meant he had a problem.
CLICK CLICK

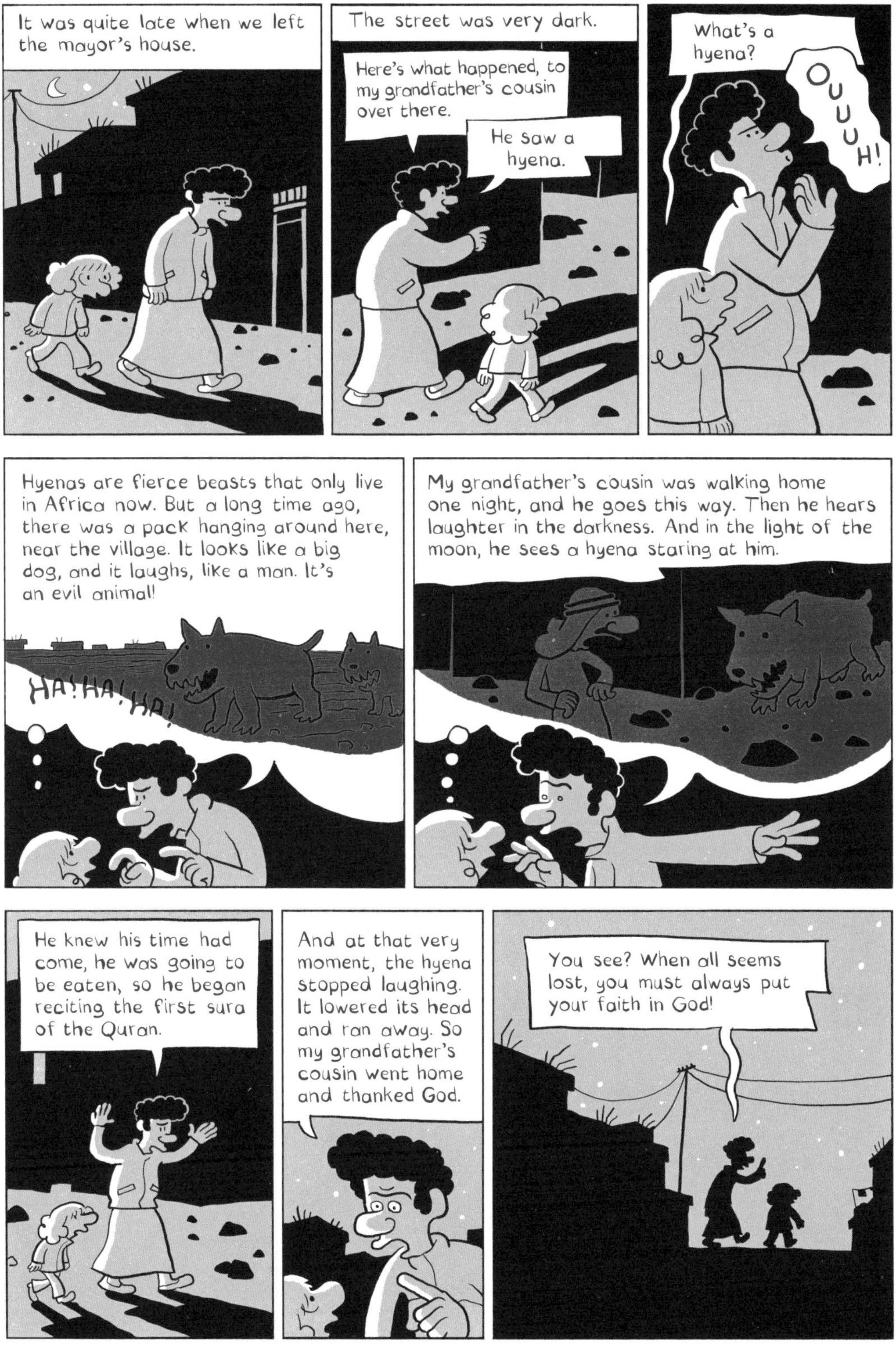
It was quite late when we left the mayor's house.
The street was very dark.
Here's what happened, to my grandfather's cousin over there.
He saw a hyena.
What's a hyena?
OUUUH!
Hyenas are fierce beasts that only live in Africa now. But a long time ago, there was a pack hanging around here, near the village. It looks like a big dog, and it laughs, like a man. It's an evil animal!
HA! HA! HA!
My grandfather's cousin was walking home one night, and he goes this way. Then he hears laughter in the darkness. And in the light of the moon, he sees a hyena staring at him.
He knew his time had come, he was going to be eaten, so he began reciting the first sura of the Quran.
And at that very moment, the hyena stopped laughing. It lowered its head and ran away. So my grandfather's cousin went home and thanked God.
You see? When all seems lost, you must always put your faith in God!

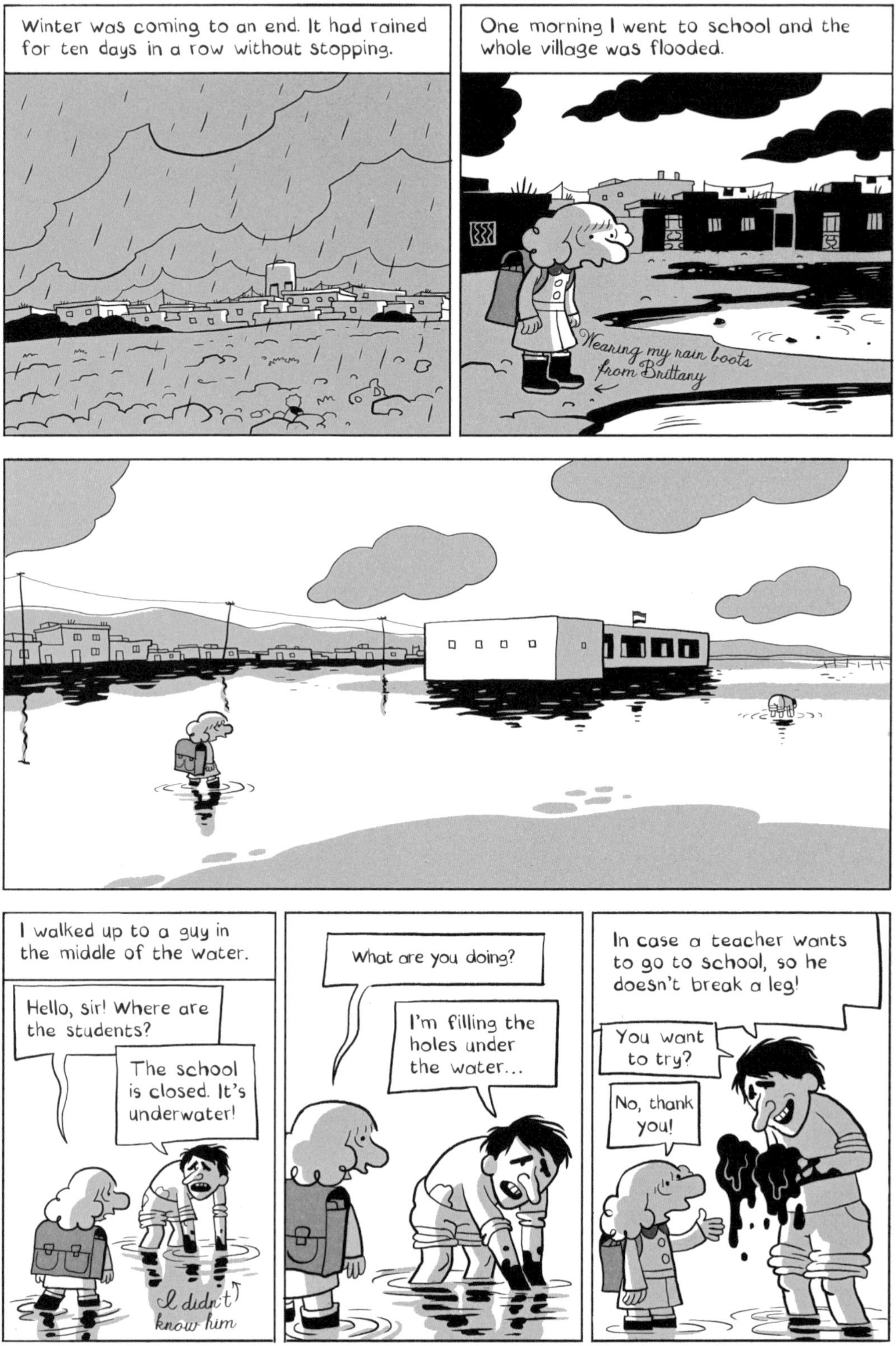
Winter was coming to an end. It had rained for ten days in a row without stopping.
One morning I went to school and the whole village was flooded.
Wearing my rain boots from Brittany
I walked up to a guy in the middle of the water.
Hello, sir! Where are the students?
The school is closed. It's underwater!
I didn't know him
What are you doing?
I'm filling the holes under the water...
In case a teacher wants to go to school, so he doesn't break a leg!
You want to try?
No, thank you!

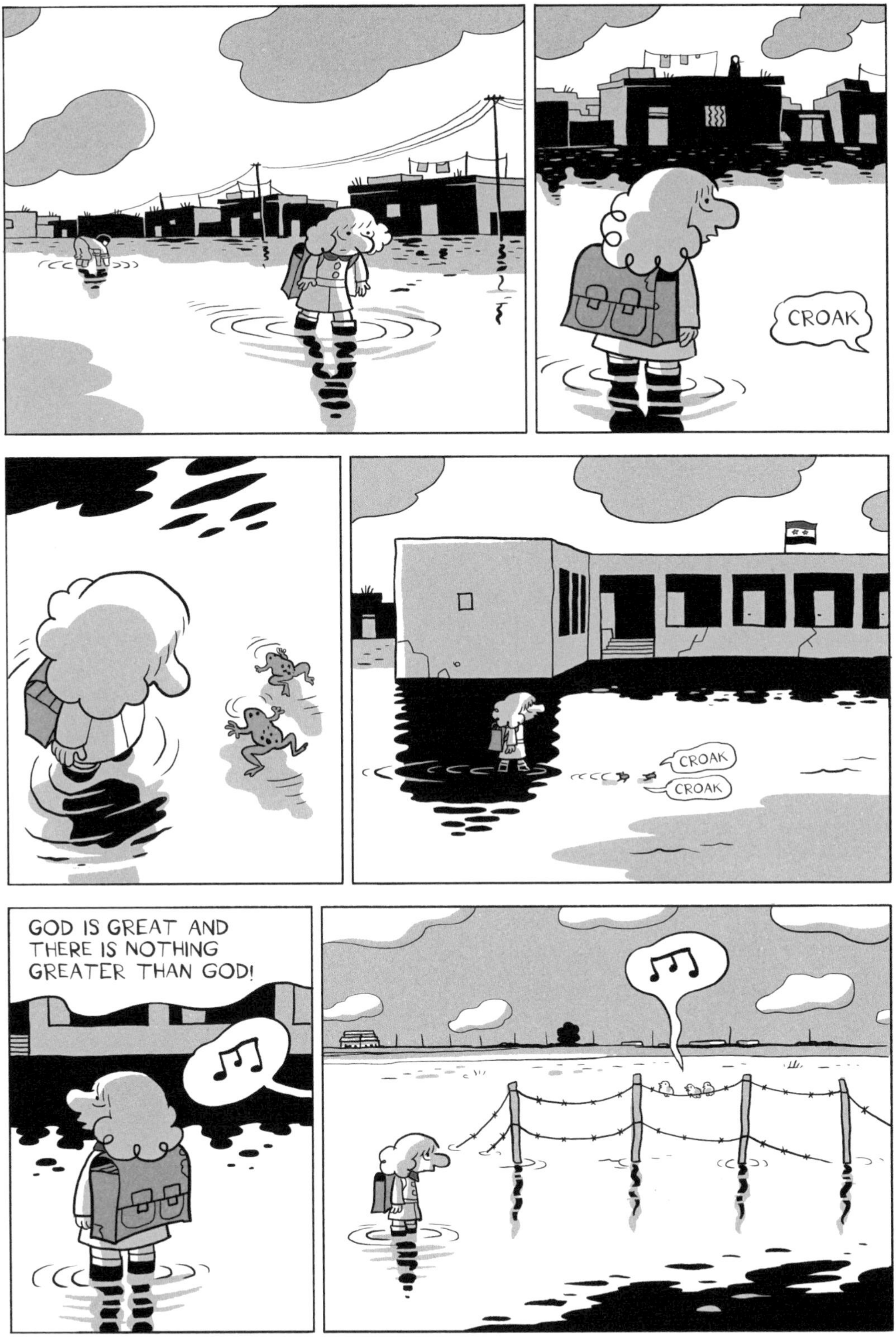
CROAK
CROAK
CROAK
GOD IS GREAT AND THERE IS NOTHING GREATER THAN GOD!

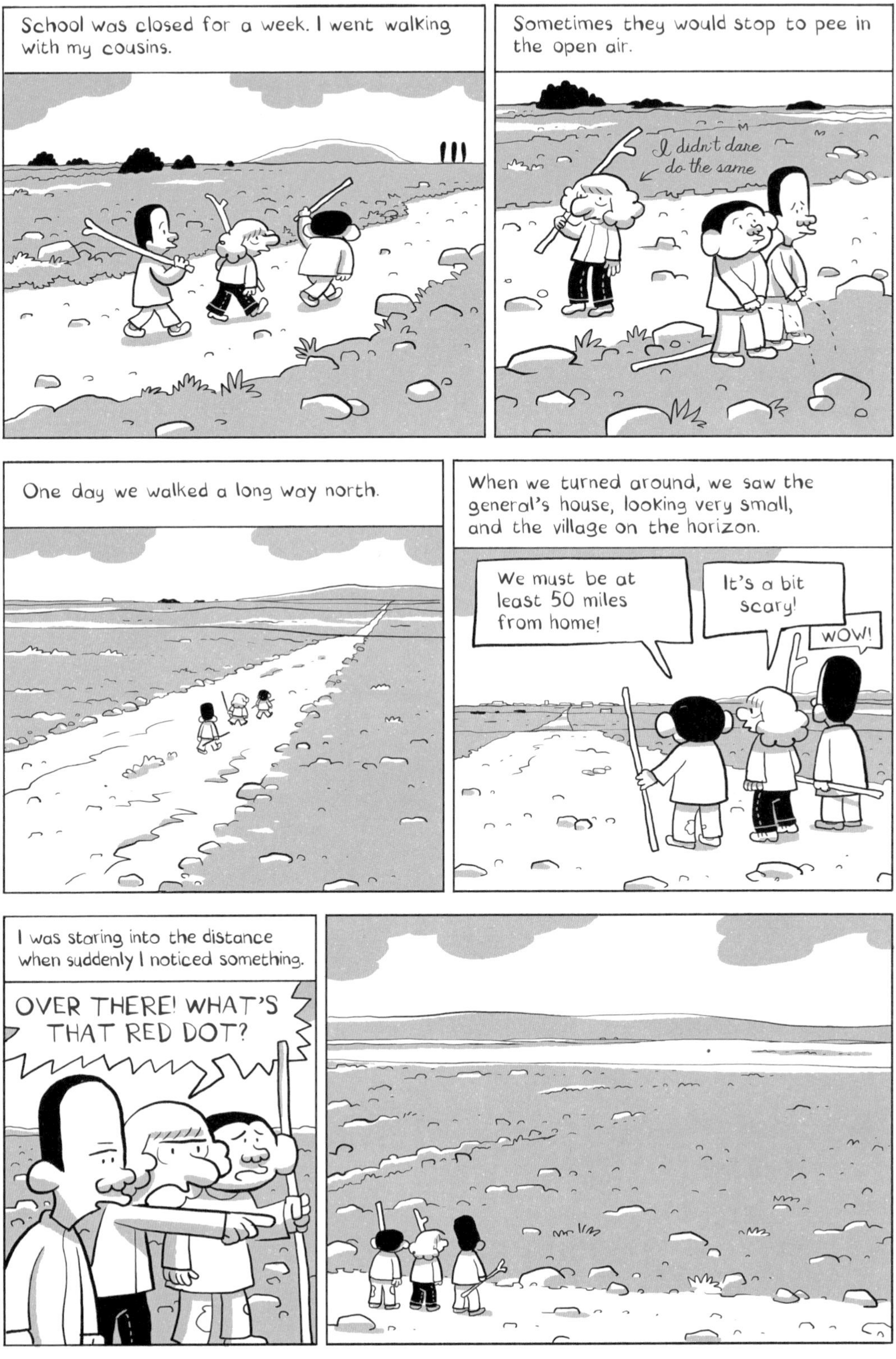
School was closed for a week. I went walking with my cousins.
Sometimes they would stop to pee in the open air.
I didn't dare do the same
One day we walked a long way north.
When we turned around, we saw the general's house, looking very small, and the village on the horizon.
We must be at least 50 miles from home!
It's a bit scary!
WOW!
I was staring into the distance when suddenly I noticed something.
OVER THERE! WHAT'S THAT RED DOT?

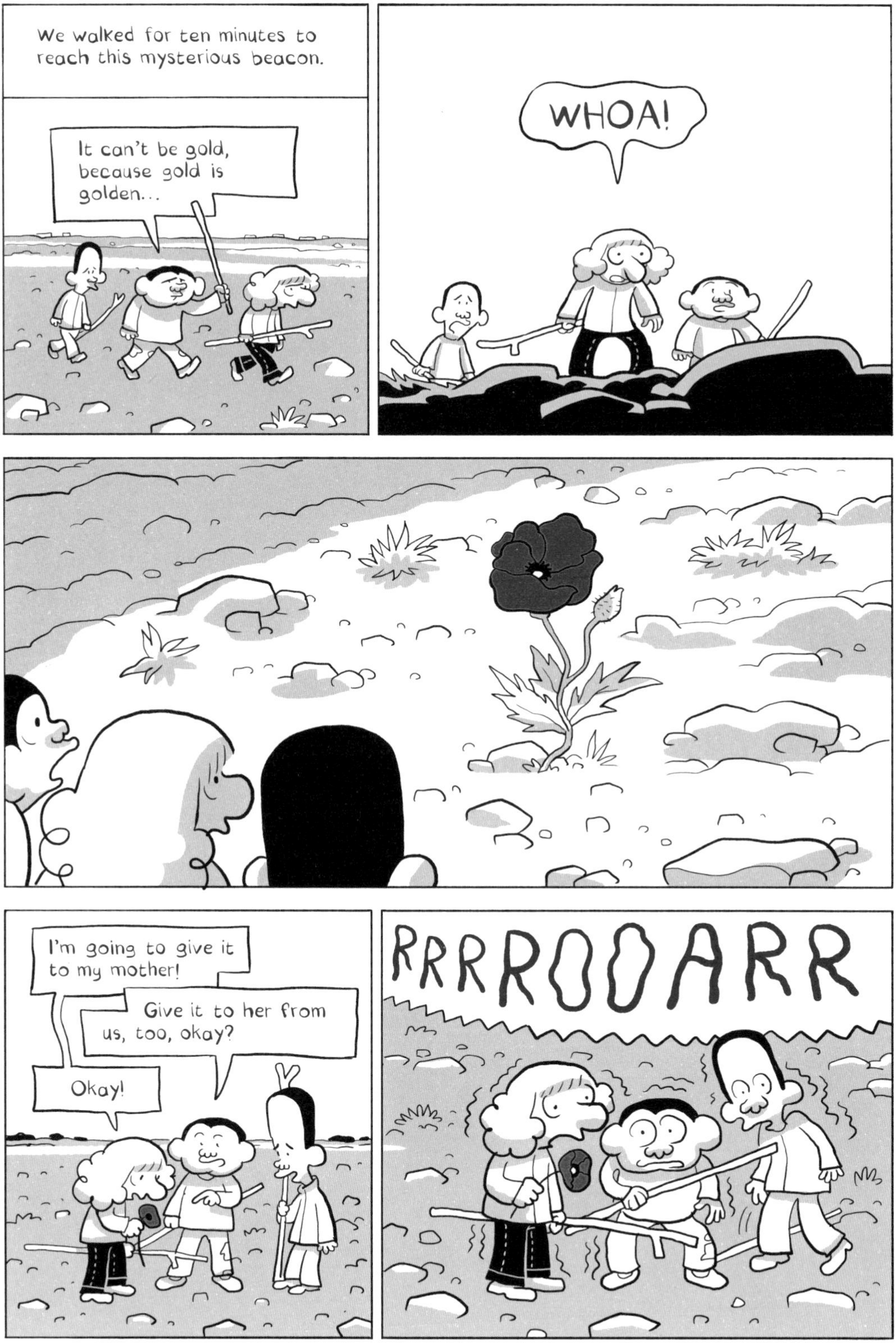
We walked for ten minutes to reach this mysterious beacon.
It can't be gold, because gold is golden...
WHOA!
I'm going to give it to my mother!
Give it to her from us, too, okay?
Okay!
RRRROOARR

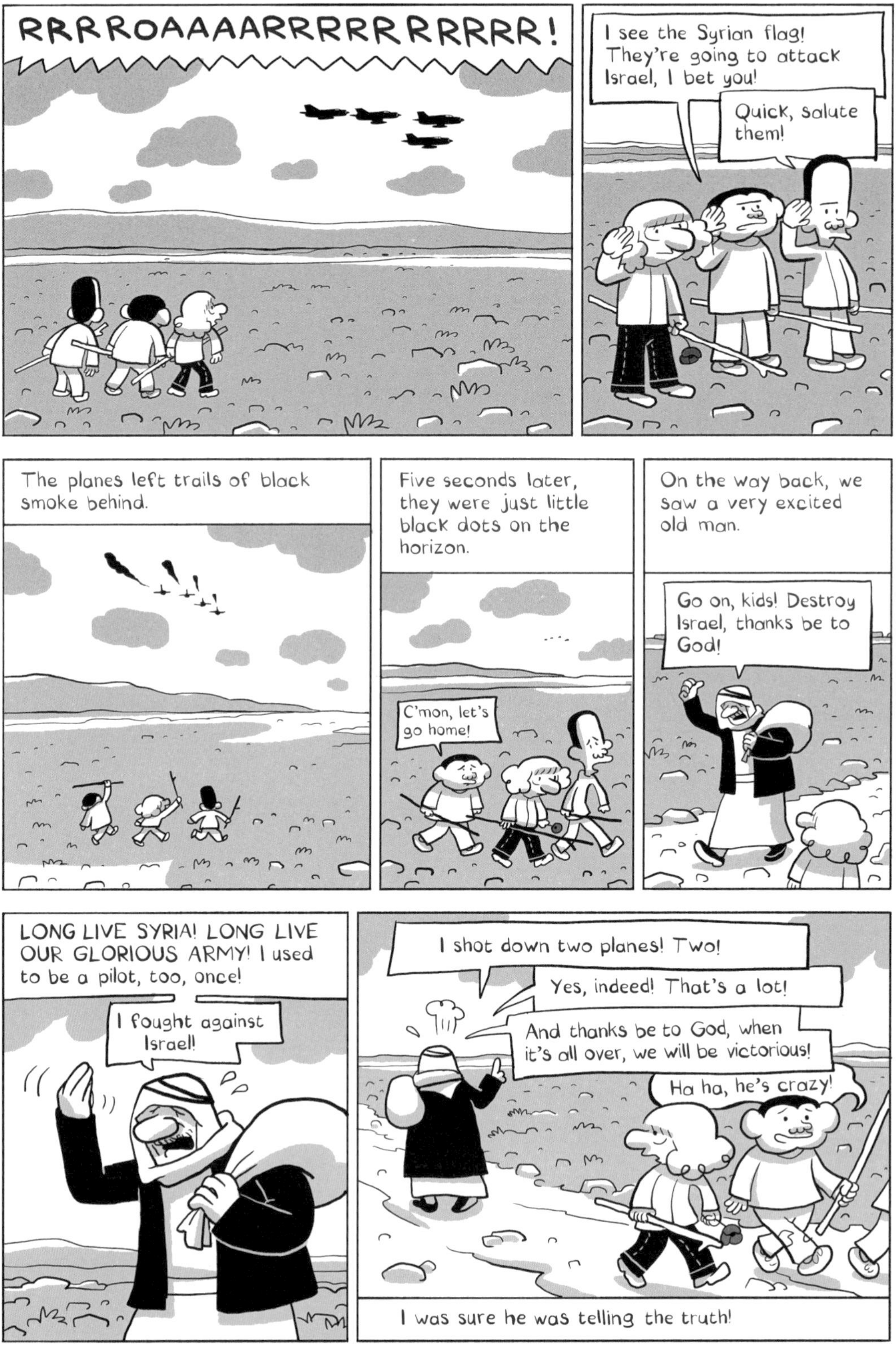
RRRROAAAARRRRRRRRRRR!
I see the Syrian flag! They're going to attack Israel, I bet you!
Quick, salute them!
The planes left trails of black smoke behind.
Five seconds later, they were just little black dots on the horizon.
C'mon, let's go home!
On the way back, we saw a very excited old man.
Go on, kids! Destroy Israel, thanks be to God!
LONG LIVE SYRIA! LONG LIVE OUR GLORIOUS ARMY! I used to be a pilot, too, once!
I fought against Israel!
I shot down two planes! Two!
Yes, indeed! That's a lot!
And thanks be to God, when it's all over, we will be victorious!
Ha ha, he's crazy!
I was sure he was telling the truth!

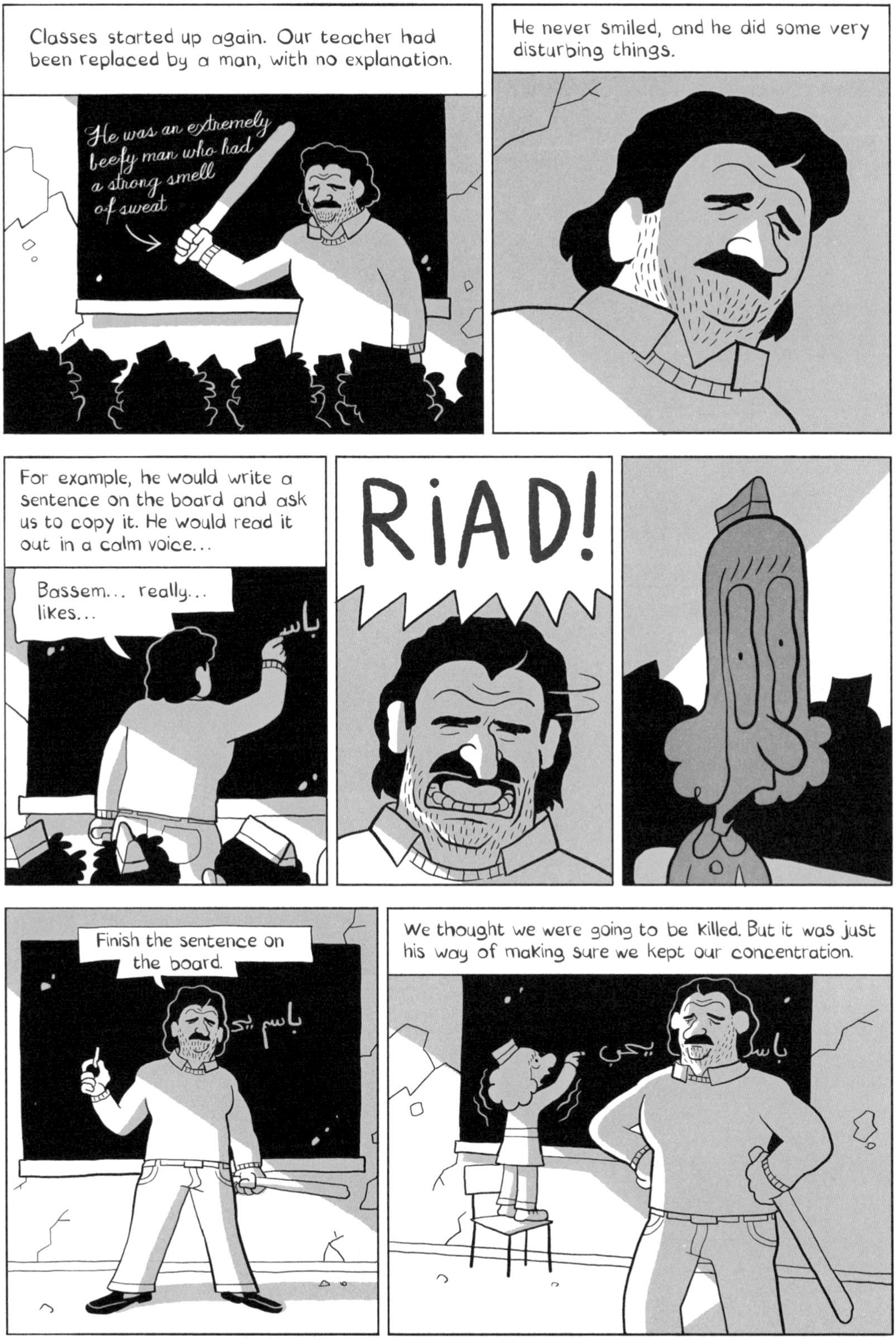
Classes started up again. Our teacher had been replaced by a man, with no explanation.
He was an extremely beefy man who had a strong smell of sweat
He never smiled, and he did some very disturbing things.
For example, he would write a sentence on the board and ask us to copy it. He would read it out in a calm voice...
Bassem... really... likes...
باس
RiAD!
Finish the sentence on the board.
We thought we were going to be killed. But it was just his way of making sure we kept our concentration.

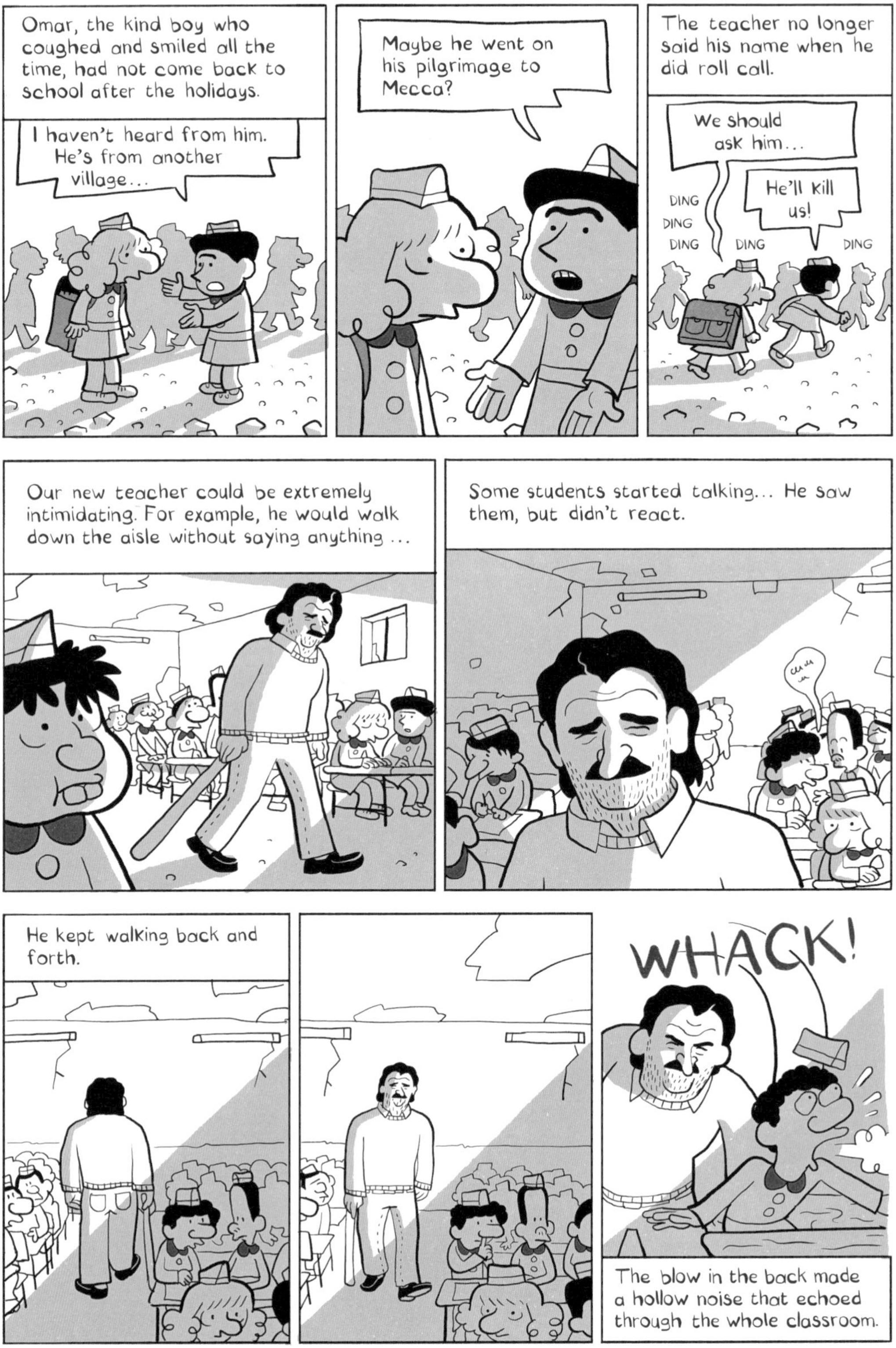
Omar, the kind boy who coughed and smiled all the time, had not come back to school after the holidays.
I haven't heard from him. He's from another village...
Maybe he went on his pilgrimage to Mecca?
The teacher no longer said his name when he did roll call.
We should ask him...
He'll kill us!
DING
DING
DING
DING
DING
Our new teacher could be extremely intimidating. For example, he would walk down the aisle without saying anything...
Some students started talking... He saw them, but didn't react.
He kept walking back and forth.
WHACK!
The blow in the back made a hollow noise that echoed through the whole classroom.

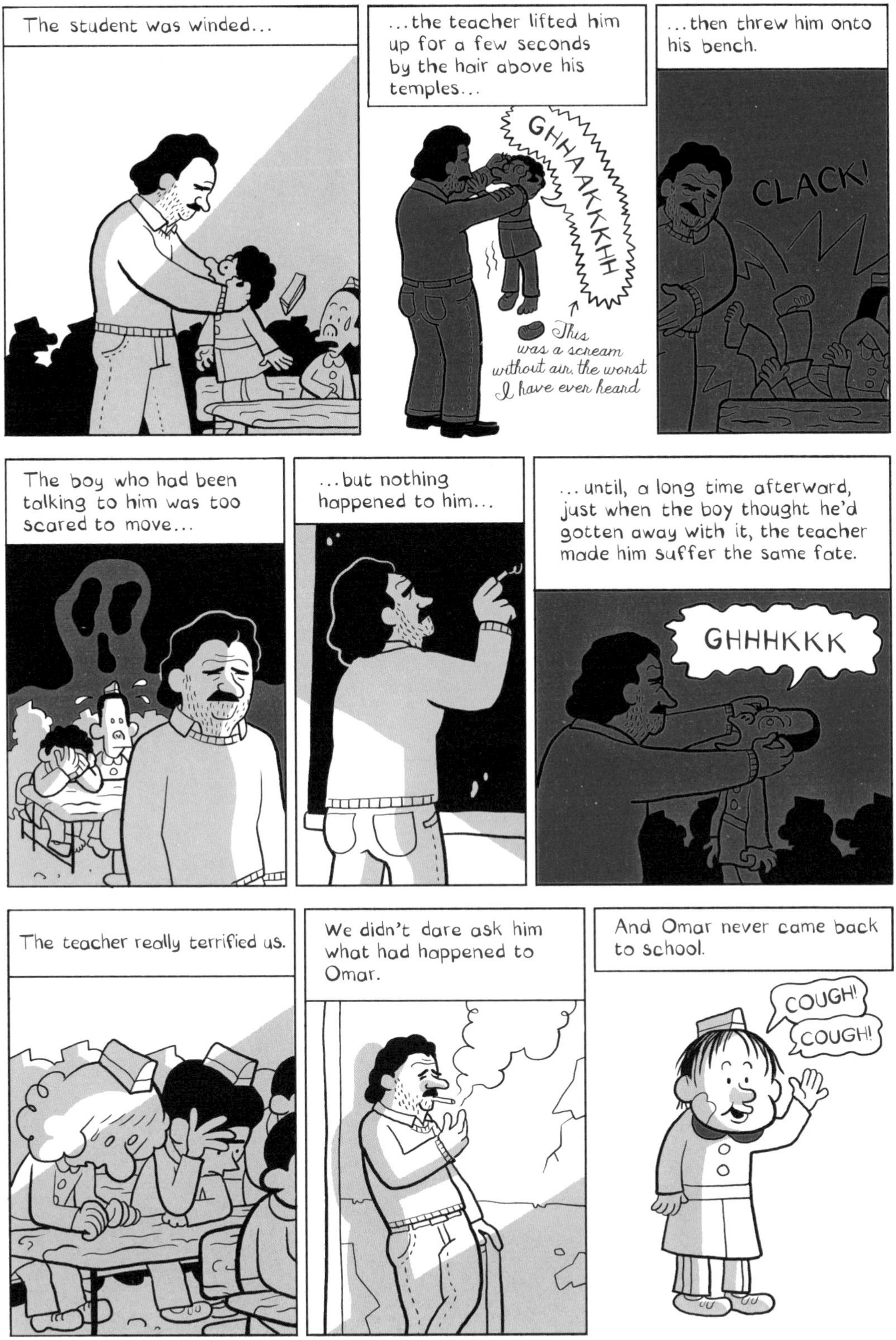
The student was winded...
...the teacher lifted him up for a few seconds by the hair above his temples...
GHHAAKKKHH
This was a scream without air, the worst I have ever heard
...then threw him onto his bench.
CLACK!
The boy who had been talking to him was too scared to move...
...but nothing happened to him...
...until, a long time afterward, just when the boy thought he'd gotten away with it, the teacher made him suffer the same fate.
GHHHKKK
The teacher really terrified us.
We didn't dare ask him what had happened to Omar.
And Omar never came back to school.
COUGH!
COUGH!

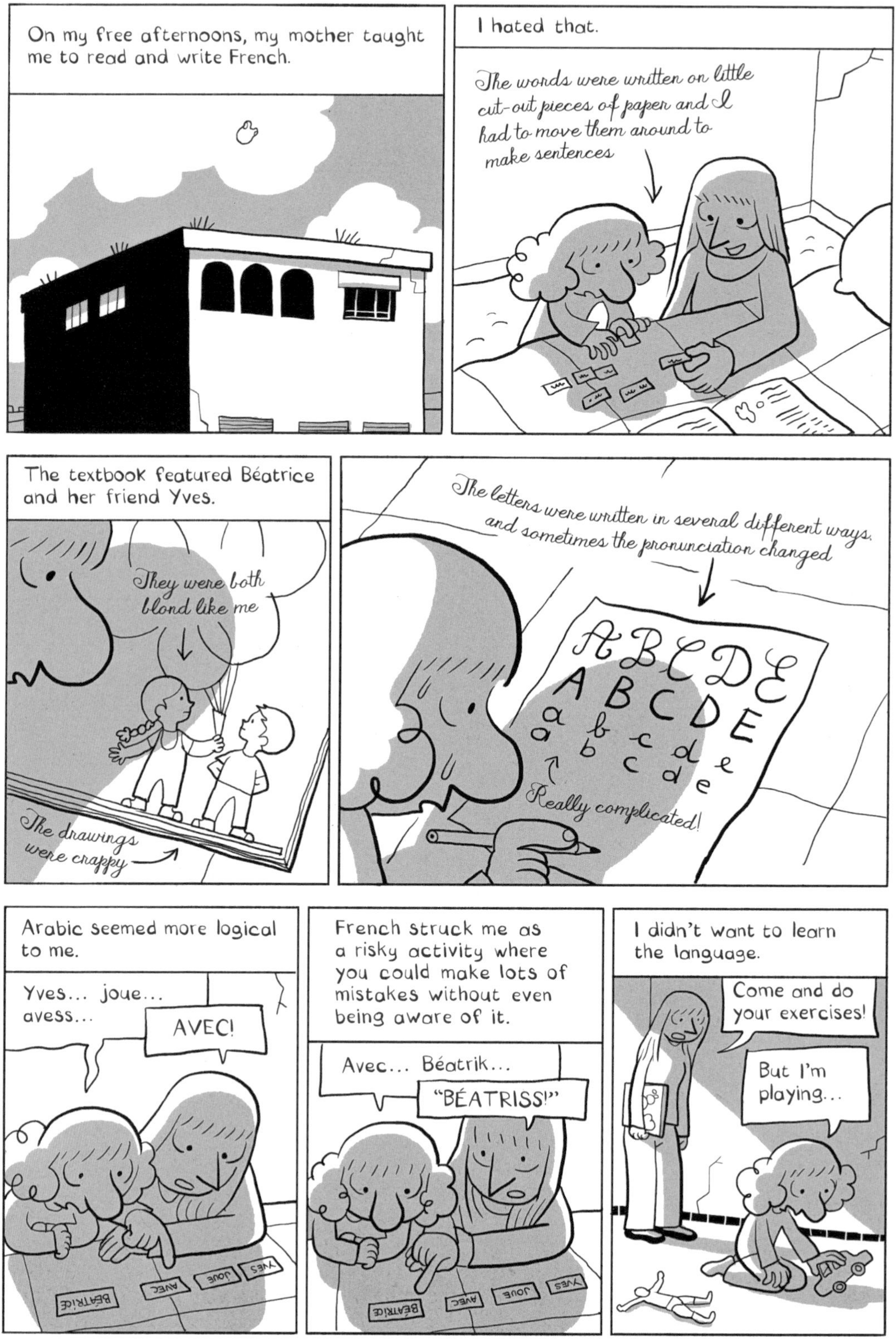
On my free afternoons, my mother taught me to read and write French.
I hated that.
The words were written on little cut-out pieces of paper and I had to move them around to make sentences
The textbook featured Béatrice and her friend Yves.
They were both blond like me
The drawings were crappy
The letters were written in several different ways, and sometimes the pronunciation changed
ABCDE
ABCDE
a b c d e
a b c d e
Really complicated!
Arabic seemed more logical to me.
Yves… joue… avess…
AVEC!
French struck me as a risky activity where you could make lots of mistakes without even being aware of it.
Avec… Béatrik…
"BÉATRISS!"
I didn't want to learn the language.
Come and do your exercises!
But I'm playing…

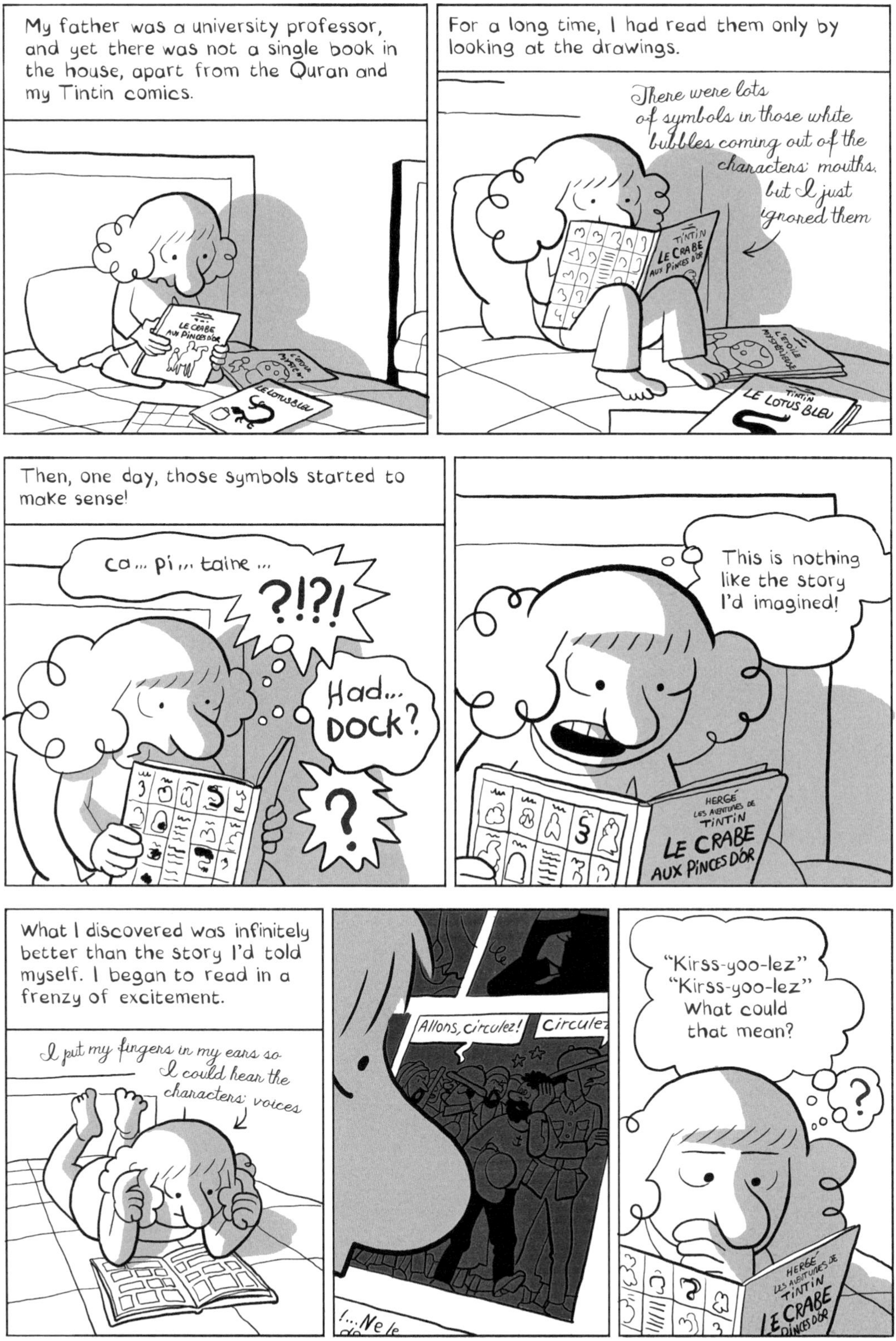
My father was a university professor, and yet there was not a single book in the house, apart from the Quran and my Tintin comics.
LE CRABE AUX PINCES D'OR
LE LOTUS BLEU
For a long time, I had read them only by looking at the drawings.
There were lots of symbols in those white bubbles coming out of the characters' mouths, but I just ignored them
TINTIN LE CRABE AUX PINCES D'OR
L'ÉTOILE MYSTÉRIEUSE
TINTIN LE LOTUS BLEU
Then, one day, those symbols started to make sense!
ca... pi... taine ...
?!?!
Had... DOCK?
?
This is nothing like the story I'd imagined!
HERGÉ LES AVENTURES DE TINTIN LE CRABE AUX PINCES D'OR
What I discovered was infinitely better than the story I'd told myself. I began to read in a frenzy of excitement.
I put my fingers in my ears so I could hear the characters' voices
Allons, circulez!
Circulez
"Kirss-yoo-lez" "Kirss-yoo-lez" What could that mean?
?
HERGÉ LES AVENTURES DE TINTIN LE CRABE AUX PINCES D'OR

Springtime arrived. There were poppies everywhere.

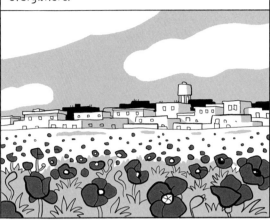

The air smelled pleasantly of warm grass.

The back wall of the mayor's house was filled with swallows.

A little yellow-breasted, black-headed bird sang all over the village.

♫ ♪ Li-Li-Li ! ♫
LALALALiLALALi!
♫ ♪ ♪

Little purple flowers grew near the river.

We walked by the edge of the Orante. The turtles stayed on the other bank, to avoid the children.

Come on, I'll show you the spring.

!!!

You can drink the water. It's delicious.

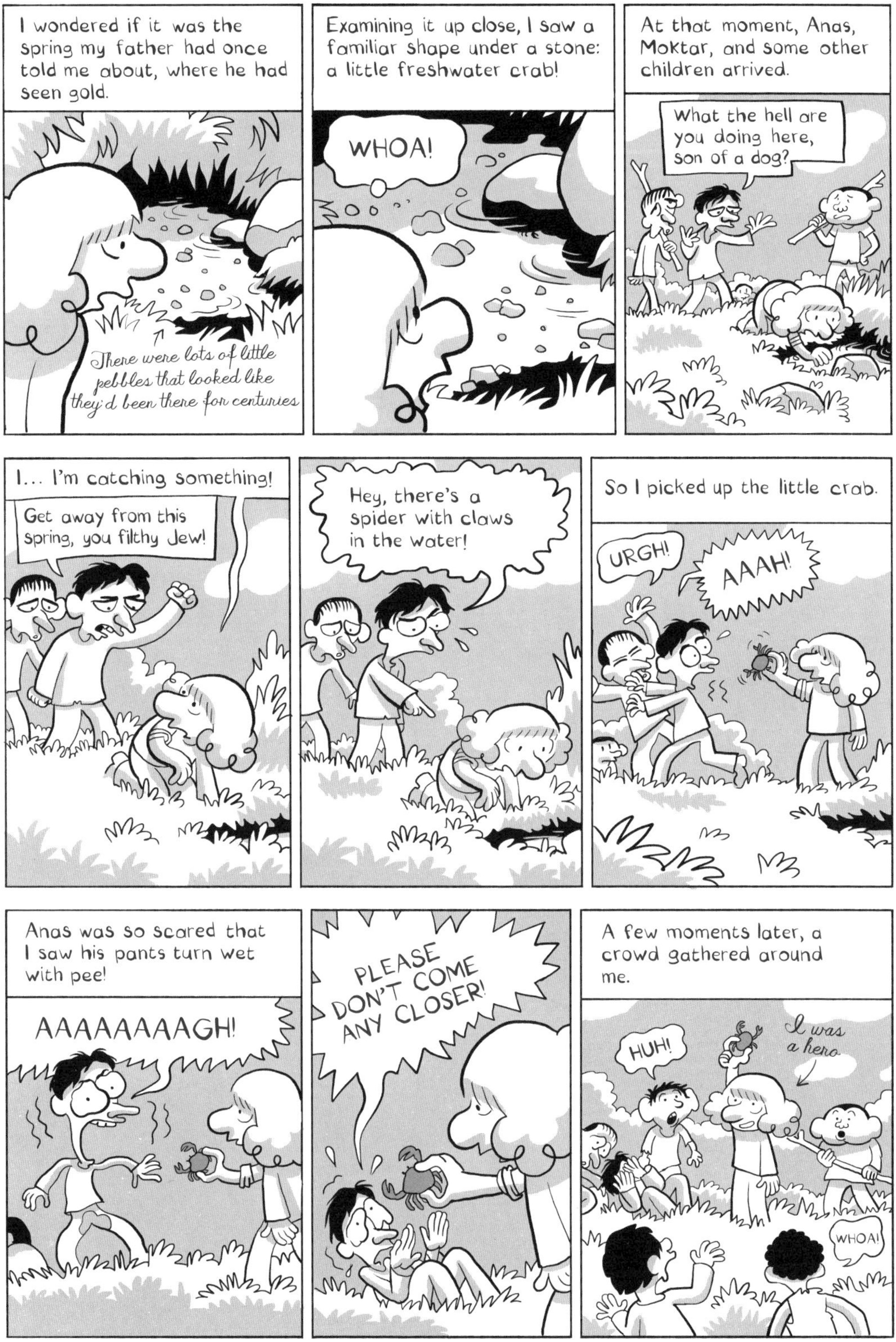
I wondered if it was the spring my father had once told me about, where he had seen gold.
There were lots of little pebbles that looked like they'd been there for centuries
Examining it up close, I saw a familiar shape under a stone: a little freshwater crab!
WHOA!
At that moment, Anas, Moktar, and some other children arrived.
What the hell are you doing here, son of a dog?
I... I'm catching something!
Get away from this spring, you filthy Jew!
Hey, there's a spider with claws in the water!
So I picked up the little crab.
URGH!
AAAH!
Anas was so scared that I saw his pants turn wet with pee!
AAAAAAAAGH!
PLEASE DON'T COME ANY CLOSER!
A few moments later, a crowd gathered around me.
HUH!
I was a hero
WHOA!

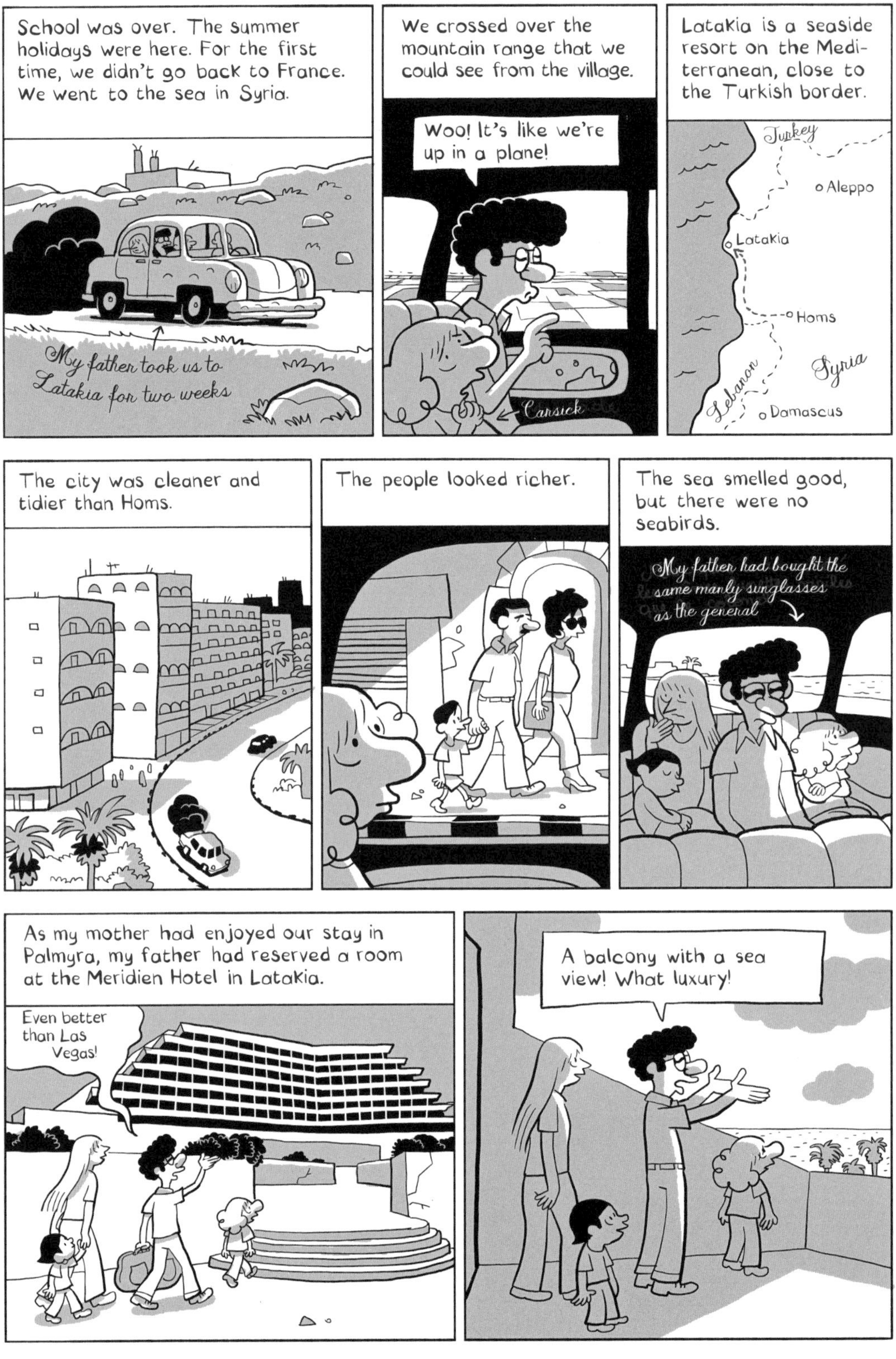
School was over. The summer holidays were here. For the first time, we didn't go back to France. We went to the sea in Syria.
My father took us to Latakia for two weeks
We crossed over the mountain range that we could see from the village.
Woo! It's like we're up in a plane!
Carsick
Latakia is a seaside resort on the Mediterranean, close to the Turkish border.
Turkey
Aleppo
Latakia
Homs
Syria
Lebanon
Damascus
The city was cleaner and tidier than Homs.
The people looked richer.
The sea smelled good, but there were no seabirds.
My father had bought the same manly sunglasses as the general
As my mother had enjoyed our stay in Palmyra, my father had reserved a room at the Meridien Hotel in Latakia.
Even better than Las Vegas!
A balcony with a sea view! What luxury!

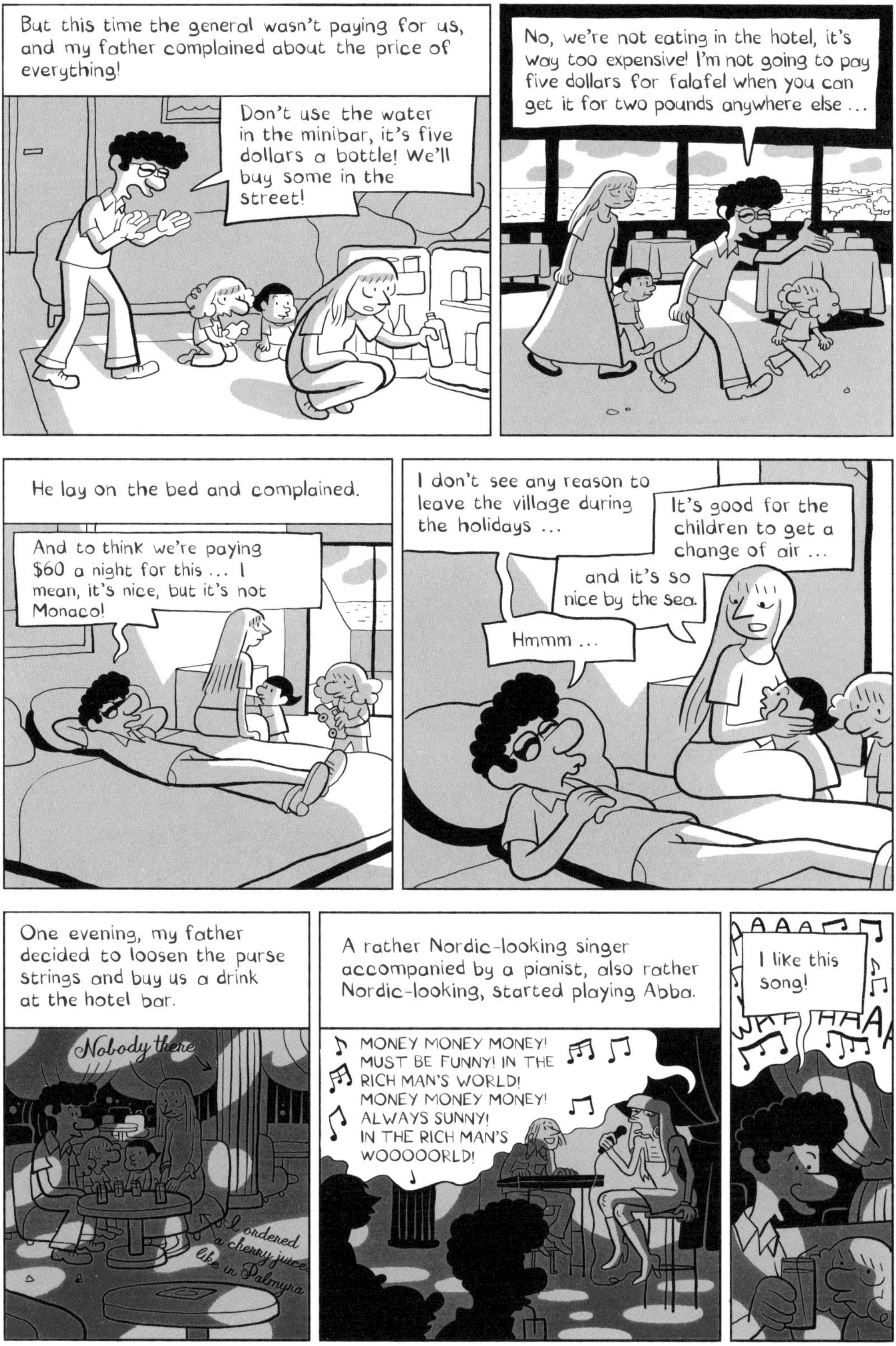

But this time the general wasn't paying for us, and my father complained about the price of everything!
Don't use the water in the minibar, it's five dollars a bottle! We'll buy some in the street!
No, we're not eating in the hotel, it's way too expensive! I'm not going to pay five dollars for falafel when you can get it for two pounds anywhere else ...
He lay on the bed and complained.
And to think we're paying $60 a night for this ... I mean, it's nice, but it's not Monaco!
I don't see any reason to leave the village during the holidays ...
It's good for the children to get a change of air ...
and it's so nice by the sea.
Hmmm ...
One evening, my father decided to loosen the purse strings and buy us a drink at the hotel bar.
Nobody there
I ordered a cherry juice like in Palmyra
A rather Nordic-looking singer accompanied by a pianist, also rather Nordic-looking, started playing Abba.
MONEY MONEY MONEY! MUST BE FUNNY! IN THE RICH MAN'S WORLD! MONEY MONEY MONEY! ALWAYS SUNNY! IN THE RICH MAN'S WOOOOORLD!
I like this song!

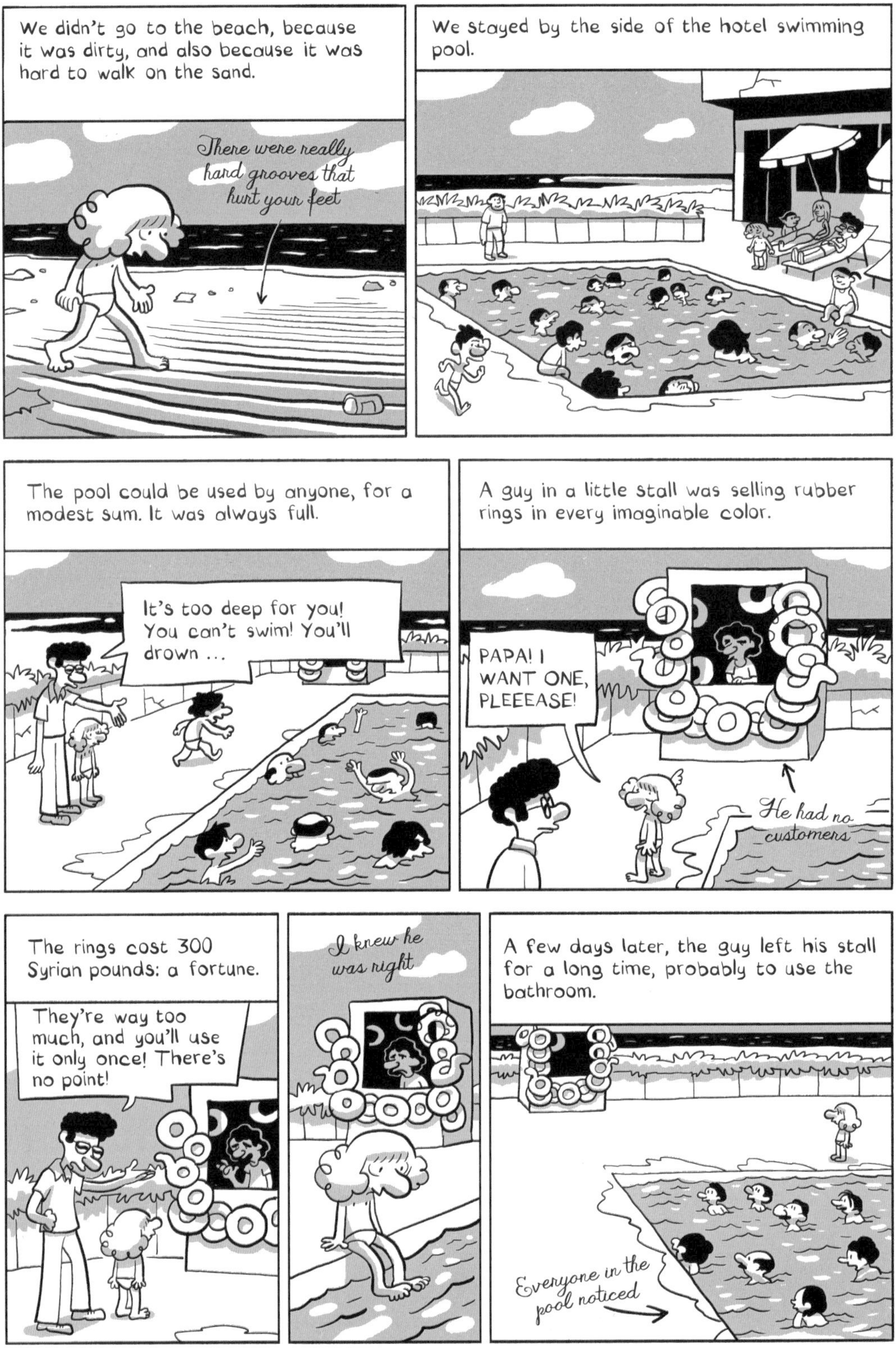
We didn't go to the beach, because it was dirty, and also because it was hard to walk on the sand.
There were really hard grooves that hurt your feet
We stayed by the side of the hotel swimming pool.
The pool could be used by anyone, for a modest sum. It was always full.
It's too deep for you! You can't swim! You'll drown ...
A guy in a little stall was selling rubber rings in every imaginable color.
PAPA! I WANT ONE, PLEEEASE!
He had no customers
The rings cost 300 Syrian pounds: a fortune.
They're way too much, and you'll use it only once! There's no point!
I knew he was right
A few days later, the guy left his stall for a long time, probably to use the bathroom.
Everyone in the pool noticed

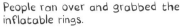

People ran over and grabbed the inflatable rings.

THEY'RE FREE TODAY!

PAPA, GO AHEAD! THEY'RE FREE!

After taking a ring, they ran off to the beach

We're not thieves!

And just because everyone does something, that doesn't mean you should do it, too!

Five minutes later, all the rings had vanished and there was hardly anyone left in the water.

The vendor came back and screamed.

AAAAAH!

He began to weep and looked around him.

SOB SOB

He started fighting with a guy who was holding one of the inflatable rings.

SON OF A DOG!

Come on, let's go!

Given how much it costs, we should make the most of our room!

151

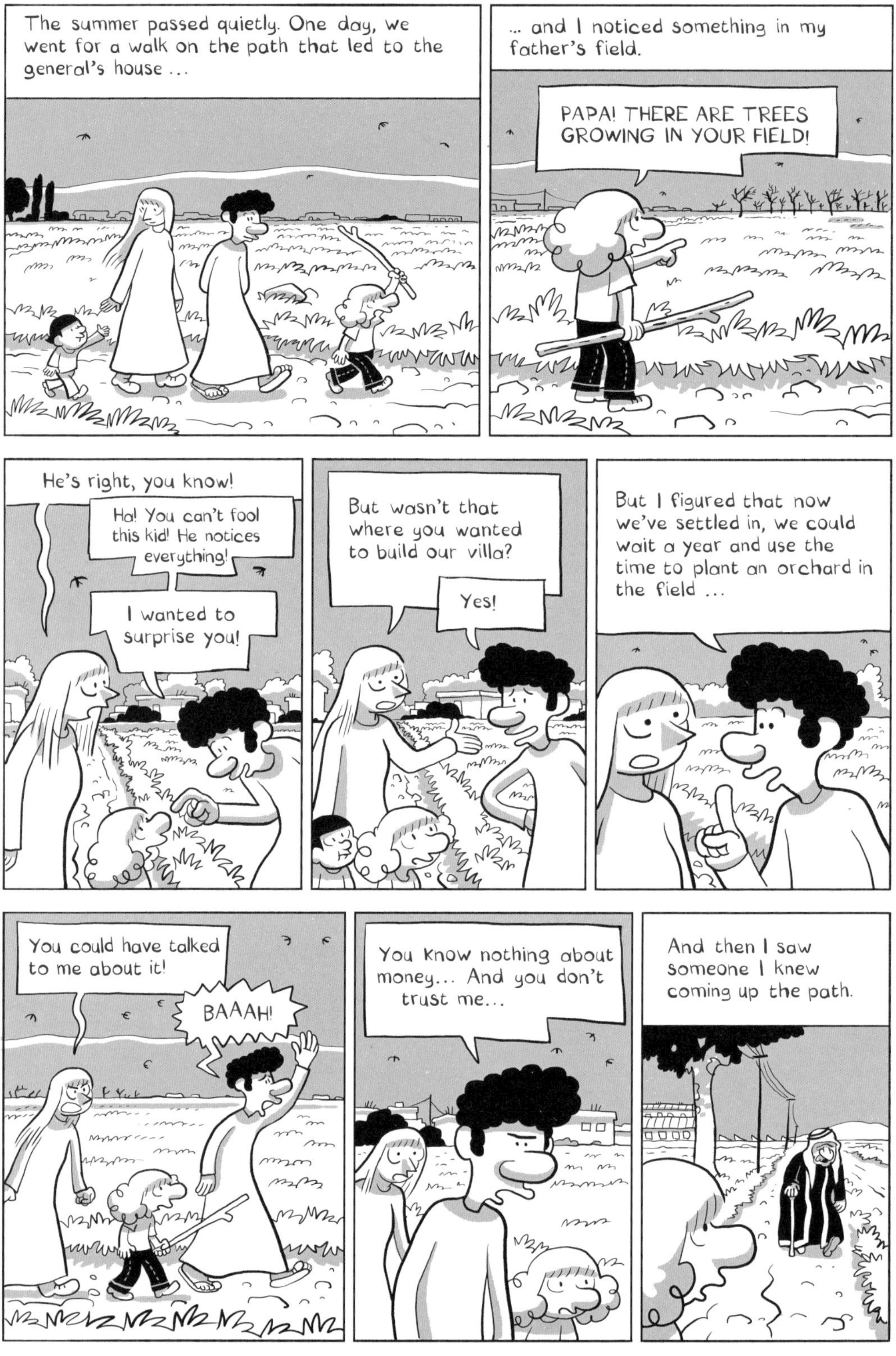
The summer passed quietly. One day, we went for a walk on the path that led to the general's house ...
... and I noticed something in my father's field.
PAPA! THERE ARE TREES GROWING IN YOUR FIELD!
He's right, you know!
Ha! You can't fool this kid! He notices everything!
I wanted to surprise you!
But wasn't that where you wanted to build our villa?
Yes!
But I figured that now we've settled in, we could wait a year and use the time to plant an orchard in the field ...
You could have talked to me about it!
BAAAH!
You know nothing about money... And you don't trust me...
And then I saw someone I knew coming up the path.

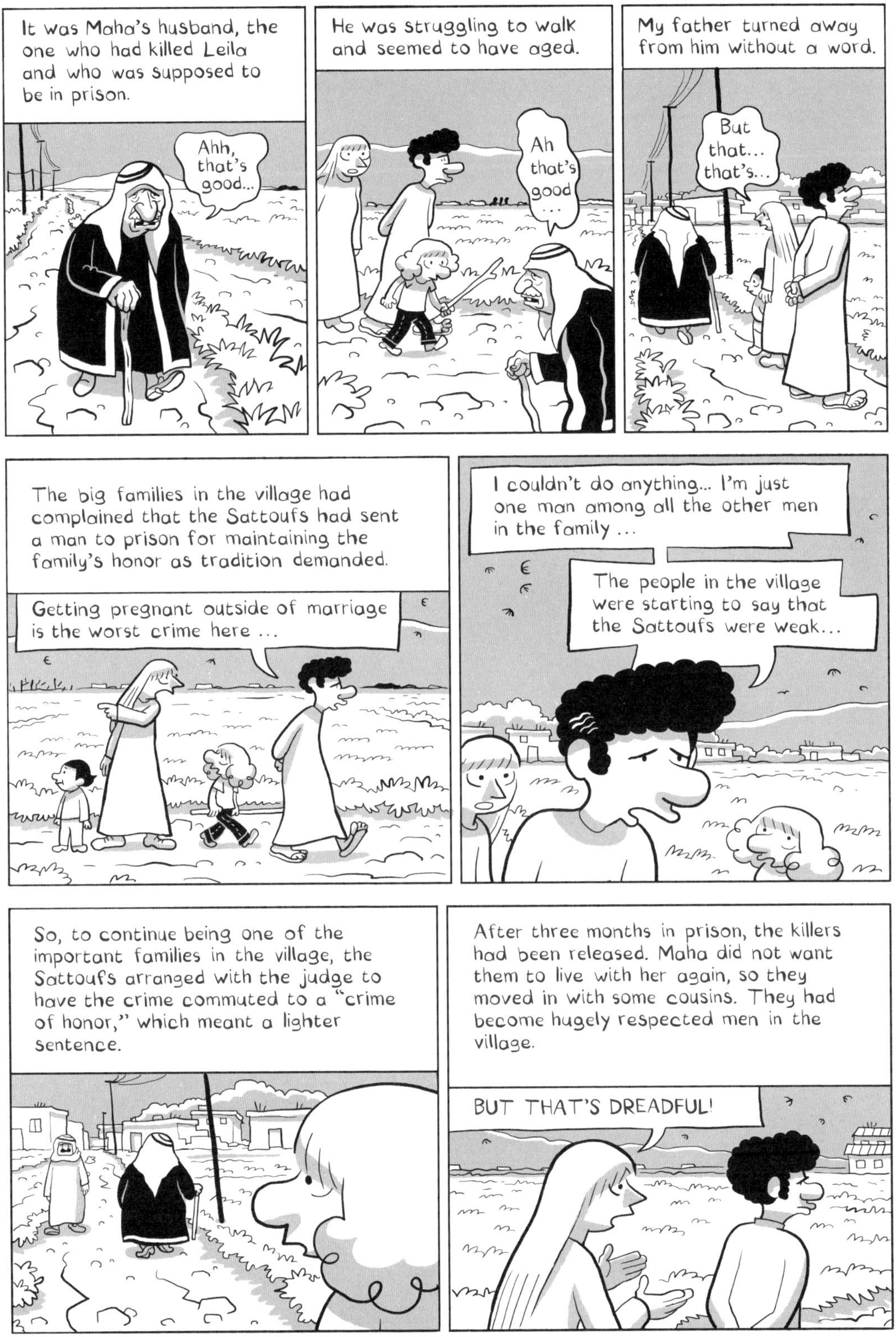
It was Maha's husband, the one who had killed Leila and who was supposed to be in prison.
Ahh, that's good...
He was struggling to walk and seemed to have aged.
Ah that's good ...
My father turned away from him without a word.
But that... that's...
The big families in the village had complained that the Sattoufs had sent a man to prison for maintaining the family's honor as tradition demanded.
Getting pregnant outside of marriage is the worst crime here ...
I couldn't do anything... I'm just one man among all the other men in the family ...
The people in the village were starting to say that the Sattoufs were weak...
So, to continue being one of the important families in the village, the Sattoufs arranged with the judge to have the crime commuted to a "crime of honor," which meant a lighter sentence.
After three months in prison, the killers had been released. Maha did not want them to live with her again, so they moved in with some cousins. They had become hugely respected men in the village.
BUT THAT'S DREADFUL!

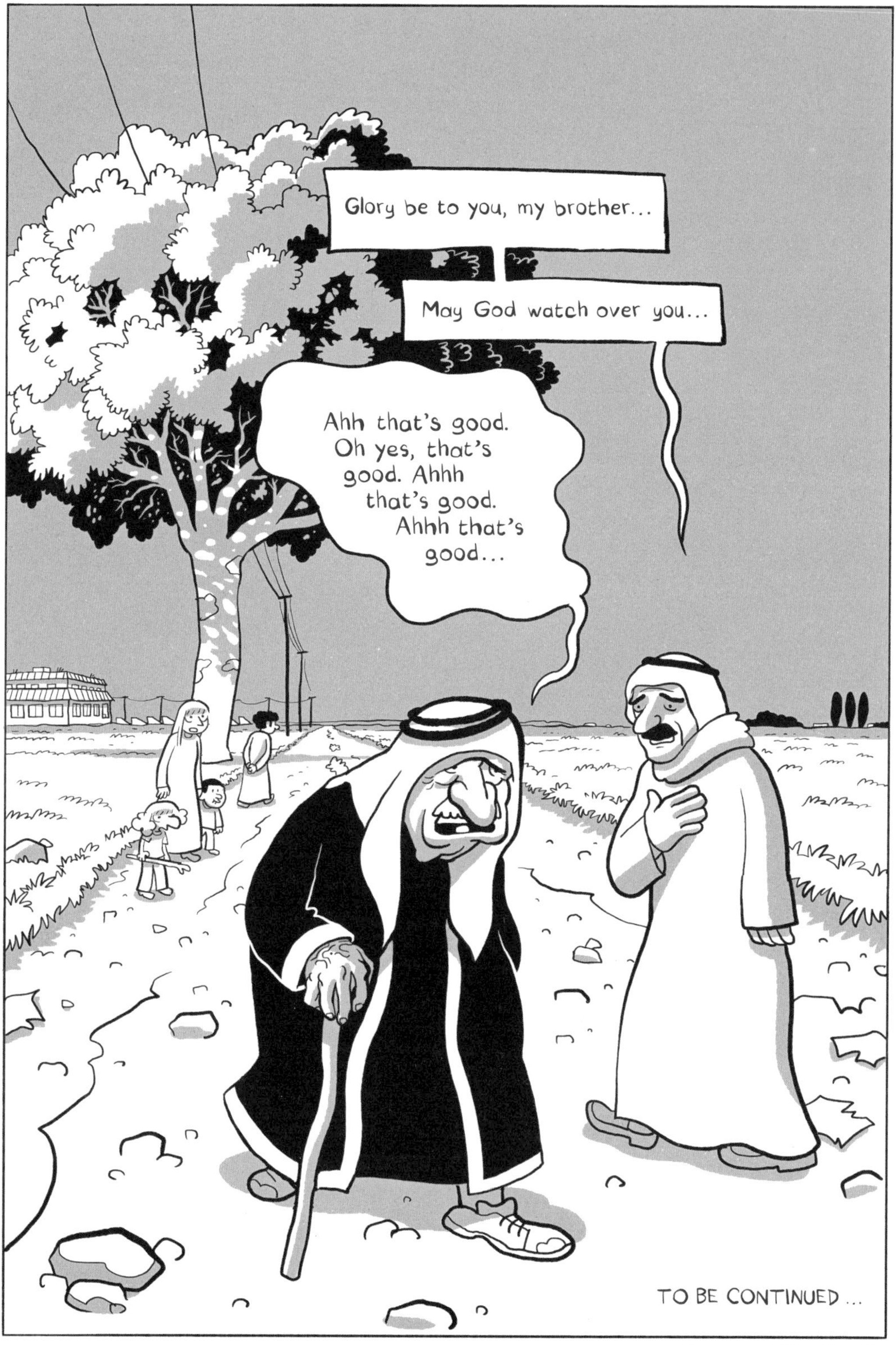
Glory be to you, my brother...
May God watch over you...
Ahh that's good. Oh yes, that's good. Ahhh that's good. Ahhh that's good...
TO BE CONTINUED...

Riad Sattouf

ABOUT THE AUTHOR

RIAD SATTOUF is the author of *The Arab of the Future,* which won the Angoulême Prize for Best Graphic Novel. He grew up in Syria and Libya and now lives in Paris. The author of four comics series in France and a former contributor to the satirical publication *Charlie Hebdo,* Sattouf is now a weekly columnist for *l'Obs.* He also directed the films *The French Kissers* and *Jacky in the Women's Kingdom.*